WITHDRAWN
UTSA LIBRARIES

The Evolving American Presidency Series

Series Foreword

The American Presidency touches virtually every aspect of American and world politics. And the presidency has become, for better or worse, the vital center of the American and global political systems. The Framers of the American government would be dismayed at such a result. As invented at the Philadelphia Constitutional Convention in 1787, the Presidency was to have been a part of a government with shared and overlapping powers, embedded within a separation-of-powers system. If there was a vital center, it was the Congress; the Presidency was to be a part, but by no means, the centerpiece of that system.

Over time, the presidency has evolved and grown in power, expectations, responsibilities, and authority. Wars, crises, depressions, industrialization, all served to add to the power of the presidency. And as the United States grew into a world power, presidential power also grew. As the United States became the world's leading superpower, the presidency rose in prominence and power, not only in the U.S., but on the world stage.

It is the clash between the presidency as invented and the presidency as it has developed that inspired this series. And it is the importance and power of the modern American presidency that makes understanding the office so vital. Like it or not, the American Presidency stands at the vortex of power both within the United States and across the globe.

This Palgrave series recognizes that the Presidency is and has been an evolving institution, going from the original constitutional design as a Chief Clerk, to today where the president is the center of the American political constellation. This has caused several key dilemmas in our political system, not the least of which is that presidents face high expectations with limited constitutional resources. This causes presidents to find extra-constitutional means of governing. Thus, presidents must find ways to bridge the expectations/power gap while operating within the confines of a separation-of-powers system designed to limit presidential authority. How presidents resolve these challenges and paradoxes is the central issue in modern governance. It is also the central theme of this book series.

Michael A. Genovese
Loyola Chair of Leadership
Loyola Marymount University
Palgrave's *The Evolving American Presidency*, Series Editor

The Second Term of George W. Bush
    edited by Robert Maranto, Douglas M. Brattebo, and Tom Lansford

The Presidency and the Challenge of Democracy
    edited by Michael A. Genovese and Lori Cox Han

Religion and the American Presidency
    edited by Mark J. Rozell and Gleaves Whitney

Religion and the Bush Presidency
    edited by Mark J. Rozell and Gleaves Whitney

Test by Fire: The War Presidency of George W. Bush
    by Robert Swansbrough

American Royalty: The Bush and Clinton Families and the Danger to the American Presidency
    by Matthew T. Corrigan

Accidental Presidents: Death, Assassination, Resignation, and Democratic Succession
    by Philip Abbott

Presidential Power in Action: Implementing Supreme Court Detainee Decisions
    by Darren A. Wheeler

President George W. Bush's Influence over Bureaucracy and Policy: Extraordinary Times, Extraordinary Powers
    edited by Colin Provost and Paul Teske

Assessing George W. Bush's Legacy: The Right Man?
    edited by Iwan Morgan and Philip John Davies

Assessing George W. Bush's Legacy

The Right Man?

Edited by
Iwan Morgan and Philip John Davies

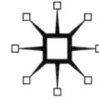

ASSESSING GEORGE W. BUSH'S LEGACY
Copyright © Iwan Morgan and Philip John Davies, 2010.
All rights reserved.

First published in 2010 by
PALGRAVE MACMILLAN®
in the United States—a division of St. Martin's Press LLC,
175 Fifth Avenue, New York, NY 10010.

Where this book is distributed in the UK, Europe and the rest of the world, this is by Palgrave Macmillan, a division of Macmillan Publishers Limited, registered in England, company number 785998, of Houndmills, Basingstoke, Hampshire RG21 6XS.

Palgrave Macmillan is the global academic imprint of the above companies and has companies and representatives throughout the world.

Palgrave® and Macmillan® are registered trademarks in the United States, the United Kingdom, Europe and other countries.

ISBN: 978–0–230–10858–5

Library of Congress Cataloging-in-Publication Data

    Assessing George W. Bush's legacy : the right man? / edited by Iwan Morgan & Philip John Davies.
      p. cm.—(Evolving American presidency series)
      ISBN 978–0–230–10858–5
      1. Bush, George W. (George Walker), 1946– 2. Bush, George, W. (George Walker), 1946– —Social and political views. 3. United States—Politics and government—2001–2009. 4. United States—Foreign relations—2001–2009. I. Morgan, Iwan W. II. Davies, Philip, 1948–
E902.A868 2010
973.931092—dc22   2010013862

A catalogue record of the book is available from the British Library.

Design by Newgen Imaging Systems (P) Ltd., Chennai, India.

First edition: November 2010

10 9 8 7 6 5 4 3 2 1

Printed in the United States of America.

Contents

List of Figure and Tables		vii
List of Contributors		ix
Introduction: Assessing George W. Bush's Legacy: The Right Man? *Iwan Morgan*		1
One	Rating Bush *Andrew Rudalevige*	11
Two	Bush's Style of Presidential Leadership *Nigel Bowles*	31
Three	Bush's Congressional Legacy and Congress's Bush Legacy *John E. Owens*	51
Four	Bush, the Judiciary, and the Conservative Constitutional Counterrevolution: Close but No Cigar *Robert J. McKeever*	79
Five	The Ethical Record of the Bush Presidency *Clodagh Harrington*	99
Six	Did Bush Pursue a Neoconservative Foreign Policy? *Timothy J. Lynch*	121
Seven	Bush's Foreign Policy Legacy: Counting the Cost *John Dumbrell*	145
Eight	Bush and Big Government Conservatism *Alex Waddan*	165
Nine	Bush's Political Economy: Deficits, Debt, and Depression *Iwan Morgan*	185
Ten	Bush's Partisan Legacy and the 2008 Elections *Philip John Davies*	207
Index		223

Figure and Tables

Figure

3.1 The Changing Ideological Position of the Congressional Parties: 91st Congress and 110th Congress — 55

Tables

1.1 Selected Rankings in Presidential Surveys, 1962–2008 — 19

3.1 Tight Inter-Party Competition and Control of the Congress and the Presidency, 2001–8 — 57

6.1 PNAC Signatories Hired and Not Hired by the George W. Bush Administration — 131

Contributors

Nigel Bowles is Honour Balfour Fellow in Politics at St. Anne's College and Director of the Rothermere American Institute, Oxford University. His numerous publications include *The White House and Capitol Hill* and *Nixon's Business: Power and Authority in the Modern Presidency*, winner of the American Politics Group's Richard E. Neustadt Prize in 2006. He is also the author of a widely read text, *Government and Politics of the United States*.

Philip John Davies is director of the Eccles Centre for American Studies at the British Library. His many publications include *Elections USA*; *US Elections Today*; *Winning Elections and Political Marketing* (coedited with Bruce Newman); *The Federal Nation: Perspectives on American Federalism*; *America's Americans: Demographic Issues in American Society and Politic*; and *Right On? Political Change and Continuity in George W. Bush's America* (all coedited with Iwan Morgan). He is chair of the American Politics Group.

John Dumbrell is Professor of Government at Durham University. His numerous books include *President Lyndon Johnson and Soviet Communism*; *A Special Relationship: Anglo-American Relations from the Cold War to Iraq*; and *The Carter Presidency: A Re-evaluation*. His most recent study is *Clinton's Foreign Policy: Between the Bushes 1992–2000*.

Clodagh Harrington is Lecturer in Politics at de Montfort University. She achieved her Ph.D. on the role of the Special Prosecutor in American politics from Watergate to the Monica Lewinsky scandal in 2006 and is currently engaged in turning that into a book.

Timothy J. Lynch is Senior Lecturer in U.S. Foreign Policy at the Institute for the Study of the Americas, University of London. He is the author of *Turf Wars: The Clinton Administration and Northern Ireland* and (with Robert Singh) *After Bush: The Case for Continuity in American Foreign Policy*, which won the American Politics Group's Richard E. Neustadt Prize in 2009; and numerous scholarly articles.

Robert J. McKeever is Head of Department of Law, Governance and International Relations at London Metropolitan University. He has published extensively on U.S. constitutional issues in scholarly journals and in various edited collections. His books include *Raw Judicial Power? The Supreme Court and American Society*.

Iwan Morgan is Professor of U.S. Studies and Director of the U.S. Presidency Centre at the Institute for the Study of the Americas, University of London. His publications include: *Eisenhower versus "the Spenders"*; *Deficit Government*; *Nixon*; and, most recently, *The Age of Deficits: Presidents and Unbalanced Budgets from Jimmy Carter to George W. Bush*, winner of the American Politics Group's Richard E. Neustadt Prize in 2010. He is chair of the executive committee of the Historians of the Twentieth Century United States.

John E. Owens is Professor of U.S. Government and Politics at the University of Westminster and Faculty Fellow in the Center for Congressional and Presidential Studies at American University. His publications include: *Congress and the Presidency*; *Leadership in Context*; and *The Republican Takeover of Congress*. His most recent work is *America's "War" on Terrorism: New Dimensions in United States Government and National Security* (coedited with John Dumbrell).

Andrew Rudalevige is Associate Professor of Political Science at Dickinson College. One of the foremost scholars of the presidency, his publications include *Managing the President's Program: Presidential Leadership and Legislative Policy Formation*, winner of the American Political Science Association's Richard E. Neustadt Award for the best book written on the presidency in 2002; *The New Imperial Presidency: Renewing Presidential Power after Watergate*; and (as coeditor) *The George W. Bush Legacy*.

Alex Waddan is Senior Lecturer in U.S. Politics at the University of Leicester. A specialist in U.S. public policy, especially pertaining to social welfare and economic issues, he has written two books, *The Politics of Social Welfare* and *Clinton's Legacy: A New Democrat in Governance*, and published numerous articles in scholarly journals, such as *Political Science Quarterly*.

Introduction

Assessing George W. Bush's Legacy: The Right Man?

Iwan Morgan

George W. Bush claimed not to care what scholars would have to say about his presidency just after his departure from office. In 2002, his chief political adviser, Karl Rove, declared, "President Bush is fond of saying that, in the short run, history always gets it wrong." In his last press conference, with his presidency widely deemed to have been a failure, a defiant Bush remarked that it was too soon to reach this verdict or any other. "There is," he insisted, "no such thing as short-term history. I don't think you can possibly get the full breadth of an administration until time has passed."[1] Without doubt, the impact and significance of a president's legacy can be properly understood only in relation to the course of history in the years after he leaves office. Nevertheless, whatever the forty-third president's misgivings on this score, an immediate estimate of his place in history is also legitimate. The recent past is too important a subject to leave to the analysts of the future. Whatever one's views on Bush's presidency, it has immense significance for America's twenty-first century development. Its legacy, therefore, merits immediate assessment, even if a definitive judgment requires the passage of time.

This analysis of Bush's legacy consists of essays written by nine UK scholars of U.S. politics and one American. Hopefully it can offer an outsider perspective that brings different insights and perhaps a more disinterested perspective in comparison to a volume on the same subject written by U.S. scholars. The project grew out of a conference, coorganized by the British Library's Eccles Centre [EC] for American Studies and the Institute for the Study of the Americas [ISA] of the University of London's School of Advanced Study in March 2009. The editors express their thanks to their colleagues in both institutions, particularly Kate Bateman and Jean Petrovic of the EC and Olga Jimenez and Karen Perkins of the ISA, for their hard work and support in making this event a success.

Our evaluation of Bush in this study is conceived within the framework of its subtitle, *The Right Man?* The contributors interpret the legacy of the Bush presidency in one or more of three ways pertaining to this: Bush's style of presidential decision making (Rudalevige; Bowles; Owens; Harrington); the ideological values that infused his public policies (Rudalevige; Owens; McKeever; Lynch; Waddan); and whether the policies he pursued at home and abroad met America's needs and advanced its interests (Rudalevige; Bowles; Dumbrell; Morgan; Harrington; Davies).

One way of approaching Bush as "the right man" is to draw on his own conviction and that of his principal advisers that expansion of presidential power was legitimate in the wake of the 9/11 terrorist attacks. In their view, the presidency's obligation to ensure the nation's security at home and abroad meant that it should not be limited by the Madisonian checks-and-balances inherent in the constitutional separation of powers. To a far greater extent than any of his modern predecessors, Bush expanded the power of his office to test and exceed the limits of America's supreme law. The rhetorical and legal justification that his administration mounted in support of this may have lasting consequences for the American system of government. Not even Richard Nixon had taken the so-called imperial presidency to the same stage of development. One cartoonist perfectly encapsulated this in drawing a somewhat primeval-looking Bush passing a portrait of the thirty-seventh president in the White House and casting a dismissive judgment on his predecessor: "AMATEUR."[2]

As a number of contributors to this volume show, Bush employed numerous ways of expanding executive power at the expense of the other branches of government. These included signing statements, claims of expanded presidential powers based on secret memoranda written by aides, withholding information that Congress needed to conduct its legislative and oversight business; and asserting commander-in-chief powers to override constitutional and legal niceties pertaining to civil liberties at home and the rights of enemy detainees taken in the "war on terror." In doing so Bush never doubted that he had the right to take the actions that he did nor that he was right to do so. In this regard his self-assurance was absolute. As he told journalist Bob Woodward of his decision to attack the Taliban regime in Afghanistan in retaliation for its support of Al-Qaeda terrorists, "There is no doubt in my mind we're doing the right thing. Not one doubt." At the end of his presidency, Bush may have grudgingly admitted to making some mistakes, but ultimately he considered himself to have been in the right on the big decisions of this presidency. Only a president with an unquestioning belief that this was the case could have remarked of his leadership approach, as Bush famously did in April 2006, "I'm the decider and I decide what is best."[3]

A second way of assessing Bush as "the right man" relates to his ideological identity. Many liberals reviled him as a made-in-Texas conservative with an unquestioning belief in the free market, a reactionary desire to roll back the cultural legacy of the 1960s, and a neoconservative outlook in foreign affairs to rebuild the world in America's image through military power. At the same time, however, conservatives were not so sure that Bush was one of them. By the midpoint of his second term, a host of right-wingers had published tracts accusing him of betraying Ronald Reagan's legacy of small government. Even his conservative supporters could not deny that Bush had expanded federal power in a wide range of policy domains, notably education, homeland security, and entitlements. In his defense, they lauded him for promoting "big-government conservatism" that accepted the impossibility of downsizing the activist state but sought to turn it to conservative ends. In their credo, Bush was building an "ownership society" that used government to enhance individual choice and enterprise. The difficulty of neatly labeling Bush's ideology extended to his administration's foreign policy. Many critics considered him blindly beholden to neoconservative principles, but neoconservatives themselves saw few parallels between his agenda and theirs.[4]

All this indicates that Bush's political beliefs were not easily pigeonholed. He was most evidently a man of the right with regard to his support for tax reduction, strong defense, social security privatization, economic deregulation, and promotion of traditional sociomoral values. On the other hand, there was much in his record that testified to ideological complexity. In foreign policy, the forty-third president sometimes talked the language of neoconservatism, but his strategy arguably harked back to an older tradition of conservative realism. On domestic issues, many of Bush's initiatives were directly at variance with Ronald Reagan's bellwether statement of conservative orthodoxy, which he made in his 1981 presidential inaugural address: "Government is not the solution to our problems; government is the problem."

Finally, some of the contributors to this volume consider whether Bush was "the right man" from the vantage of whether his policies were the right ones to address the problems facing the United States on his watch. In the case of some presidents, such an assessment has to allow for the fact that a goodly number of their legislative proposals were blocked or substantially amended by Congress. Harry

S. Truman, Jimmy Carter, and Bill Clinton provide the most obvious examples on this score. In Bush's case, however, he was remarkably successful in achieving his principal policy aims. A pliant legislature generally gave him most of what he wanted—and in some instances when it opposed him, Bush's expansive concept of executive power facilitated unilateral attainment of his ends. Failure to enact Social Security reform and immigration reform arguably constituted the only significant legislative defeats that he suffered over the course of his presidency.

While Bush was largely successful in implementing his agenda, its merits are very much open to question. On the big issues that defined his presidency—and are likely to do so far into the future—the contributors to this volume offer an unambiguously negative assessment. Bush can point to the lack of further attacks on the homeland after 9/11 as arguably his greatest achievement (even if the total number of worldwide terrorist attacks significantly increased on his watch). It is doubtful, however, that this was attributable to his expansion of executive power beyond the letter and spirit of the Constitution in order to prosecute the war on terror. More pertinently, his administration's actions on this score highlighted the ethical, legal, and political dangers associated with the imperial presidency and set precedents for future presidential conduct that America may well have cause to regret. In foreign policy, the strikes against Bush on his legacy scorecard included the diminution of America's soft power; a war in Iraq that was launched with questionable cause and without a viable exit strategy; a war in Afghanistan that was supposedly won but where a regrouped enemy posed a renewed threat by the end of Bush's tenure; and failure to participate meaningfully in international efforts to deal with climate change. On the economy, Bush's tax cuts produced huge budget deficits, but not the sustained economic growth that he had promised they would deliver. Moreover, his insistence that the free market was the agency of prosperity rang hollow when serious recession and financial crisis required huge government intervention to save the economy from collapse in 2008.

In the first chapter of this volume, "Rating Bush," Andrew Rudalevige brings together the themes and issues discussed above. After reviewing the benefits and shortcomings of presidential rating systems and examining why some presidents fare better than others in the eyes of history, he offers an insightful early return on Bush. While taking issue with those who have decried him as the worst president in history, Rudalevige argues that his successes were short-term ones that had problematic long-term consequences. In his view,

Bush's main policy achievements were largely tactical in nature but tended to undermine strategic progress, were often based on insufficient scrutiny and faulty intelligence, and tended to eschew the really tough choices that are necessary for a president to "do good."

In "Bush's Style of Presidential Leadership," Nigel Bowles examines the forty-third president from the perspective of Richard Neustadt's classic construction of presidential power. Like Rudalevige, he faults Bush for his short-term outlook and his tendency to take decisions without fully weighing the payoffs and costs at different points. Drawing on Neustadt's concept of presidential power as primarily that of persuasion, he also finds Bush excessively reliant on the power of command based on contentious claims of his authority. In Bowles's opinion, this approach did not serve well either Bush's own needs or those of his nation because presidential authority comprises a complex texture of negotiation, education, and thinking in time that requires reasoning backward from intended objectives to means for their attainment.

In "Bush's Congressional Legacy and Congress's Bush Legacy," John Owens illustrates how Bush adopted a highly "presidentialist" style of leadership toward the legislature. Capitalizing on the war on terror, he dominated national and homeland security policymaking, conventionally domains of executive ascendancy, to an unprecedented degree. What truly made his presidency historically distinctive, however, was his aggressive assertion of unilateral powers based mainly on claims of inherent constitutional prerogatives. In contrast to Neustadt's prescription, what Bush demonstrated in Owens's view was that a president's power is based not only on persuasion but also on the extent to which Congress and the courts allow him to assert his authority. Nevertheless, assertive presidentialism also had clear drawbacks. As Bush discovered, it did not generate the political legitimacy necessary to safeguard his policy legacy. Moreover, it established dangerous precedents that could permanently change the equilibrium of the constitutional order if not resisted.

In "Bush, the Judiciary, and the Conservative Constitutional Counterrevolution: Close but No Cigar," Robert McKeever notes that judicial selection was one policy domain in which Bush was unambiguously conservative. The forty-third president sought completion of the judicial counterrevolution that conservatives had long anticipated. Around the midpoint of his presidency, it appeared that he was poised to achieve this end through his success in appointing conservatives to the district courts, circuit court of appeals, and the Supreme Court. However, McKeever's careful analysis of key judgments over Bush's entire presidency in the contested domains of abortion, affirmative action and race, civil liberties, the death penalty, and gay rights indicates that there was little or no change in legal and constitutional doctrine in any of these areas. The Supreme Court, in particular, remained an undependable ally of the conservative cause because the swing vote of Anthony Kennedy effectively determined its balance of power and prevented a marked shift to the right in its judgments on the aforementioned issues.

In "The Ethical Record of the Bush Presidency," Clodagh Harrington considers one of the most troubling aspects of the Bush legacy. Not since Richard Nixon had an American president come under such criticism for abuse of power. While acknowledging that Bush operated in difficult and challenging security circumstances, Harrington's review of his administration's actions based on assertions of inherent executive power produces a highly negative evaluation of his legacy. In her assessment, presidential unilateralism, the abuse of civil liberties, the sanction of torture and rendition of war on terror detainees, and executive misconduct in the "Plamegate" scandal threatened the constitutional order and the rule of law. Perhaps more than anything else, images of the torture of Abu Ghraib detainees, which did untold damage to America's reputation abroad, became the defining symbol of the disregard for ethics. For Harrington, the lesson of the Bush years is that the unrestrained imperial presidency constitutes a threat to the democratic values that are America's greatest source of strength.

In "Did Bush Pursue a Neoconservative Foreign Policy?" Timothy Lynch builds a case to answer this question in the negative. Commencing with a working definition of neoconservatism, Lynch tests the influence of this doctrine at two levels of analysis—personnel and grand strategy—and finds the Bush administration lacking on both scores. In a lively review that challenges some conventional assessments, he argues that Bush's foreign policy did not have a single ideological character. In his assessment, it paid only limited heed to neoconservative ideas and showed much greater affinity with conservative realism. Accordingly the war on terror manifested far more historical continuity than discontinuity with the U.S. foreign policy tradition. From Lynch's perspective, the resultant lack of neoconservative imperial will ultimately proved damaging because the military interventions in Iraq and Afghanistan did not take sufficient account of the problems of regime change.

In "Bush's Foreign Policy Legacy: Counting the Cost," John Dumbrell evaluates how "reputation" is measured in foreign policy on the basis of leadership, vision, crisis management, organizational capacity, and consistency. Using this index, he argues that assessments of Bush are likely to remain negative in the short to medium term at least, but that the president showed some capacity in his second term to learn from his first-term shortcomings. With regard to Bush's legacy, his inheritance to the Obama administration is markedly inferior to the one bequeathed him by the Clinton administration. To an extent this can be attributed to the post-9/11 context of global affairs, but Dumbrell faults Bush for failure to uphold American soft power, military overstretch, and the weakening of America's international economic position. In many respects, he suggests, Bush's widely perceived shortcomings as a foreign policy leader constituted his most helpful legacy to his successor by creating the opportunity for agenda change.

In "Bush and Big Government Conservatism," Alex Waddan examines whether the forty-third president was truly a new kind of conservative who accepted the reality of big government. His analysis points to confusion and inconsistency rather than clarity in the Bush record. Bush was a traditional conservative in his dedication to free-market economic policies and in his outlook on sociomoral issues. In contrast, the much touted "compassionate conservatism" that promised federal funds for churches and other private charities to help the poor proved a damp squib. The "opportunity society" initiatives to built individual choice into public programs had more substance but ultimately lacked coherence. In essence, therefore, Bush's legacy was a problematic one for the conservative movement. As he left office, it was still seeking a politically marketable answer to the question of what role government should play in the complex economy and society of the early twenty-first century.

In "Bush's Political Economy: Deficits, Debt, and Depression," Iwan Morgan examines presidential economic policy. Bush's legacy of recession, financial crisis, and massive public debt contrasted sharply with his own inheritance of prosperity and surplus budgets. While acknowledging that Bush cannot be held wholly or even mainly responsible for the woes of the economy, Morgan shows that his tax cuts failed to lay the promised foundations of sustained prosperity and resurrected the problem of huge budget deficits. Economic growth, therefore, became dependent on a real estate boom fuelled by cheap credit, but the bubble burst with disastrous consequences in 2007. Problematic in itself, Bush's economic legacy poses serious questions about the magic of the free market. Accordingly, his presidency could mark the end of the Age of Reagan rather than its consolidation and expansion, but such an outcome would depend on the capacity of his successor to affirm and institutionalize a more positive economic role for the state.

In "Bush's Partisan Legacy and the 2008 Elections," Philip John Davies examines Bush's failure to build a new Republican majority, one of his most cherished goals. GOP success seemed assured at the midpoint of his presidency, thanks in large part to the partisan benefits of the war on terror, but it rested on narrow foundations and proved short lived. In his second term, Bush's inept response to Hurricane Katrina and the unpopularity of his prolonged occupation of Iraq pulled down his approval ratings. This made him a drag on the congressional GOP, thereby contributing to its loss of control of both houses of Congress in 2006. The economic downturn, which accelerated the decline in Bush's poll ratings, then gave the Democrats the opportunity to regain control of the White House. The 2008 election was certainly no landslide of 1932 proportions but constituted a significant repudiation of the incumbent president and his party. As Davies notes, the irony of the Bush era in electoral terms was that aspirations of majority status evinced at its start by Republicans were voiced at its end by Democrats, a transformation that the forty-third president had inadvertently helped to bring about.

George W. Bush had taken office in 2001 in the unpromising circumstances of being the first president since 1888 to be elected without winning a popular-vote majority. Undeterred by this, he had no intention of pursuing a modest agenda because of doubts about his legitimacy. As Office of Management and Budget director Mitch Daniels correctly predicted in mid-2001, "It's not going to be a presidency of miniature gestures."[5] Soon afterward the terrorist attacks of 9/11 changed the context of American politics and public policy, thereby giving Bush the opportunity to become a transformative president along the lines of Franklin D. Roosevelt and Ronald Reagan. In the end, he fell well short of this ambition, in large part because of the consequences of his first-term recklessness. Whether or not his presidency is judged a failure, its significance cannot be doubted because it raised questions of deep importance for America's twenty-first century political development. As such Bush's record in office will be debated for years to come. Hopefully this volume can contribute usefully to that discussion and thereby confound Bush's insistence that history in the short term has no merit.

Notes

1. Karl Rove, "What Makes a Great President?" Address to the University of Utah's Rocco C. Siciliano Forum, November 12, 2002, http://hnn.us/

articles/1529.html; "The President's News Conference, January 12, 2009," in John T. Woolley and Gerhard Peters, *The American Presidency Project* (Santa Barbara: University of California), www.presidency.ucsb.edu
2. The cartoon by Ben Sargent appeared in the *Austin American-Statesman*, March 27, 2007. For reproduction and discussion of it, see Daniel Frick, *Reinventing Richard Nixon: A Cultural History of An American Obsession* (Lawrence: University Press of Kansas, 2008), 235–36.
3. Bob Woodward, *Bush at War* (New York: Simon and Schuster, 2002), 256; "Bush: 'I'm the Decider' on Rumsfeld," *CNN International*, April 19, 2006, http://edition.cnn.com/2006/POLITICS/04/18/rumsfeld
4. For particular examples of each school of thought, see Michael Lind, *Made in Texas: George W. Bush and the Southern Takeover of American Politics* (New York: Basic Books, 2003); Richard A. Viguerie, *Conservatives Betrayed: How George W. Bush and Other Big Government Republicans Hijacked the Conservative Cause* (Los Angeles: Bonus Books, 2006); Fred Barnes, *Rebel-in-Chief: Inside the Bold and Controversial Presidency of George W. Bush* (New York: Three Rivers Press, 2006); Max Boot, "Think Again: Neocons," *Foreign Policy*, January/February, 2004.
5. Quoted in Dan Balz, "Next on Bush's Agenda: Bigger Policy Changes," *Washington Post*, May 6, 2001, A1.

Chapter One

Rating Bush

Andrew Rudalevige

In the United States we like to "rate" a President. We measure him as "weak" or "strong" and call what we are measuring his "leadership." We do not wait until a man is dead; we rate him from the moment he takes office.[1]

So begins Richard Neustadt's classic 1960 book *Presidential Power*. Fifty years later, seeped as we are in a media-driven political culture devoted to the instant analysis of who's hot (and not)—to the "horse race," the "top ten list," and a proliferation of league tables—his emphasis seems more apt than ever. Efforts to rate and order presidencies have become something of a cottage industry in their own right.[2] Even pundits outside the United States have entered the field; in advance of "the world's most important general election" in 2008, the *Times* of London, in what might be considered a belated declaration of American dependence, put out a list of its own.[3]

Presidents themselves usually disavow the exercise. "You asked about legacy and all that business," Bush said in May 2008, "which I don't worry about, by the way. I'll be long gone before some smart person ever figures out what happened inside this Oval Office."[4] Still, even Bush had his preferred reference point for that "smart person" to use in framing judgment. That was Harry Truman, a president widely unloved by the electorate at the close of his term but one whose stock has risen steadily since, as his longer-term decisions seemed to bear fruit over time.

Others, though, suggested less flattering parallels—between Bush and Lyndon Johnson, say, with Iraq standing in for Vietnam, or between Bush's forceful promotion of democracy abroad, and the crusading internationalism of Woodrow Wilson.[5] And given that such widely varying analogies are all vaguely plausible, we can see why the editors of a recent volume entitled *Judging Bush* observed that "evaluating presidents is a notoriously hazardous and often sloppy enterprise."[6] Partly, as with the Truman analogy, this is a matter of timing and time horizons. Dwight Eisenhower, too, saw his rankings rise over time (in his case, to match his extant public popularity) as a fuller internal record of his presidency became available. Neustadt, for one, had downplayed Eisenhower's executive skills, but early judgments can mislead, even within a single individual's tenure in office. Indeed, the assessment of the Bush legacy at the start of 2005—as observers lauded the Republican majority realignment apparently achieved—contrasts rather sharply with the picture four years later.[7] If journalism is the first draft of history, we find ourselves now at best, in William Galston's useful phrase, "between journalism and history."[8]

The deeper problems with rankings, though, lie in the nature of the enterprise itself. They are inherent in the difficulty in choosing the right standards for measurement and in assigning credit or blame to isolated individuals in the separated system of American governance. What outcomes did George W. Bush personally effect? Which of those should receive more weight in our retrospective assessment? Can we give credit for a good decision, even if it had a bad outcome? And is a decision or outcome "bad" if it conflicts with a later code of morality or with a latter-day judge's ideological preferences? Wrapped up in these complications, ratings schemes have often foundered on the uncharted shoals of bias or causality.

Yet we cannot avoid using presidential ratings or creating our own, any more than Neustadt could: he ended the passage quoted at the outset with the assertion that "We are quite right to do so." In his view, the ratings task was necessary because the presidential office "has become the focal point of politics and policy in our political system."[9] That has hardly changed.

In fact, since Neustadt wrote these words, the importance of presidential performance to policy and polity has become only more acute. Presidents are at the center of the action, each potentially a hugely consequential force not just in American politics but in global politics as well (as the fact of the *Times* ranking concedes). We crave some assessment of their leadership. We are, indeed, compelled to make the attempt, if only to put to use the lessons learned. And since doubts about the utility of rankings will not deter partisans or pundits—nor for that matter history—from rating the Bush record, it is incumbent upon scholars to begin the process early on, by seeking to lay out transparent terms of reference and judgment.

What follows seeks to establish some of that groundwork. It describes some of the systems used by American historians and political scientists to rate presidents and rank them relative to one another, using such criteria as leadership qualities, accomplishments, political skills, and character. Then, by way of foreshadowing the wide range of issues covered in the remainder of this volume, it turns to George W. Bush. Upon what dimensions might his complex and consequential presidency be rated? How does he compare to his predecessors? Indeed, will he be seen as "Near Great"? "Average"? As "the worst president ever" (as historian Sean Wilentz has contentiously charged)?[10] Do these extremities coalesce around any sort of consensus? How should we decide how to decide, when rating the Bush presidency?

The Rating Game

In 1948, *Life* magazine published a survey of fifty-five historians conducted by Arthur M. Schlesinger Sr. The group had been asked to grade each American president on a scale that would soon become the industry standard, capitalization and all: as Great, Near Great, Average, Below Average, or as a Failure. Schlesinger repeated the exercise in 1962. Then, in 1996, a similar poll was conducted by his son, Arthur M. Schlesinger Jr., a well-known historian in his own right.[11]

Each iteration of the Schlesinger rankings received widespread attention. Each attracted both imitators and detractors. Indeed, the detractors often did the imitating, since they aimed to fix the shortcomings they saw in the rankings as presented.

One criticism assailed the very idea of making the fine distinctions that rankings imply. It is worth keeping in mind that the presidential incumbents are, almost to a person, outliers—located on the far positive reaches of any scale measuring American political aptitude and skill. This creates a problematic bell curve when they are isolated into a single population. We might see the top and bottom as clearly differentiable, but is there any meaningful gap in performance between someone ranked #15 and someone ranked #25 in such a small set of observations?

Still, more commonly critiques focused on the purported Democratic bias of the sample of academics consulted by both Schlesingers. To be sure, it is difficult to separate out one's ideological leanings or policy preferences from one's assessment of the quality of choices driven by ideological leanings and policy preferences. And since the Schlesingers chose partisan respondents, some argued, the result was skewed to favor left-leaning presidents who favored expansionist policies and activist government. To redress this, a 2000 poll sponsored by the Federalist Society and the *Wall Street Journal* aimed at "explicitly balanc[ing] the group to be surveyed with approximately equal numbers of experts on the left and the right," an exercise reprised by the *Journal* in 2005. Political scientist Alvin S. Felzenberg produced yet another ranking intended to avoid "the enduring limitation" caused by "bias on the part of the evaluators," this time at book length in time for the 2008 election.[12]

Other competing surveys focused their critiques instead on the grounds on which presidents were assessed. In the Schlesinger surveys, these were translucent. In fact Schlesinger Jr. argued that judgment was necessarily subjective—that historians, charged with grading greatness, had little choice but to follow Supreme Court Justice Potter Stewart's guide to defining pornography: "I know it when I see it."[13]

There is something intuitive to this, to be sure (and in certain administrations the link to Stewart's observation has been perhaps too close for comfort). But it nonetheless begs certain questions. Fred Greenstein, concerned that "presidential greatness... is a value judgment," went on to suggest that the concept was not empirical enough to usefully assess.[14] If this is too severe, his observation should at the very least compel us to be more transparent about what we value, and should value, in the realm of political leadership. Yet even then we must keep in mind that such values may change over time, politically if not morally and often both: the institution of slavery and the treatment of Native Americans, for two, loom rather nastily over the earlier presidents. The comparative salience of even less normative issues, as abetted by most raters' imperfect knowledge of American history—a quick read of past State of the Union messages suggests an array of crises now widely forgotten—also makes a difference for our accuracy in judging the past. As the novelist Thomas Hardy observed, "The figure at hand suffers on such occasions, because it shows up its sorriness without shade; while vague figures afar off are honored, in that their distance makes artistic virtues of their stains."[15] We constantly judge the past by the present, as well as the reverse.

Along these lines we must always recall that different presidents enter office under very distinct political circumstances, circumstances that expand or constrict the options available for presidential achievement. Bill Clinton moaned to his advisers that no one could be a great president without a war or other national emergency, a thought channeled by Obama chief of staff Rahm Emanuel a decade later when he urged his boss to "never waste a crisis."[16] William Lammers and Michael Genovese set "opportunity levels" as a crucial background variable in their comparative assessment of presidential leadership.[17]

More systematically, Stephen Skowronek (though he does not set out explicitly to rank presidents) notes that disruption is a near-perquisite for a presidential place in history. He has explored the role of "political time" in this dynamic, arguing that the meshing of a given president with prevailing policy coalitions leads to very different prospects for successful policy change. A president like Franklin Roosevelt, entering office during national economic crisis and with World War II on the horizon, with the opposition platform in disarray, has very different chances to reorder the polity than someone like Jimmy Carter, grafted to the tail end of a disintegrating Democratic realignment. Roosevelt is a president of "reconstruction," keeping company with Washington and Abraham Lincoln; Carter, like John Quincy Adams and Herbert Hoover, was able to achieve only "disjunction." These combinations of circumstances—of presidential opportunity tied to policy and electoral mandate—recur through time; history may not repeat itself, but (in Mark Twain's quip) "it rhymes." Accordingly, Skowronek's framework encompasses not only the "politics presidents make" but also the politics that make presidents.[18]

So in assessing presidents we must control for the times. But that very fact, interestingly, implies the importance of the individual as well. Consider: would Clinton, or Carter, automatically have become a great president—remembered as is FDR—if they had won election in 1932 instead of 1976 or 1992? Or were FDR's own personality and skill-set necessary, if not sufficient, resources for success in those troubled times? (And would FDR's skills, however considerable, have conquered Clinton's personally regretted lack of externally imposed crisis?[19] Moreover, would FDR be remembered so fondly had he left office after two terms with the Great Depression unconquered instead of carrying on to success as a war president?)

More broadly, then, even as we assume that the substantive and political setting matters to any individual president, we should seek to distinguish a particular incumbent from a generic alternative. What is the "value added" of having a specific person in the Oval Office, controlling for context? We can put the question in very tangible terms without casting too far back in history: how would the U.S. response to the September 11 terrorist attacks have differed had the Floridian butterfly ballot fluttered toward Democratic presidential candidate Al Gore? Comparing Gore versus Bush, we might assume that certain parts of history would have gone along similar lines, but that others would likely have diverged significantly. The variance represents the Bush difference.

Such queries require counterfactual speculation, of course, and despite the best efforts of sophisticated statistical simulations, we cannot rerun history with a new presidential variable plugged into our predictive equation. Even if we could, we would run into another methodological road-block: the all-too-frequent assumption of presidential *causation*, when the only relationship between a president and an event is *correlation*. As Donald Rumsfeld famously briefed, "Stuff happens"—but the fact of its happening during a president's term does not mean the president made it happen. There is a wide range of governmental outputs, and outcomes, though not all of them attributable to presidential action even if he did in fact prefer that outcome.

All this should encourage us to seek nuance, to be as cautious about our causal claims and evidence as we would be in a more obviously empirical exercise. For one, we should focus on the skills and traits brought to bear by individual presidents against the historical backdrop to their administration. Works like Fred Greenstein's *The Presidential Difference* aim at just this. Greenstein rates the modern presidents on six scales, incorporating (1) communications skills; (2) organizational skills; (3) political skills; (4) policy vision; (5) cognitive style (dealing less with IQ than with the ability to take in and process complex arguments and information); and (6) emotional intelligence.[20] Felzenberg, who is more overtly concerned than Greenstein to rank presidents against each other, takes a like approach but with quite different tests. He grades presidents on their vision, character, and competence—"the ability of a president to achieve his policy objectives and to respond effectively to unforeseen events"—as well as on the substance of those policy achievements, in the economic and national security arenas and in the realm of "preserving and extending liberty."[21] Each incumbent received a mark from one (failure) to five (excellent) in each area, and the aggregate of the grades then produced an overall set of rankings. Against their backdrop of "opportunity levels," Lammers and Genovese likewise assess leadership styles and skills across four dimensions: advisory processes, administrative strategies, public leadership, and congressional relations.[22]

These individual judgments dovetail in method with the large-sample 2000 and 2009 "President's Day" surveys conducted by the cable television public affairs network C-SPAN. Rather than asking for a single mark of "great," "near great," and so on, along the "know it when you see it" axis, the 2009 version asked sixty-five scholars of the presidency to grade all forty-two individuals who have served as president[23] on no fewer than ten "attributes of leadership." These cut across a wide range of areas encompassing not only skills and policy arenas but also perceptions: public persuasion, crisis leadership, economic management, moral authority, international relations, administrative skills, relations with Congress, vision/agenda setting, "pursuing equal justice for all," and broad "performance within context of the times."[24]

Yet another taxonomy comes from the editors of the recent volume entitled *Judging Bush*. Surveying the rankings literature in some depth, they prioritize different aspects of competence, expressed through policymaking, political skills and organization, character, and opportunity level. Four types of competence are proposed: (1) strategic; (2) political; (3) tactical; and (4) moral. The first refers to a president's influence on the polity over the long term, in a policy sense, while "political" competence is reserved for his ability to reshape the electoral regime in the older sense of realignment theory. Tactical competence assesses the president's ability (supported by his staff organizations) to make informed and rational decisions, and his administration's ability to carry out governmental duties and processes. "Moral" competence, finally, is both negative and positive—indicated by a given administration's ability to avoid scandal, but also by its proactive general trustworthiness.[25]

All of these categorical approaches invite us to consider not only the multiple skills required for success in the job but also the multiple dimensions to any presidency. How do we feel about personal behavior, for instance, as opposed to the content of that person's public policy? Should we judge a president on his skills, or on the ends to what those skills are put?

As Felzenberg notes, apropos of the *Judging Bush* approach, "a president can be extraordinarily competent in some aspects of their [sic] job and extraordinarily incompetent in others."[26] Woodrow Wilson promoted freedom and self-determination abroad—but not for African Americans at home. Lyndon Johnson had immense legislative achievements in domestic policy and civil rights—only to see them drown in the Gulf of Tonkin. Nixon went to China, but his men went to the Watergate. As Bill Clinton left office, two-thirds of Americans approved of his performance as president—but three-quarters also thought he "lack[ed] high moral or ethical standards."[27]

Providing a series of categories allows presidential raters to make some distinctions along these lines, allowing us to praise Johnson's commitment to voting rights while decrying his decision to escalate in Vietnam. Indeed, the very decision process that determines which categories "count" is useful in making transparent both our expectations of the office and what we value in political life.

But in itself this does not relieve us of the burden of judgment. While there is undeniable value in forcing transparency of assumption and assessment, as with any quantitative test the utility of the results hinges on the quality of the questions. Remember that ratings across a long list of categories that are compacted, equally weighted, into a single score, assume that each category is of equal importance—both across a presidency, and across time. Does "performance within the context of the times" have the same value as "administrative skills" or "relations with Congress" (indeed, does the former subsume the others in any case?) Do "economic management" and "moral authority" count simply as two equivalent questions on a multipart exam? Should a bad television presence cancel out a good nuclear crisis? It is more satisfying to rank across different dimensions; but if each category is equally weighted, in mathematical terms the result may be equivalent to the less formal calculation of overall "greatness." Indeed, the latter may allow for a more realistic mental weighting across the categories that integrates historical context more thoroughly. Marc Landy and Sidney Milkis have a short and sweet assessment: whether the president transforms how Americans view their government entails winning a "struggle for its constitutional soul."[28] You know that, presumably, when you feel it.

The Bottom Line

Despite all these complexities and caveats, the various rankings correlate quite closely, especially (perhaps, again, reflecting the tight distribution of presidential talent) at the top and bottom of the lists.

As table 1.1 show, the "best" presidents are almost inevitably comprised of some ordering of George Washington, Abraham Lincoln, and Franklin Roosevelt, with Thomas Jefferson and Theodore Roosevelt normally close behind. These are the contenders for the political equivalent of Olympic gold. The worst—those who never get beyond the rear of the field—include some combination of Franklin Pierce, James Buchanan, Warren Harding, Andrew Johnson, and Richard Nixon. Ronald Reagan, whose poor showing (#25) in the 1996 Schlesinger poll prompted outrage from conservatives, appears at #8 in the 2000 Federalist Society/*WSJ* iteration. Yet

Table 1.1 Selected Rankings in Presidential Surveys, 1962–2008

Rank	Schlesinger, Sr. 1962	Schlesinger, Jr. 1996	Federalist Society 2000	C-SPAN 2009
Top Six	Lincoln	Lincoln	Washington	Lincoln
	Washington	Washington	Lincoln	Washington
	F. Roosevelt	F. Roosevelt	Washington	F. Roosevelt
	Wilson	Jefferson	Jefferson	T. Roosevelt
	Jefferson	Jackson	T. Roosevelt	Truman
	Jackson	T. Roosevelt	Jackson	Kennedy
The Next Four	T. Roosevelt	Wilson	Truman	Jefferson
	Polk	Truman	Reagan	Eisenhower
	Truman	Polk	Eisenhower	Wilson
	J. Adams	Eisenhower	Polk	Reagan
Bottom Four	Pierce	Nixon	A. Johnson	Harrison
	Buchanan	A. Johnson	Pierce	Pierce
	Grant	Buchanan	Harding	A. Johnson
	Harding	Harding	Buchanan	Buchanan

overall the two surveys have a rather astonishing correlation of 0.94 (where 1.00 would mean identical data).[29] The C-SPAN version also varies little, elevating John F. Kennedy into the top six but otherwise proving quite similar to the Schlesinger and Federalist Society takes. Felzenberg's individualized take is more idiosyncratic, with his grading curved to a wide conception of personal freedoms—both in the sense of civil liberties and in promoting unfettered economic competition—that upgrades presidents like Reagan (tied for third), U.S. Grant (seventh), and Calvin Coolidge (twelfth) and punishes FDR (sixth), Jefferson (fourteenth), and especially Andrew Jackson (twenty-seventh). But even here Lincoln is still first, and Buchanan last.[30]

Rating Bush

And so we come to the forty-third president. George W. Bush has appeared, to date, in only one of these surveys—the 2009 C-SPAN historians' poll, taken one month after he left office. There, Bush was rated a rather dismal thirty-sixth of forty-two. This is far below the recent presidents he tried hardest not to be, including his father, George H. W. Bush (#18), and Bill Clinton (#15)—as well as those he did want to be, such as Ronald Reagan (#10) and the nineteenth-century Republican realigner, William McKinley (#16).[31]

This may be the first word but it hardly seems likely to be the last. If Bush's late-term invocation of Truman had a desperate ring about it, it is nonetheless true that time horizons matter and future perceptions of the past will change. Even more crucial is the sort of analysis called for above—a weighting, rather than a simple averaging, of the components of presidential leadership in the context of history. Interestingly, as noted earlier, the C-SPAN poll asked respondents to gauge presidents across ten different categories of leadership. With the financial system left in turmoil, thirteen-digit federal deficits, and unemployment rates brushing double digits, one might not expect a high mark in, say, economic management (where he came in at number 40.) But Bush was also ranked in the bottom half of all presidents in every other category, peaking in the mid-20s in the categories of "Vision/Setting an Agenda," "Pursued Equal Justice for All," and "Crisis Leadership."

These categories show why even breaking down ratings into clearer dimensions can be problematic in practice. After all, few accused Bush of having no vision, though many intensely disliked that vision. Crisis leadership depends in part on how one defines the terms of- and perhaps crucially, the duration of—a crisis. Does "equal justice for all" extend only to oppressed minorities, or also to suspected terrorists? And so on. Even in the arena of economic management it is hard to declare with certainty that only Herbert Hoover and James Buchanan did worse than Bush, given the various Panics and Crashes that punctuated eighteenth- and nineteenth-century American history. The categories force a black and white judgment where grays and shadows abound.

Indeed, the full picture is complex, and sometimes paradoxical. Bush was a big-government conservative, an MBA "decider" trapped in a White House echo-chamber, a "uniter" who polarized the nation and the world. He was a president who could be both eloquent and incomprehensible, a would-be party-builder who scored rare personal triumphs in the 2002 midterms but was barely invited to his party's 2008 national convention. He alienated members of Congress who nonetheless voted again and again to enact his wishes (and failed to vote to overturn his unilateral actions). He was personally compassionate but nourished blinkered ideological factions that defeated some of his important proposals. He pushed policies with both big costs and potentially big benefits—but whose benefits and costs were not assessed simultaneously.

As noted earlier, some observers see Bush as an utter failure; others see him as consequential, if flawed; still others deem him a paragon of moral clarity who boldly "earned his Great President badge."[32] And given the shifts of policy across the two Bush terms—take, for instance, the case of North Korea—no single conclusion can stand for the whole. We might appropriately (though neither man would likely appreciate the comparison) be put in mind of another American "W," the poet Walt Whitman. "Do I contradict myself?" Whitman wrote. "Very well then I contradict myself (I am large, I contain multitudes)."[33] The Bush administration, too, contained multitudes, not all of which are even visible yet: because policies take time to work themselves out, and because the administration *was* consistent in its desire to avoid oversight and act on its own discretion.

Where does this leave us, in our efforts? We might start to extricate ourselves with a tally sheet of sorts. The Bush record is extensive, and some of it has been overshadowed by the glare from Iraq and the war on terror. A straightforward list may make the point best: whether or not one agrees with the direction or substance of any given policy change, each is undeniably consequential.

Thus, during his term, Bush achieved:

- Major revisions of the tax code, with separate tax-cutting legislation passed in each of his first six years in office;
- Major education policy changes, in the No Child Left Behind Act that reauthorized the Elementary and Secondary Education Act and, later, in the reauthorization of the Higher Education Act;
- A major expansion of a signature Democratic "Great Society" initiative, adding prescription drug coverage to the Medicare health insurance program for the elderly;
- Two justices confirmed to seats on the U.S. Supreme Court, along with three hundred and fifty additional judges also holding lifetime appointments to other levels of the federal bench;
- Promotion of the Partial Birth Abortion Ban and its successful defense before the Supreme Court, as well as the issuance of an executive order preventing most federal funding for stem-cell research;
- A large-scale AIDS relief and antimalaria program, especially in Africa, as well as disaster relief after the 2004 Boxing Day tsunami and a broad restructuring of foreign assistance programs generally into the Millennium Development Corporation;
- A quadrupling of the number of countries with which the United States has free-trade agreements;

- A massive bank bailout bill in the wake of the near-collapse of the financial system toward the end of his term;
- The largest changes to the federal bureaucracy since the passage of the National Security Act of 1947—namely creation of the Department of Homeland Security and, with enactment of the Intelligence Reform Act, the office of Director of National Intelligence;
- Implementation of the "President's Management Agenda," and changes to extant centralized regulatory review procedures, so as to tighten White House control over that bureaucracy;
- Two iterations of the Patriot Act that greatly broadened federal law enforcement power;
- Amendments to the Foreign Intelligence Surveillance Act, enhancing presidential discretion to conduct surveillance of terror suspects;
- The Military Commissions Act, which (until partially revised by a Supreme Court decision) made important changes endorsing the president's approach to the mechanisms for detaining and trying detainees in the war on terror, notably those held at Guantanamo Bay, Cuba;
- A landmark nuclear cooperation agreement with India and agreement with Libya to end its nuclear research;
- Withdrawal from the Anti-Ballistic Missile (ABM) treaty regime;
- Overthrow of the Taliban regime in Afghanistan and Saddam Hussein's regime in Iraq, with national elections subsequently held in both countries. In February 2009, as Bush left office, 84 percent of Iraqis polled responded that their localized security conditions were at least "quite good," nearly double the response as recently as August 2007.[34]

That last item should perhaps be taken to include the generous legislative grants of power that authorized the president's response to the September 11 attacks (a measure that cannot be read as limited to Afghanistan), and the "preauthorization" of the Iraq war approved by Congress in October 2002. And along those lines, we must also note the item that tops the Bush administration's own listing of its record in its "legacy booklet," published by the White House at the end of 2008: namely, that "for more than seven years after September 11, 2001, [Bush] prevented another attack on our homeland."[35] (The use of the active voice here, of course, gets to some of the ambiguities of causality discussed earlier. But the basic point is a simple fact.)

The list should also probably account for the things that Congress did *not* do, especially with regard to Bush's aggressive use of unilateral action to achieve policy preferences without the tedious "process" in which legislators delight. (When Congress did act on such matters, as with the Military Commissions Act, it tended to endorse presidential actions rather than check them.) It may be enough to note that when the 108th Congress adjourned in December 2004, Bush became the first full-term president in 175 years not to have vetoed a single bill. That no-veto streak would eventually stretch past five years, into 2006, before the return of a Democratic majority to Capitol Hill ratcheted up interbranch conflict. But when asked at a midadministration press conference about using the veto to curb spending, the president sounded bemused: "they passed bills that met our budget targets. And so how could you veto...if the Congress has done what you've asked them to do?"[36] How indeed? Bush and a steadfast Republican leadership in Congress, especially in the House, showed that a firm grip on the legislative and public agendas can produce meaningful policy change.

Despite all this, after the 2006 elections—with two full years left in his term—Bush was treated as the lamest of lame ducks, and as early as the fall of 2007 magazine covers (in this case the *Atlantic*) began to trumpet feature stories detailing the "Lessons of a Failed Presidency." After all, immediately prior to the 2008 election, more than nine in ten Americans felt that the country was "on the wrong track."[37] Bush left office with a 22 percent approval rating; a national poll conducted for NBC News and the *Wall Street Journal* a month after the election, when public sympathy for an outgoing incumbent often kicks in, found that two-thirds of Americans still disapproved of what Bush was doing. In the poll, large majorities criticized Bush's handling of the economy, foreign policy, and the Iraq war—only 18 percent of respondents said they "were going to miss him" when he left office. Asked about Bush's greatest successes in office, a plurality of 35 percent noted the lack of terrorist attacks within the United States since September 2001, and 25 percent the removal of Saddam Hussein from office in Iraq. But the third-place finisher, the only other answer to receive double-digit support, was not even on the list read out by the pollsters. This is because that answer—volunteered by 17 percent of respondents—was "none."

Not unrelated to this, nearly half of those asked said that Bush would be remembered as "definitely worst than most" of the recent presidents and another 30 percent said he would be remembered as "not as good as most." Just 2 percent said he was "one of the very best."[38] Editorial cartoons at the end of the term tended to serve as quick visual shorthand of this conventional wisdom.[39]

This negativity, of course, reflected a less positive list of large-scale events on the administration's watch, some of them the flip side of the achievements tallied above. For instance,

- The violent bursting of two bubbles, in housing prices and speculative banking, with the near-collapse of the financial markets and the regulatory regime (the Standard and Poor's 500 stock index was at 1,342 when Bush took office and at 850 when he left. Much of this decline was back-loaded: investment indices declined by 40 percent or more in 2008);
- The dubious use of unilateral powers to, at worst, undermine the rule of law, including the designation of U.S. citizens as enemy combatants; de facto suspension of habeas corpus; the installation of military tribunals to try these and other "enemy combatants"; the use of domestic wiretapping surveillance without judicial warrant, in contravention of statute; and the use of rendition and aggressive interrogation techniques that in the eyes of many amounted to torture;[40]
- Little substantive attention to global warming, or (despite high-profile rhetoric) to energy independence issues, and administrative actions that actually forestalled such efforts;
- Failure to achieve stated major administration priorities such as Social Security reform, restructuring of the tax system, or revamping immigration;
- A shift from the FY2001 budget surplus of $127 billion (1.3 percent GDP) inherited by the administration to massive annual budget deficits and a concomitant increase in the public debt from 33.1 percent GDP in FY2001 to a projected 65 percent GDP ten years later;
- A secrecy regime that prevented the public disclosure of public records;
- Failure to capture or kill Osama bin Laden;
- Failure to deter Iranian or North Korean efforts to continue their nuclear programs;
- Failure to anticipate or adequately respond to the destruction of much of the city of New Orleans (and of large swaths of the Gulf Coast generally) by Hurricane Katrina in the autumn of 2005;
- The elephant in the room, or rather the desert: Iraq. According to the Brookings Institution's "Iraq Index," as of July 2009, Operation Iraqi Freedom has cost some $653 billion,[41] as well

as the lives of 4,300 American troops, 9,100 Iraqi military and police personnel, and more than 100,000 Iraqi civilians; 142,000 U.S. troops remained in Iraq at the end of the Bush presidency, nearly 70 months after the infamous "mission accomplished" declaration of May 1, 2003. The 2007 "surge" was a success, in that it depressed the level of violence across Iraq; whether Iraqis took advantage of that space to reach the political accommodation needed for longer-term security is an open question.

Much future judgment of the Bush administration rests on developments in this last arena. Balancing the costs and benefits of the Iraq invasion is, of course, an ongoing exercise. But that analysis seems to have been neglected by the upper echelons of the administration itself: the lack of attention to the needs of the occupation phase of the mission, and the selective use of attractive intelligence to justify a predetermined conclusion, are well-documented.[42]

This links to another charge that appears to have some validity: that Bush received a suboptimal flow of information and advice, shielded from real-world events and opinions by a comfortable "bubble" of yes-men (and women) and handpicked audiences. This was amplified by the administration's aggressive, and effective, politicization of the executive branch. Perhaps the abiding emblem of this combination became his congratulatory exhortation to Federal Emergency Management Agency director Michael Brown, who had come to FEMA from the International Arabian Horse Association without a background in emergency management. "Brownie," said the president, "you're doing a heck of a job."[43] The residents of the Gulf Coast, and ultimately of the United States, begged to differ.

Final Thoughts: The Easy Way Out?

Reading even this partial, contradictory tally sheet should remind readers of the complications involved in rating a presidential record. The raw material must be refined by assessing questions of causality and responsibility; of the appropriate length of the apt time horizons; of the difficult calculation of costs versus benefits at various points as policies proceed; and, again, of the need to weight, not just average, an administration's achievements and demerits.

Those tasks burden the chapters that follow. Here I will merely return to a point stressed earlier, that our presidential ratings must come from standards that define the value we place on values. How we reach collective judgment says as much about us as about a given president. As James Pfiffner has argued, "It matters much less how we rank a president, than that we deliberate about which important values we ought to use to understand our past and shape our future."[44] I would suggest several guidelines for so doing. We should ask how, for instance, an administration's commitments matched up with the resources made available to implement them. How did the opportunities taken compare to the opportunity costs they incurred? And how does the short term stack up against the long?—for surely one's political legacy must be intertwined with, if not equivalent to, the legacy left to future generations.

If these are the right questions, they suggest at least a preliminary means of sorting and sieving the jumbled Bush record. To wit—perhaps ironically, given his administration's stated faith in the redemptive verdicts of future historians—the Bush record may come to be seen as a model of short-term success at the cost of long-term sustainability. Too often the president achieved impressive immediate results, only to see those very tactical gains undermine strategic progress. If the president had something his father lacked—the "vision thing," in spades—the "prudence" gene that might have institutionalized that vision seems to have skipped a generation.

In the electoral arena, for instance, notable early gains that produced the first unified Republican government since the 1950s were swept away in 2006 and 2008: the GOP realignment so devoutly sought by Karl Rove was swept away with it. Part of the problem was perhaps that others close to the president (Vice President Dick Cheney, for one) cared little about that goal; but the larger issue was surely that, in the face of a profound desire for national unity spurred by the 9/11 attacks on New York and Washington, the administration "put terrorism and war to work in an electoral rather than a historical context," using them to drive wedges rather than build a new and lasting coalition.[45] Policy commitments, too, were entered into without sufficient scrutiny of their spillover effects. President Bush's version of the unitary executive, in which dissent was taken for disloyalty, and in which contempt for Congress construed consultation as weakness, exacerbated matters. The manipulation of partisan polarization provided, at first, electoral and roll call majorities, but it had diminishing returns.[46] Ignoring the uses of soft power wound up making it harder to utilize hard power, across the branches of government and across the oceans; moral high ground has, after all, tangible uses.

This suggests a sort of myopia that will puzzle future raters of the Bush record. In President Bush's January 2009 farewell address, he noted that while "you may not agree with some tough decisions I have made...I hope you can agree that I was willing to make the tough decisions."[47] Yet if 9 percent of federal spending is now required simply to pay the interest on the national debt, have not those tough decisions in fact been deferred to a future generation? It is easier to cut taxes and increase spending rather than the reverse; it is easier to delegate powers to the president's unilateral discretion than to deliberate on the proper scope of those powers and the ends they might achieve. It is easier to prevent debate than to allow it, easier to demonize than to deliberate, easier to stop opponents from participating than to risk their upsetting your priorities. It is easier to declare a war of "us" versus "them," rather than to persuade them to be us. And frankly, it is easier to torture evil people than to allow them to remain spitefully silent.

President Bush was hardly the "worst president ever," with all that implies. He was hardly alone in favoring short-term over long-term gains: in so doing he probably accurately reflected his times, and our culture. Yet if, as Michael Genovese concludes, the ultimate task for a president is to "do good,"[48] living up to that obligation requires making truly tough decisions and engaging in persuasion as well as pronouncement. Indeed, taking the easy way out makes the job harder—not for future raters but, far more importantly, for future presidents.

Notes

1. Richard E. Neustadt, *Presidential Power* (New York: Wiley, 1960), 3.
2. For a helpful survey of what is available, see Meena Bose, "Presidential Ratings: Lessons and Liabilities," in Meena Bose and Mark Landis, eds., *The Uses and Abuses of Presidential Ratings* (New York: Nova Science, 2003), 3–26.
3. Abraham Lincoln finished on top. Jeremy Griffin and Nico Hines, "Who's the Greatest? The *Times* US Presidential Ranking," *Times*, October 28, 2008, http://www.timesonline.co.uk/tol/news/world/us_and_americas/us_elections/article5030539.ece (Accessed June 24, 2009).
4. From an interview with the Israeli media, May 12, 2008, http://www.haaretz.com/hasen/spages/982914.html (Accessed June 18, 2009). Skeptics might note that the Bush administration's devotion to secrecy might make that smart person's job the more difficult.
5. See Colin Campbell, Bert Rockman, and Andrew Rudalevige, "Introduction: Legacies and Leadership in Context," in Campbell, Rockman, and Rudalevige, eds., *The George W. Bush Legacy* (Washington DC: CQ Press, 2008), 1–20.

6. Neil Reedy and Jeremy Johnson, "Presidential Greatness Reconsidered," in Robert Maranto, Tom Lansford, and Jeremy Johnson, eds., *Judging Bush* (Stanford CA: Stanford University Press, 2009).
7. See, for example, Michael Nelson, "George W. Bush: Majority President," in Nelson, ed., *The Elections of 2004* (Washington DC: CQ Press, 2005), 2.
8. William A. Galston, "Between Journalism and History: Evaluating George W. Bush's Presidency," in Maranto, Lansford, and Johnson, *Judging Bush*, 273–93.
9. Neustadt, *Presidential Power*, 3.
10. Sean Wilentz, "The Worst President in History?" *Rolling Stone*, April 21, 2006.
11. An expanded version of the last study, with citations to its predecessors, is Arthur Schlesinger, Jr., "Rating the Presidents: Washington to Clinton," *Political Science Quarterly*, 112, Summer 1997, 179–90.
12. James Lindgren, "Ranking Our Presidents: How Did 78 Scholars Decide How to Rank the Presidents from Washington to Clinton?" (Washington DC: Federalist Society, November 16, 2000), http://falcon.arts.cornell.edu/govt/courses/F04/PresidentialRankings.pdf (Accessed June 5, 2009); Alvin S. Felzenberg, *The Leaders We Deserved (And a Few We Didn't): Rethinking the Presidential Rating Game* (New York: Basic Books, 2008), 3; and see also Felzenberg, "'There You Go Again': Liberal Historians and *The New York Times* Deny Ronald Reagan His Due," *Policy Review*, 82, March/April 1997.
13. Schlesinger, Jr., "Rating the Presidents," 179; and see *Jacobellis v. Ohio*, 378 US 184 (1964).
14. Quoted in James P. Pfiffner, "Ranking the Presidents: Continuity and Volatility," in Bose and Landis, *Uses and Abuses*, 27.
15. Thomas Hardy, *Tess of the d'Urbervilles*, Chapter 39; Schlesinger, Jr., similarly noted that "presidents sometimes do more for the reputation of their predecessors than they do for their own." See "Rating the Presidents," 183.
16. Clinton quoted in Dick Morris, *Behind the Oval Office* (New York: Random House, 1997), 307–8; Emanuel quoted in Mike Dorning, "Rahm Emanuel: President's Chief of Staff Has Lost None of His Drive," *Chicago Tribune*, April 26, 2009, http://www.chicagotribune.com/news/politics/obama/chi-rahm-emanuel-26-apr26,0,4148537.story (Accessed July 3, 2009).
17. William W. Lammers and Michael A. Genovese, *The Presidency and Domestic Policy: Comparing Leadership Styles, FDR to Clinton* (Washington DC: CQ Press, 2000).
18. Stephen Skowronek, *The Politics Presidents Make*, 2nd ed. (Cambridge MA: Harvard University Press, 1997).
19. Clinton, of course, created his own crisis as partial compensation.
20. Fred I. Greenstein, *The Presidential Difference: Leadership Style from FDR to George W. Bush*, 2nd ed. (Princeton: Princeton University Press, 2004).

21. Felzenberg, *Leaders We Deserved*, 109.
22. William W. Lammers and Michael A. Genovese, *The Presidency and Domestic Policy: Comparing Leadership Styles, FDR to Clinton* (Washington DC: CQ Press, 2000).
23. Recall that Grover Cleveland served two separate terms, thereby making Bush the forty-third president ("43," to distinguish him from his father, "Bush 41.")
24. http://www.c-span.org/PresidentialSurvey/Overall-Ranking.aspx (Accessed June 24, 2009).
25. Reedy and Johnson, "Presidential Greatness Reconsidered," in Maranto, Lansford, and Johnson, *Judging Bush*.
26. Felzenberg, *Leaders We Deserved*, 111.
27. Gary Langer, "Poll: Good Job by the Bad-Boy President Shows Wide Split along Professional, Personal Lines," *ABC News*, January 17, 2001, http://abcnews.go.com/sections/politics/dailynews/poll_clintonlegacy010117.html (Accessed July 16, 2009).
28. Marc Landy and Sidney M. Milkis, *Presidential Greatness* (Lawrence: University Press of Kansas, 2000).
29. See Lindgren, "Ranking our Presidents," 4 (note 7). This figure varies depending on how Schlesinger's categories are translated mathematically. Standardizing those categories so that each is separated by one point gives a correlation of .956 and an r^2 of .913.
30. Felzenberg, *Leaders We Deserved*, 378.
31. Regarding Reagan see, for example, Lou Cannon and Carl M. Cannon, *Reagan's Disciple: George W. Bush's Troubled Quest for a Presidential Legacy* (New York: PublicAffairs, 2008) and regarding McKinley, see Joshua Green, "The Rove Presidency," *Atlantic* (September 2007), 60.
32. David Gelernter, "Bush's Greatness," *Weekly Standard* 10, September 13, 2004.
33. Whitman, *Complete Poetry and Collected Prose* (New York: Library of America, 1982), 246.
34. Brookings Institution, *Iraq Index*, July 16, 2009, 49. The index is compiled from numerous sources and updated by Michael E. O'Hanlon and Jason H. Campbell, http://www.brookings.edu/saban/~/media/Files/Centers/Saban/Iraq%20Index/index.pdf (Accessed August 15, 2009).
35. *Highlights of Accomplishments and Results: The Administration of George W. Bush, 2001–2009* (Washington, DC: White House, 2009), 39, http://georgewbush-whitehouse.archives.gov/infocus/bushrecord/documents/legacybooklet.pdf (Accessed August 15, 2009).
36. "Presidents Holds Press Conference," Office of the White House Press Secretary, December 20, 2004.
37. See *New York Times*/CBS poll results, http://documents.nytimes.com/latest-new-york-times-cbs-news-poll#p=1 (Accessed June 18, 2009).
38. Hart/McInturff, *Survey #6091* conducted for NBC News/*Wall Street Journal* (Washington, DC: December 5–8, 2008), Questions 3, 4a, 4b, 4c, 4d, 26, 27, 28a.

39. A broad selection may be found at http://www.cartoonistgroup.com/bysubject/subject.php?sid=245 (Accessed July 16, 2009).
40. See Jane Mayer, *The Dark Side* (New York: Doubleday, 2008); James P. Pfiffner, *Power Play: The Bush Presidency and the Constitution* (Washington DC: Brookings Institution Press, 2008).
41. Note that White House economic adviser Lawrence Lindsey was fired in 2002, at least in part for suggesting that the Iraq War might cost between $100 and $200 billion; the administration maintained instead that Iraq, through oil revenues, would pay for its own liberation.
42. See, for example, James P. Pfiffner, "Intelligence and Decision-Making before the War in Iraq," in George C. Edwards III and Desmond King, eds., *The Polarized Presidency of George W. Bush* (Oxford: Oxford University Press, 2007), 213–42.
43. "President Arrives in Alabama, Briefed on Hurricane Katrina," Office of the White House Press Secretary, September 2, 2005.
44. Pfiffner, "Ranking the Presidents."
45. Joshua Green, "The Rove Presidency," *Atlantic,* September 2007, 72.
46. See Andrew Rudalevige, "Diminishing Returns: George W. Bush and Congress, 2001–08," in Maranto, Lansford, and Johnson, *Judging Bush*.
47. George W. Bush, "Farewell Address to Nation," January 15, 2009, in John T. Woolley and Gerhard Peters, *The American Presidency Project* (Santa Barbara: University of California), www.presidency.ucsb.edu
48. Michael A. Genovese, *Memo to a New President: The Art and Science of Presidential Leadership* (New York: Oxford University Press, 2008), 219–20. Genovese proposes asking whether a given policy resonates with the "touchstone documents of our nation," from the Declaration of Independence to the Four Freedoms.

Chapter Two

Bush's Style of Presidential Leadership

Nigel Bowles

> I believe the President's job is to confront problems, not to pass them on to future Presidents and future generations. That's the job of a leader. That's how I have led, and that's how I will continue to lead.
> —George W. Bush, "Remarks at a Victory 2004 Luncheon in Bridgeton, Missouri," May 14, 2004

What does George W. Bush's style of presidential leadership—his orientation to office and his framing, ordering, and taking of decisions—disclose about his presidency? I approach the question through a simplified version of Richard Neustadt's framework for the analysis of presidential leadership by consideration of his authority, professional reputation, sense of purpose, and temperament. Documentary records that are relevant and available are thin. Accordingly, we work with what we have: the president's public statements, which are available electronically from the *American Presidency Project* Web site (hosted by the University of California, Santa Barbara); newspapers and magazines; the memoirs of participants; the records of journalists; and secondary academic literature.

Neustadt argues that a president's "effective influence," or his "power," derives from three related sources. The first comprises the president's bargaining advantages that offer the possibility of his persuading others in the so-called Washington community that what he wants them to do is what they ought in any case to do for their own reasons. The second concerns the expectations that those people have about his capacities and his will to use the various advantages that they believe him to have. And the third entails those people's judgments of how voters regard him and of how they may regard their legislators if they do what he wants. Among the advantages that Neustadt argues that a president has are his "human qualities," a "sense of purpose," and a "feel for power," conditioned by sources of "confidence, itself fashioned from experience and temperament."[1]

Authority

Neustadt distinguished between formal "powers" (authority), "professional reputation" within the Washington Community of presidency watchers, and "prestige" or public support. He defined power as "personal influence of an effective sort on governmental action," differentiating it from the "formal 'powers' vested in the Presidency" by constitution, law, or custom. He insisted upon the need to be "meticulous about distinguishing personal influence from constituted authority," and considered the presidency's limitations in authority so pronounced that "weak" was its fundamental and primary descriptor.[2]

Would Neustadt have drawn an inference comparably broad or strong had he or a successor analyst within his intellectual tradition relied for evidence on the presidential style of President George W. Bush? Can the claim that the presidency is "weak in authority" be sustained in the early twenty-first century? President Bush pressed relentlessly to surmount not just constitutional constraints upon executive authority's scope and exercise, but also statutory ones. His pressure upon both changed policy and politics, not least in strengthening congressional and public doubts about the utility and acceptability of the use of military force in Iraq, the torture of suspects, and extensive surveillance of American citizens. Acceptable or not, effective or not, the president's actions for three reasons were revolutionary neither in scope nor effect. First, a president's executive order is open to being modified or even formally revoked, as President Barack Obama showed by his actions on his first day in office. Second, irrespective of whether a president's use of authority is contentious, its results may damage his professional reputation at home and abroad—as President Bush discovered. Third, partly in consequence of the second, Bush's successors are constrained to act in light of knowledge of the costs to him of his use of authority. That use embraces not only abuse of authority during his presidency but his failure to draw upon ample reserves of lawful authority to bring the full force of presidential assistance to bear immediately upon the human disaster that Hurricane Katrina caused. In security policy, President Bush laid claim to Article II powers that the framers did not grant; in the major emergency that devastated thousands of lives in Louisiana, he failed to use such powers that constitution and statute did grant him. Most of what follows in this section is concerned with expansive claims in the first category of cases rather than with his inertia in the second. But the contrast matters for revealing that Bush's stance toward authority was both instrumental and a matter of expedient calculation.

In security policy, Bush conducted himself with a view to challenging the constraints that the separation of powers imposes upon presidents. If "revolutionary" exaggerates, "expansive" does not. There is in Bush's leadership style toward security matters a Caesarist impulse, if not a Caesarist transformation of the presidential office. He attempted to effect major changes by the contestable and contested use of formal authority in his abrogation of the Anti-Ballistic Missile Treaty; by Executive Order 13223, limiting the disclosure of presidential records; by extending the president's claim of executive privilege with respect to Department of Justice records about FBI corruption; by his support for Attorney General John Ashcroft's policy advising federal agencies to limit to the fullest extent possible the disclosure of information pursuant to freedom of information requests; by Executive Order 13292, delaying the release of certain classified documents granting the government expanded authority to reclassify documents previously released.[3]

Bush's presidential style of action in security policy nevertheless comports with two secular developments that affected the constitutional powers of the presidency: first, the spirit of expanded executive claims of inherent authority apparent since Truman sought in 1950 to extend the authority granted him in Article II; and second, the nearly parallel inclination of the U.S. Congress to fail to do what Article I requires of it. Nothing in what Bush attempted would have surprised Neustadt, partly because he had observed Richard Nixon's dispositions toward opponents, Congress, the Constitution, and the law. But in light of assessments of Truman's overreaching and the severity of his judgments about Johnson and Nixon, Neustadt is likely to have considered that Bush's claims to extraordinary authority had no constitutional merit; and that Bush's pursuit of them would damage him in the long run. What is likelier to have disappointed Neustadt was that Congress did not resist more tenaciously signing statements, treaty abrogations, and a strange narrative about a unitary executive that the framers did not create, for which there was no support in Philadelphia in 1787, and that most presidents have not supposed that they possessed.

Some Bush appointees reckoned that a contentious reading of certain clauses in "Federalist No. 70" gave a sufficient account of the nature of executive authority. Why trouble with the different arguments and tenor of the rest of that paper or of the *Federalist Papers* as a whole? The administration's claim that the executive is "unitary" rests upon the propositions that the president's control over the entire executive branch is complete and exclusive; and that neither Congress nor the judiciary may properly interfere with actions that the president might take under his authority so conceived. The claim lacks warrant. Neither Articles I, II, and III, nor the *Federalist Papers* nor Madison's *Notes on the Federal Convention* lends it support.

The fragility in constitutional law of Bush's claims is one thing. Surprise that infringement should be attempted is another. In reality, the forty-third president's expansive claims to authority not granted him by the Constitution should not occasion this response. Beginning with Harry Truman, claims of such authority by successive occupants of the Oval Office eventually gained acceptance through the exhaustion of resistance. Truman's merited defeat in the steel seizure case (*Youngstown Sheet & Tube Co. v. Sawyer*, 343 US 579 [1952]) stands out not because it marked the halting of such presidential claims but because it is an exception to their secular growth. In matters of authority, presidents have moved to occupy territory that the Constitution denies them but that Congress has failed to defend.

A president's commands have the potential to change the political landscape. As Neustadt observed, "When what we once called 'war' impends, he now becomes our system's Final Arbiter... Command may have a narrow reach but it encompasses irreparable consequences."[4] The war in Iraq illustrates his point that command comes at a political price. Commands, in whatever form, offer a president under pressure the illusion of prospective closure to complex political problems. By the standard of what he thought he could get away with rather than of what the Constitution permitted, Bush's presidential leadership style indicates that presidents might be able to extend their effective reach more freely than Neustadt anticipated that any president would dare or any Congress would allow. But it also points to the temporal limitations of reliance upon command: what appeared to voters so successful between mid-September 2001 and the midterm elections of 2002 did not so appear to them between 2005 and 2009. Wise presidents think about the risks involved in the invocation of such authority, not just now but tomorrow and in years to come. In other words, they think about probable patterns of retrospective judgments of their use of command with greater political imagination than Bush appears to have done.

Yet inaction carries risks, too, as Bush rightly understood. Whether further horrors might have been visited upon the United States after September 2001 had he not acted as he did in matters of domestic security cannot be known. Alas, there are fewer political rewards for laying claim to the possibility of having avoided disaster than for surmounting it. But the president's recumbent leadership style in Hurricane Katrina's literal and metaphorical wake revealed the destructive costs of failure to use the authority constitutionally his. In this regard, Bush's behavior contrasts sharply with that of Lyndon Johnson, who, faced with the immensely damaging Hurricane Betsy in 1965, flew to New Orleans within five hours of first speaking about the disaster to Senator Russell Long (D-LA) about its impact upon his state.[5]

Professional Reputation

As a source of presidential power, a president's professional reputation comprises three elements: the judgments that members of the Washington Community make of him (are they, for example, themselves persuaded that he has the skill and will to use his advantages in a particular instance?); how their judgments of him shape his influence over them; and what they expect the president to do and why—in other words, what they think he might dare to do and what they *perceive* to be happening.

Political judgments of presidents, no less than of other politicians, are matters of perception and intertemporal calculation. Here is where the lack of access to private papers of most members of the Washington Community in 2009 matters most, because a full assessment of their perceptions of the president's skill and will and of their expectations of him and of his daring and imagination is not possible in this circumstance. All we have to work with are clues rather than definitive evidence.

Intellectual capacity is but part of professional reputation within Washington, but has figured large among Bush's critics. Bush certainly knew little about the world before holding national office. Pressed by a journalist in the 2000 election campaign to name the presidents of Taiwan and Chechnya, the general who had led a recent coup in Pakistan, and the prime minister of India, Bush haltingly identified only the president of Taiwan. Vice President Gore's spokesman tartly observed, "I guess we know that 'C' at Yale was a gentleman's 'C.'" Nevertheless, other aspirant presidents have not been similarly tested, and too much weight has been placed on this example. More worrying is that Bush also did not know what all his post-Eisenhower predecessors certainly did before entering the White House—that Germany was a member of NATO.[6]

We cannot reasonably infer from Bush's ignorance of international affairs that as a candidate he was unintelligent. It seems likelier that following defeat by Kent Hance in the election for the nineteenth U.S. Congressional District of Texas in 1978, he tried hard to hide his cognitive intelligence. The excellence of his university background conferred not an advantage but a handicap in that contest, as anticipated by his opponent (the only person ever to defeat Bush in an election). Hance used Bush's superior education against him: "In the Panhandle, if it's Texas Tech versus Yale, Tech will beat Yale every time. That's not even a close game." Bush appears to have resolved that he would not let opponents play the same card against him in future campaigns.[7]

Bush's inarticulateness in public provided rich material for opponents, commentators, and late-night comedians. Those who conversed with him in private reported differently, finding him more intellectually aware and supple than his public performances typically suggested. Bush also had that rare but excellent quality among male politicians of acknowledging when he did not fully understand a point being made to him. It would be surprising if a legislator's diary or papers disclosed a president who in private impressed them as Theodore Roosevelt or John Kennedy usually did their own contemporaries. Yet it would be unsurprising if their papers were to reveal someone who succeeded in that politically useful task of defying, in Philip Shenon's words, "his critics' lowered expectations."[8] When he chose to, Bush was also capable of learning quickly. His failure to appreciate the nature or scale of terrorist threats to the United States before September 2001 was a policy error with profound consequences. But he rapidly grasped their significance after September 11. Bush's increasingly firm grasp of policy that fall resulted partly from his twenty-four meetings with the National Security Council between 9/11 and his formidable performance at the press conference of October 11. The president's redirection of his administration after September 11 could not have been accomplished without intense and organized application on his part. Bush knew that such engagement was a prerequisite of his not merely being in command but of convincingly *showing* himself to be so. This demonstrated his understanding of the broader political truth: the Washington Community watches constantly for signs and clues of the president's purpose, capacities, intentions, and imagination. As Bush himself put it,

> Part of being a leader is: *people watch you*. I walk in that hall, I say to those commanders—well, guess what would happen if I walk in and say "Well, maybe it's not worth it." When I'm out in the public, I fully understand that the enemy watches me, the Iraqis are watching

me, the troops watch me, and the people watch me. The other thing is that *you can't fake it.* You have to believe it. And I believe it. I believe we'll succeed.[9]

This insight eluded smarter presidents than Bush—especially Herbet Hoover and Jimmy Carter, reputed to be among the most intelligent occupants of the Oval Office. In contrast to the forty-third president, their intellectual acuity did not enable them to understand the political importance of scrupulously remembering that the shaping of others' perceptions drives the crafting of professional reputation. Disastrously wrong as he got it after Katrina in 2005, Bush's building of his reputation after September 2001 was greater than his allies had feared or his opponents had imagined possible.

In New York on September 14, 2001, with the acrid smell of destruction hanging in the city's air, Bush appeared transformed by the shattered physical and political landscapes. Living there at the time, I watched a president who showed a vibrant capacity to empathize with terrorism's victims. On live television that day, he paused for what seemed an eternity before finally responding to an onlooker who claimed not to hear him speaking to them through a bullhorn at Ground Zero. Eventually, displaying acute political intuition, Bush replied, "I can hear you. The rest of the world hears you[,] and the people who knocked these buildings down will hear all of us soon!"

Here was a politician with the dual capacity to surprise his audience by the demonstration of hitherto hidden qualities and—crucially against the backdrop of a shattered city—to reassure the nation. This was a cathartic moment in Bush's relations with voters and, therefore, with the Washington Community. He responded to a public yearning for strong leadership, for the articulation of national purpose, and supplied it in different forums: amid the rubble of south Manhattan; earlier that same day in a packed National Cathedral in Washington; then in a commanding address to a joint session of Congress; and a month later in his powerful White House press conference where he put both cognitive intelligence and political grasp on public display. Here was a president who appeared to have the capacity to change the perceptions not only of the public (as the extraordinary rise in his public opinion poll ratings showed) but of the Washington Community (as their assessments of him changed with this most startling of unexpected events). Between the first and the fourth weeks of September, the president's approval ratings rose from 55 to 90 percent.[10]

The history of the American presidency is replete with examples of incumbents who, despite having the potential advantage flowing from their position, failed to turn crisis to advantage. In contrast, between 2001 and 2003, Bush did not miss the opportunity presented by terrorist attacks upon New York and Washington. Moreover, the change in his approach and evident self-confidence became immediately apparent. Within a month of the attacks, answers to Neustadt's question pertaining to members of the Washington Community— What do they think him capable of? What do they think he might dare do?—had changed. Now he not only knew General Musharraf's name, but also what he wanted him (and everyone else with whom he had dealings) to do, and why and when he wanted him to do it, as the successful military campaign against the Taliban rapidly unfolded. Here was a president who appeared to have mastered the politics of his circumstances; reset his nation's agenda and that of the world; reframed the terms of political debate; and thereby reordered the Washington Community's perception of him and of his potential. In recent decades, perhaps only Ronald Reagan's extraordinary boldness in attempting to reach a transformative agreement with Soviet President Mikhail Gorbachev at the 1985 Geneva summit to reduce strategic nuclear weapons by one half exceeds the capacity that Bush demonstrated in 2001 to reclaim the policy and political initiative on new terms.[11]

The charge that Bush's presidential leadership style is undercut by analytical weakness sweeps too broadly to convince for analytical capacity is only part of the point. If it were more, the reputations of Franklin Roosevelt, Harry Truman, and Lyndon Johnson would not have been so high with the Washington Community—or future historians. None of them was analytically gifted in any academic sense. More important are the dual qualities of an intelligence of imagination, namely a capacity to perceive possible futures from a failed present, and an organizational intelligence, without which intelligence of imagination risks being throttled in the veto-rich matrix structures of American politics. British scholar-politician David Marquand once observed that a successful political leader's mind at work "is more akin to the imagination of a creative artist than to any faculty that intellectuals possess." By that criterion, Bush's conduct of himself in office in post-9/11, 2001, and for much of 2002 was impressive. Thereafter (and especially after the launching of the war against Iraq), it was, with the exception of his ordering of the surge in Iraq, less impressive than any president since Johnson after failure in Vietnam hardened into probability in 1966.

That was reflected in Bush's insistence aboard the *USS Abraham Lincoln* on May 1, 2003, that the Iraq War mission was "accomplished";

his tone-deaf response to the Katrina disaster in 2005 when the emotional intelligence of September and October 2001 deserted him completely; and by his apparent intellectual, political, and emotional bemusement in the face of catastrophic financial collapse in 2008. As the president later recognized, the *Abraham Lincoln* episode greatly damaged his reputation. Whilst he referred that day explicitly to the end of "major combat operations," the stage-managed triumphalism on the flight deck was a self-inflicted wound, the more remarkable for one who only eighteen months earlier had shown so clear a grasp of the importance of shaping the Washington Community's perceptions. Bush's recasting of his professional reputation did not endure, not least because of a nearly monotonic decline in his public support that fell from 86 percent in December 2001 to 66 percent a year later before recovering to 77 percent in April 2003 when a victory in Iraq briefly seemed possible. From July 2003, his support never again reached 60 percent, falling to barely 50 percent at the time of his reelection in November 2004, and declining below (and staying below) that point from the spring of 2005. His support hovered around 40 percent in 2006, continued to drift downward throughout 2007, and reached a nadir of 23 percent in 2008. His final evaluation of 22 percent in January 2009 was the lowest in the history of presidential polling—beneath even Richard Nixon's at the depths of Watergate.[12] No professional reputation can survive such erosion of public prestige.

Human Qualities: Sense of Purpose

Neustadt found indications of a sense of purpose "in irreversible commitments to defined courses of action..., personal involvement, in terms of what the man himself is seen to say and do, so plain and so direct that politics—and history—will not let him turn back." Bush's presidency clearly supplied such examples: education reform; successive reductions in marginal tax rates; antiterror policy; and in the war against, and then within, Iraq from 2003. The combination of resolution and apparent moral confidence in these cases discloses an executive style characterized by an unusually clear sense of purpose with attendant short-term political benefits, as the midterm elections of 2002 showed.

These examples show that Bush's sense of purpose becomes synonymous with what political analyst Michael Freeden means by "ideology," namely "recurrent, action-oriented, patterns of political argument."[13] That understanding of ideology has applications to

Bush's executive style: first, to the content of policy and, second, to the processes of government in a separated system. Among twentieth-century presidents, only Woodrow Wilson and Ronald Reagan have recurrently oriented and sustained patterns of political argument to executive action as George W. Bush did. The presence of such an ideology does not, of course, give assurance that such action will be effective in achieving intended outcomes. Yet Bush welded just such a durable and overarching ideology to his resolve to use the presidency to effect change in education policy and in taxation. His ideology did not easily comport with the broader lines of ideological division within American politics. For example, his drive to reduce marginal rates of taxation certainly enthused conservative Republicans, but his education reforms did not. This does not make his sense of purpose nonideological for his patterns of political argument were strikingly recurrent, displaying consistency in strategic political action on taxation and education reform from his governorship through his presidency. His interest being strategic, he deployed those patterns of argument that he judged had the potential for him to encapsulate and project executive action in the cause of achieving fiscal and educational policy change through legislation.

Elsewhere in his presidency, Bush's ideological orientation to the processes of government in a separated system set himself apart from the great majority of his modern predecessors. As political scientist James Pfiffner has observed, it exhibited an understanding of and an approach to constitutional and statute law that, when it suited him, were disdainful, disregarding, and dismissive. In Bush's creation of military commissions within the executive branch, denial of habeas corpus to U.S. citizens, suspension of the Geneva Conventions, sanction of torture in interrogating detainees, and deployment of the National Security Agency to monitor electronic communications of American citizens, Pfiffner argues that he "abrogated the rule of law by taking actions not authorized by law and sometimes directly against the law."[14] How, in a law-governed system of separated powers, did a president whose sense of purpose extended to abrogation of congressional statutes and constitutional law manage to do what he did? An explanation might begin with an examination of the flaccidity of the response of successive congresses to not only Bush's style of government but also those of his predecessors. The point is demonstrated not primarily in the weakness of Congress between 2001 and 2009 but at what is commonly taken to be the apogee of its influence in 1973–74. Congressional response to Nixon's abuse of the war power was supine even then: the War Powers Resolution of 1973 comprised an implicit acceptance that the presidency enjoyed constitutional authority in respect of the deployment of forces abroad that the Constitution did not grant it.[15]

Human Qualities: Feel for Power

Neustadt understood "feel for power" in historical context, asking how close a president comes "to the realities around him." How did Bush fare on this score? His feel for power was that of an executive, a characteristic derived from observation of and some participation in his father's political career; his own legislative inexperience; and his action-oriented political temperament. Of the seven aspects of governing styles that Charles Jones finds characteristic of legislators—"representative, reactive, responsive, collaborative, open and sharing, compromising, and narrowly accountable to constituencies," Bush displays none of the first six, and only manifests the seventh in limited fashion. Conversely he manifests all six characteristic of executives—"proactive, hierarchical, contained, programmatic, resolute and broadly accountable."[16] Moreover, he supplemented those qualities with an apparent ease in the role of decision maker that has by no means been common among presidents, and which his acquisition of a Harvard MBA did nothing to diminish. Evaluating his own abilities, he observed, "If I have any genius or smarts, it's the ability to recognize talent, ask them to serve and work with them as a team… When they give advice I trust their judgment." When they disagree, "the job is to grind through these problems, and grind through these scenarios and hopefully reach a consensus of six or seven smart people, which makes my job easy."

The feel for power requires a president to be able to judge the dynamics, contingencies, and imperatives of a separated system. With the exception of his attempted Social Security reforms, Bush's feel for power appears to have been sufficient for his domestic purposes. In tax policy, for example, he achieved far greater success in 2001 and 2003 than most members of the Washington Community had thought possible when the intensely divided 107th Congress assembled in January 2001. The final version of the Economic Growth and Tax Relief Reconciliation Act that the president signed into law on June 7 (P.L. 1836) was an extraordinary political victory against the congressional odds. In aggregate, the reductions in taxes for which the bill provided amounted to $1.35 trillion over the decade 2001–10, with a reduction in the top rate of tax from 39.6 to 35 percent. The president and his advisers judged the bill's content finely, and won substantial votes on the conference committee's report. The 240–154 margin in the House drew support from 211 Republicans, 28 Democrats, and 1 independent. The vote in the Senate was 58–33, with 12 Democrats supporting the Conference Report, and just 2 Republicans opposing it.

As indicated by Bush's tax strategy, a president's feel for power may be judged by disposition, by the character of the process of presidential-congressional interaction, or by results. His strikingly metallic disposition was on early display when addressing tax strategy in a press conference just two days after inauguration:

> *The President*: I think that it's important for me to explain my position. It's important for me to hear other's positions. It's important for me to understand where there's resistance and why. But it all happens with good, honest discussion, a frank discussion about positions. I look forward to explain to any Member that's concerned about tax relief and why, why I proposed it. And I think the evidence is going to become more and more clear that the economy is—it's not as hopeful as we'd like, which I hope will strengthen my case.
>
> Q. Mr. President, you talked about frank and honest discussions. Are you willing to give on either one of those issues, or is there a—
>
> *The President*. Well I'm certainly not willing to negotiate with myself. [*Laughter*] Particularly in your column. [*Laughter*][17]

In 2003, with smaller margins of victory in both the House and the Senate, where a tie was broken by Vice President Cheney's casting vote, Bush won passage of the Jobs and Growth Tax Relief Reconciliation Act that reduced taxation on capital gains and dividends, accelerated tax reductions provided for in 2001, and eased the burden of the Alternative Minimum Tax. Both tax bills vindicated his feel for power since he came much closer to judging accurately the realities of his position and the possibilities for significant change in fiscal policy than did many of his contemporaries.

If the president's disposition were tested solely by reference to his fiscal initiatives in 2001 and 2003, analysts would be justified in inferring it to have been characterized by unusual resolution—with as much attention paid to his identification of ideological enemies as to his ideological supporters, and by a remarkable capacity in the 2003 case to count precisely who would support him and at what price. If his disposition were tested by his No Child Left Behind (NCLB) Act, signed into law in 2002, different inferences would be drawn. In fiscal policy, he confronted liberal and moderate Democrats, using their opposition to him as vindication of the changes that he sought. In his education reforms, he embraced those Democrats and created a coalition of striking breadth. Inclusive and cooperative reform directed to the public good and, in particular, to improving children's educational opportunities was a staple theme of Bush's numerous public statements and remarks about education in 2001. So, too, were frequent and generous references to the ideological diversity of senior congressional figures whose support he had successfully curried. He missed no opportunity to thank publicly Representatives John Boehner (R-OH) and George Miller (D-CA), both of the House Committee on Education and the Workforce, and Senators Tim Hutchinson (R-AR), Judd Gregg (R-NH), and Edward Kennedy (D-MA), all members of the Senate Committee on Health, Education, Labor, and Pensions, whose active political support he needed for legislative victory.[18] In all, he took his stump education speech to thirteen public meetings outside Washington; broadcast two radio addresses; offered prepared remarks on education reform to reporters in Washington on eighteen occasions; and made four statements on the legislation.

Miller and Kennedy were crucial political allies of the president on NCLB, both as symbols of a bipartisan movement for reform and as capable and experienced legislators. Without their tactical and political support, not least their resistance to the lobbying efforts of the National Education Association and the American Federation of Teachers, Bush knew that his initiative would fail. Barely a year after sending Congress a statement of his "goals and principles" (deferring to it the drafting of legislative language, and compromising by withdrawing his support for vouchers), the president held an elaborate signing ceremony. Bipartisan majorities had voted for a major extension of federal regulation: more than four-fifths of House Republicans, and more than nine-tenths of Senate Republicans, voted for the legislation on final passage. In Andrew Rudalevige's words, opposition was "limited to an odd amalgam of the discontented far Left and far Right."[19] Even House Majority Leader Tom DeLay (R-TX) voted for a bill he later described as "awful," swept along by White House pressure, a mood of intense bipartisanship in the months after 9/11, and the evident willingness of most of his Republican colleagues to follow the president's lead.

In these three cases, Bush had shown a feel for power unusually flexible in its form, adjustable to contrasting demands, and startlingly successful. In short, to use Neustadt's own laudatory term, he preserved his power prospects with a political agility largely missing from his use (and abuse) of his commander-in-chief authority in prosecuting the war on terror from 2003 onward and as domestic leader after Katrina in 2005.

Sources of Confidence: Experience

Neustadt refers in *Presidential Power* to those "three things that a President brought with him to the job: a sense of purpose, a feel for power, and a source of confidence" and proceeds to argue "that the first two were conditioned by the third, and that self-confidence was fashioned from experience and temperament." What are we to make of the combination of experience and temperament in Bush's case, of its implications for his confidence, and so for his sense of purpose and feel for power, and of their implications for his executive style?

Bush was something of a late developer as a member of a dynasty with a tradition of success in business and commitment to public service. While building up the family fortune, the preceding generations had transmitted a distaste for display, affectation, or presumption coupled with exceptional expectations. As he might have written of other great New England families, political scientist Hugh Heclo observes that of all the arenas in which they expected achievement, public life was preeminent and provided an "...arena for this most important of all revelations about a person."[20] Seeking to escape the cultural limitations of Yankee Republicanism within which his own father had flourished, George H.W. Bush became a highly successful businessman in west Texas, but long remained vulnerable in Texas politics to charges of being "carpet-bagger" and an eastern blue-blood to boot. Even when seeking the presidency in 1988, he encountered Texas Governor Ann Richards's derisive comment to the Democratic convention, "Poor George: he couldn't help it that he was born with a silver foot in his mouth." The populist attacks on his father and his own experience in his first run for office in 1978 instilled in George W. Bush a determination, as one commentator put it, not to be "...out-Christianed or out-good-old-boyed again."[21]

Early political defeat did nothing to diminish Bush's view that loyalty was a singular virtue or to quell his ambitions for office. Nevertheless, the qualities of patience, indirection, and willingness to "go slow" in building a reputation within the U.S. House or U.S. Senate were not ones that he possessed. As his father had himself discovered, the action-oriented life of executive decision making fitted his temperament and skill-set rather better. His business experience first in oil, where success initially proved elusive, and then, in particular, with the consortium that owned the Texas Rangers baseball team, endowed him both with a profile and a network of his own that was distinctive from what he derived from his Bush family connexions. Roland Betts, the major investor in the Rangers, had long encouraged Bush to set himself apart from his father by striking out on his own: As he recalled, "Baseball was it. He became our local celebrity. He knew every usher. He signed autographs. He talked to fans. His presence meant everything. His eyes were on politics the whole time, but even when he was speaking at Republican functions, he was always talking about the Rangers."[22] Talking about the Rangers at Republican functions in Texas was not only a vote-maximising strategy but also a manifestation of Bush being at ease with himself in a cultural and political context set in counterpoint to his family's history and experience. What his grandfather, Senator Prescott Bush (R-CT), neither could nor would have done became to George W. Bush a vehicle for self-realization and political advancement.

Sources of Confidence: Temperament

Bush's own perceptive reflections on the political importance of others' ceaseless perceptions, evaluations, and reevaluations of a president reveal him as a politician who acquired an iron will and self-discipline. Those two qualities appeared relatively late in his life, but were prerequisites for his plausibility as a gubernatorial and presidential candidate. Nor was either his will power or his discipline an affectation: he gave up drinking in 1986, and smoking shortly thereafter. He has returned to neither. For all his alleged incuriosity, his intelligence reveals itself in ways often more useful to politicians—not least in his exceptional ability to remember names and faces. From ushers at Texas Rangers baseball games to foreign leaders, once he had committed names and faces to memory, he remembered them. He did so because he could, because he realized the political value of doing so, and because it enabled him to compete intensely with those who might challenge him. Competition was central to his self-image and to his understanding of his life's purpose. As exaltation of personal competition was fundamental to his family's ethos, he exulted in its practice. A Texas journalist friend thought him "...irreverent, unself-conscious, and intensely competitive. If you are his adversary, he delights in your discomfort—yet he expects you to recognize that it is something of an honor to be invited to play the game."[23]

Will, discipline, and competitiveness sit alongside firm religious attachment. Although much remarked upon, the quality has attracted less scholarly comment than its constituent importance to his temperament warrants.[24] Bush entitled his prepresidential memoirs *A Charge to Keep*, the first four words of the title of one of Charles Wesley's hymns, especially celebrated within the Methodist movement to which he belongs.[25] The title omits the crucial ending *I Have*, but Bush internalized the complete first line and resolved to give expression to it during his political career. Bush wrote in *A Charge to Keep* that Wesley's hymn "...speaks of purpose and direction," and is associated with a verse from St. Paul's First Epistle to the Corinthians: "Now it is required that those who have been given a trust must prove faithful." Like Jimmy Carter's memoirs, his own provides compelling evidence of a religious temperament. In the opening paragraph, Bush identifies the first of the three most important "moments of recognition" in his life as "Renewing my faith." His book bristles with a sense of purpose informed not only by religious *belief* but also by religious *conviction:*

> I build my life on a foundation that will not shift. My faith frees me. Frees me to put the problem of the moment in proper perspective. Frees me to make decisions that others might not like. Frees me to do the right thing, even though it may not poll well. Frees me to enjoy life and not worry about what comes next. I've never plotted the various steps of my life, certainly never campaigned for one office to try to position myself for the next. I am more spontaneous than that. I live in the moment, seize opportunities, and try to make the most of them.[26]

George W. Bush spoke not just of his faith but of his actions as consistent with his faith in a way that—among other twentieth-century presidents—only Wilson and Carter were wont to do. Significantly, Wilson's view of the proper relationship between the political and divine spheres was quite different from Bush's. Where Wilson thought that politics and religion, the "two great empires of human feeling," should be kept firmly separate, Bush said that he drew them together not only in his own mind but also in his understanding of the world.

Conclusion

Two questions arise about presidential leadership style from Bush's drawing together of the two empires that Wilson separated. The first addresses value consistency and the second purely political reasoning. With respect to the first, insofar as Bush drew politics and Methodism together, how did he reconcile Methodist values with permitting torture of detainees? And with respect to the second, did his view of the world facilitate his thinking appropriately, rigorously, and imaginatively about his power prospects and the U.S. national interest?[27] How, for example, did he reason through his decision to disregard the legal prohibition upon torture? Given that Bush was untroubled on this subject by considerations of ethics—Methodist or otherwise, by the constitution, by international law, or by domestic statute, I infer that his reasoning comprised a utilitarian calculus in which he anticipated that the probable benefits of torture would exceed probable costs. To convince, such a calculus must discount for anticipated benefits and costs not just in the short-run but in the long-term—and not just in respect of foreign forces but of American. If America's president endorses the use of torture when law and Army regulations prohibit it, what are the probable benefits and costs not just now but tomorrow and (well) beyond? Did Bush's style of presidential leadership lead him to consider this question intertemporally? If he did, what did he think the payoffs and costs might be to him, to his professional reputation, to the probabilities of the Iraq venture's success, and to the international reputation of the United States at different future points? What greater risks of torture did he think that members of the U.S. military would run in two, five, and ten years' time because he had permitted torture of foreign forces after 2002? If he did not think about those payoffs and costs at different points, what does that tell us about the values underpinning his decisions and the sophistication of his reasoning?

    The damage that torture in particular and the failed venture in Iraq more generally did to reputation can be measured in the estimations of him in the Washington Community and among public opinion. Crucially, however, his presidential leadership style points to the limitations of presidential politics as command—to an understanding of the presidency as a site of effectively unlimited and unaccountable power without reference to its basis in constitutional and legal authority.

    In security policy, Bush's leadership style indicates that presidents might come to depend upon command in its various forms more systematically than Neustadt anticipated, its limitations of politics and policy notwithstanding. To the latter extent, Bush belatedly became aware of two traps. The first was one into which Richard Nixon fell of confusing what Neustadt termed "the first bite of invoked authority" with effective use of power viewed not just prospectively by the president but retrospectively by him and the Washington Community upon which his political effectiveness depends. The second was not to bring the full authority of his office to bear upon Katrina for which only the panoply of powers that his office (and his office alone) possessed would suffice. On such unwarranted claims and unused authority did Bush's professional reputation in part come to rest.

In a damning report that underlined the shortcomings of Bush's executive style, the Iraq Study Group (ISG) declared: "Many Americans are dissatisfied, not just with the situation in Iraq but with the state of our political debate regarding Iraq. Our political leaders must build a bipartisan approach to bring a responsible conclusion to what is now a lengthy and costly war. Our country deserves a debate that prizes substance over rhetoric, and a policy that is adequately funded and sustainable. The President and Congress must work together. Our leaders must be candid and forthright with the American people in order to win their support."[28] James Baker, the ISG cochair and guiding light, effectively instructed the president to follow all seventy-nine recommendations: "I hope," he tartly observed, "...we don't treat this like a fruit salad and say, 'I like this, but I don't like that.'"

The ISG report was a proxy for the Washington Community's judgment on Bush's professional reputation. By implication, it found his failings to be those of inadequate judgment, impatience, and unawareness of the complexities of choice making. The Community's judgment of him was already settled by the time of the report's publication: its immunity to alteration was apparent from his gaining so little either in reputation or prestige from the relative success of the surge strategy that comprised his response to the ISG recommendations. That his decision in this regard was arguably both courageous and justified by events neither could nor did enable him to recover a reputation that was by then fixed. The fundamental inference remains: George W. Bush's presidential style of reliance upon contentious claims to authority, not obviously his, could suffice neither for him nor for American needs because authority, an entitlement to act, is always but part of a more complex texture of political action comprising listening, negotiation, education, and thinking in time—reasoning backward from intended objectives to means for their attainment.

Notes

1. Richard E. Neustadt, *Presidential Power and the Modern Presidents* (New York: Free Press, 1990), 203.

2. Quoted in Charles O. Jones, "Richard E. Neustadt: Public Servant as Scholar," *Annual Review of Political Science*, 6, 2003, 11.
3. T. J. Halstead, "The Law: Walker v. Cheney: Legal Insulation of the Vice President from GAO Investigations," *Presidential Studies Quarterly*, 33, September, 2003, 635–48.
4. Richard E. Neustadt, "Afterword: 1964," *Presidential Power* (New York: John Wiley, 1964), 201.
5. President Johnson and Russell Long, phone conversation, September 10, 1965, 2:26 pm, #8847, WH6509.03, LBJ Library; President Johnson, Robert Phillips, and Senator Russell Long, phone conversation, September 14, 1965, 6:10pm, #8858, WH6509.03, LBJ Library. (I am indebted to Gareth Davies for drawing my attention to these conversations.)
6. Jacob Weisberg, *The Bush Tragedy* (New York: Random House, 2008), 146; Ivo H. Daalder and James. M. Lindsay, "Bush's Foreign Policy Revolution," in Fred I. Greenstein, ed., *The George W. Bush Presidency: An Early Assessment* (Baltimore: Johns Hopkins University Press, 2003), 202–3.
7. Nicholas D. Kristof, "Kerry's Blue-Collar Bet," *New York Times*, July 7, 2004.
8. Philip Shenon, *The Commission: The Uncensored History of the 9/11 Investigation* (New York: Twelve, 2008), 341.
9. Robert Draper, *Dead Certain: The Presidency of George W. Bush* (New York: Simon and Schuster, 2007), x–xi; emphasis in the original.
10. ABC News/*Washington Post* poll, January 13–16, 2009.
11. Memorandum of Conversation between President Reagan and President Gorbachev, Geneva, November 19, 1985, Ronald Reagan Presidential Library.
12. CBS News/*New York Times* poll, January 16, 2009.
13. Michael Freeden, "The Ideology of New Labour," in Andrew Chadwick and Richard Heffernan, eds., *The New Labour Reader* (Oxford: Polity, 2003), 44.
14. James Pfiffner, *Power Play: The Bush Presidency and the Constitution* (Washington DC: Brookings Institution Press, 2008), 234.
15. Public Law 93–148, 93rd Congress, H. J. Res. 542, November 7, 1973.
16. Charles O. Jones, "Governing Executively: Bush's Paradoxical Style," in John C. Fortier and Norman Ornstein, *Second Term Blues: How George W. Bush Has Governed* (Washington, DC: AEI and Brookings, 2007), 114.
17. "The President's Press Conference," January 24, 2001, in John T. Woolley and Gerhard Peters, *The American Presidency Project* (Santa Barbara: University of California), www.presidency.ucsb.edu
18. Kennedy became committee chairman in May 2001 following the assumption of Independent status by Senator James Jeffords (R-VT), which cost the GOP control of the upper chamber.
19. Andrew Rudalevige, "The Politics of the No Child Left Behind Act," *Education Next*, Hoover Institution, http://www.educationnext.org/20034/62.html.

20. Hugh Heclo, "The Political Ethos of George W. Bush," in Greenstein, *The George W. Bush Presidency*, 25.
21. Kristof, "Kerry's Blue-Collar Bet."
22. Joe Nick Patoski, "Team Player," *Texas Monthly*, June 1999.
23. Paul Burka, "The W Nobody Knows," *Texas Monthly*, June 1999.
24. D. Jason Berggren and Nicol C. Rae, "Jimmy Carter and George W. Bush: Faith, Foreign Policy, and an Evangelical Presidential Style," *Presidential Studies Quarterly*, 36, November 2006, 606–32.
25. George W. Bush, *A Charge to Keep* (New York: W. Morrow, 1999), 45.
26. Ibid. 6.
27. John Milton Cooper, *The Warrior and the Priest: Woodrow Wilson and Theodore Roosevelt* (Cambridge, MA: Belknap Press, 1983), 171.
28. James A. Baker, III, and Lee H. Hamilton, *The Iraq Study Group Report* (New York: Vintage Books, 2006), 4.

Chapter Three

Bush's Congressional Legacy and Congress's Bush Legacy

John E. Owens

Critical to the assessment of every modern president's legacy has been his success in leading Congress and his impact on presidential-congressional relations. In Abraham Lincoln's day, a presidential message to the legislature "may be a shot in the air without practical result."[1] In contrast, the "modern" occupant of 1600 Pennsylvania Avenue—from Franklin Roosevelt to Barack Obama—is expected to formulate a legislative agenda and to see this through to enactment.[2] Owing to the separated nature of the U.S. system of government, however,[3] there is a second question that requires an answer in any meaningful analysis of a president's relations with the Congress: how successful was the Congress in checking and balancing the president?

George W. Bush entered the White House with a bold policy agenda, as well as some very distinctive views about the role of the presidency. He wanted to be a transformational president who changed the nation's political course, rather than merely a transactional leader engaged in seeking mutual payoffs with followers. He was also a risktaker who wanted to pursue bold and inspiring policy goals. He further aspired to provide what political scientist Stephen Skowronek calls "leadership by definition" by demonstrating steadfastness, perseverance, confidence, and direction.[4] The minimalist role of resolving disputes among political actors and interests basically wedded to the policy status quo held no interest for the forty-third president.[5] Neither was Bush a traditional antistatist Republican in manner of Ronald Reagan or Newt Gingrich. Rather, he espoused a somewhat ill-defined "compassionate conservatism," which seemingly accepted the long-standing federal commitments to social security, health care, education, but aimed to reinvent them by expanding individual choice, enhancing individual responsibility, and "empowering people."

Analyses of presidential-congressional relations have predominantly focused on *legislating* within the framework of the Madisonian system of government.[6] This reflected the influence of Richard Neustadt's classic formulation that presidential power in the pluralistic American polity was essentially that of persuasion rather than command.[7] Unsurprisingly, therefore, scholars have found the preponderance of power between the coequal separate institutions to be fluctuating rather than fixed, with the president and Congress holding ascendancy in different periods and sharing it in others.[8] However, the exclusive focus on law-making produces an incomplete perspective on presidential-congressional relations, particularly in the Bush era. More than any recent predecessor, the forty-third president claimed and used his unilateral powers without significant challenge from Congress.

The Electoral and Congressional Context

Understanding a president's congressional legacy—and the Congress's presidential or executive legacy—requires the understanding of the strategic context in which the different institutions acted and interacted.

Bush became president in controversial circumstances: his Democratic opponent received more popular votes, but he won an Electoral College majority thanks to a Supreme Court ruling that awarded him Florida's disputes votes. This inevitably weakened his political legitimacy, as underlined by a preinauguration poll registering the highest ever level of *disapproval* of any new president since polling began: 31 percent of respondents held that Bush had "won on a technicality," 24 percent thought he "stole the election," while 38 percent thought Al Gore the "real winner."[9] In addition to lacking a credible mandate, Bush's prospects of leading the Congress seemed further hampered by his party's loss of congressional seats for the third election in succession. The 2000 election left the Republicans with only a twelve-seat majority in the House and in a fifty–fifty tie with Democrats in the Senate, where their majority depended on Vice President Dick Cheney's casting vote. Moreover, less than five months into the new Congress, the GOP lost control of the Senate following the defection to Independent status of James Jeffords (VT). Further testifying to Bush's parlous position on the eve of the 9/11 attacks on New York and Washington, a Gallup poll found that only 51 percent approved "of the way [he was] handling his job as president," while 39 percent disapproved.[10]

The subsequent shift in the political agenda to focus on the war on terror and national security produced dramatic improvement in Bush's approval ratings. This also benefited the GOP, which increased its House majority and regained control of the Senate in the 2002 midterm elections, the first time since 1934 that a president's party had increased its congressional strength in his first term. These developments did not signify that Bush had become president of all the people in the fullest sense. A mid-2003 opinion poll found that 38 percent of respondents—including most Democrats and half of independents—continued to withhold their approval of his presidency.[11] In 2004, however, Bush went on to win reelection, albeit by the narrowest popular vote margin secured by an incumbent, and the GOP increased its majorities in both chambers of Congress. This was the first time since 1928 that the Republicans had retained control of both White House and Congress in national elections.[12]

Bush's popular standing went into freefall in his second term, however. The botched response to Hurricane Katrina, and public concern over mounting American casualties in Iraq sent his approval ratings plummeting to 38 percent in late 2006. Then, with the U.S. economy in sharp contraction, Bush's *disapproval* rating rose to a remarkable 71 percent in 2008.[13] Popular approval of his party also went into steep decline.[14] Between 2003 and 2008, GOP identification declined from near parity with the Democrats to its lowest mean percentage since Reagan's first term, giving Democrats an enormous 28 points advantage.[15]

The broader context for Bush's strategic predicament was the intensification of the trend evident since the 1970s of party-activist and office-holder polarization. In the early twenty-first century, those on opposing sides of a major issue occupied separate political universes, making it much more difficult for them to understand and empathize with each other's preferences. While voters remained somewhat less polarized, the party identifiers within the electorate still tended to be more homogeneous in their views and more divergent in their partisanship than in the past. This development is the subject of considerable scholarly debate. Contending explanations include the southern realignment, redistricting, local contexts, and, most importantly, growing social and economic inequality in the United States within individual states.[16] Increased partisan polarization resulted in the decline of split-ticket voting and greater synchronization of ballots in House, Senate, and presidential elections.[17]

It also the main reason why (1) majorities in the House and Senate have narrowed in recent years; (2) single-party control of government was difficult to achieve; and (3) congressional parties are now much more ideologically divergent than at any time since the last days of Reconstruction.

Single-party Republican control of government lasted for some fifty-two months of Bush's presidency and GOP margins were very tight in both congressional chambers during this time. As the congressional parties grew more ideologically homogenized, they came to occupy separate ideological spaces. As figure 3.1(a) demonstrates, thirty years ago there was some overlap in the two main parties' range of ideological preferences (measured by DW-NOMINATE scores). This was a terrain occupied by conservative and centrist Democrats from the South and centrist Republicans from the Northeast.[18] However, figure 3.1(b) illustrates that there was complete partisan separation in the 110th Congress (2007–8). Democrats had steadily become more homogeneously liberal owing to their loss of Southern seats, while Republicans were even more homogenously conservative as a result of rollback in Northeast.[19]

The effects of increased polarization in Congress can be seen not only in enhanced partisan voting but also in growing partisan control of the legislative agenda. Increasingly powerful majority leaders used restrictive rules with greater efficiency to shape the House's agenda in line with the majority party's expectations and policy preferences. In the Senate, where institutional rules give the minority party greater influence, majority leaders used cloture motions to achieve similar effects, albeit with less success.[20] Not surprisingly, in the context of more ideologically homogeneous congressional parties, more powerful majority leaders willing and able to exploit procedural rules to achieve partisan outcomes, and typically narrow pluralities, the probability of congressional-presidential agreement in writing major legislation has significantly *increased* under conditions of unified party government but significantly *decreased* under conditions of split-party government.[21] By the same token, we should expect the president's propensity to claim and use unilateral powers to bypass the Congress and the legislative process to institute policy, and the Congress's propensity to conduct oversight of the president's administration of policy to vary depending on the configuration of partisan control of the different branches of government. Under conditions of unified partisan control, congressional majorities are *less* likely to conduct critical oversight of the administration, while the reverse is true of opposition party congressional majorities.[22]

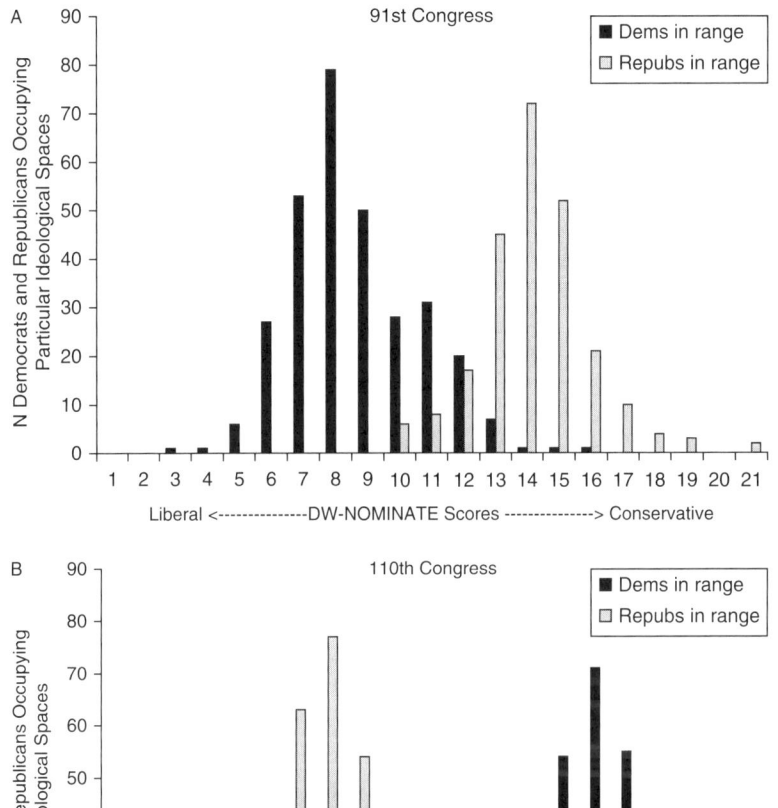

Figure 3.1 The Changing Ideological Position of the Congressional Parties: 91st Congress and 110th Congress.

Bush's *Presidentialist* Approach to the Separated System

In light of the strategic context that Bush encountered on taking office, it would have been understandable had he pursued a cautious governing strategy that reached "across the aisle" to moderate Democrats in order to enhance his legitimacy and broaden his support, but this was not the approach he followed.

Despite initial promises that he would be a "uniter, not a divider," the forty-third president pursued a strongly partisan, divisive, governing strategy that changed little over his time in office despite shifts in partisan control of Congress, illustrated in table 3.1, and declining public approval. His was a *presidentialist* as well as a partisan strategy[23] that paid scant respect to congressional privileges and prerogatives and maximum regard to the president not being seen as being beholden to Congress. As Bush told his chief of congressional liaison, "we will not negotiate with ourselves, ever... People will move toward us and continue to move toward us."[24] This is not to say that Congress never entered into the Bush White House's strategic calculus, or that legislators were never consulted. Rather, for most of the Bush presidency, the Congress was an inconvenience, a body that merited consideration only when new legislation or other means of implementing policy was unavoidable. Reflecting on this strategy, Vice President Dick Cheney—its foremost exponent—declared in 2009: "From the very day we walked in the building...[W]e had an agenda; we ran on the agenda, we won the election—full speed ahead."[25]

The foundations of Bush's *presidentialist* philosophy—or "ultra-separationist" interpretation of the presidency[26]—lay in political and legal doctrines and practices developed in the Nixon, Reagan, Bush 41, and Clinton administrations.[27] Influenced by Cheney and other conservative "old hands" from previous Republican administrations, Bush and his advisors held that the presidency had been emasculated by congressional resurgence after the *débacles* of Vietnam, Watergate, and Iran-Contra.[28] They concluded that Bush needed to reassert the prerogatives of the presidency and govern "executively"—with or without the Congress. The president needed to take primary, if not exclusive, responsibility for defining public policy—rather than the Congress and the president together in Madisonian fashion—by capitalizing on his constitutional position as chief executive[29] to extend executive and presidential power.

This approach to the presidency and the separated system melded well with Bush's own views on leadership. Bordering on "the hurried,"

Table 3.1 Tight Inter-Party Competition and Control of the Congress and the Presidency, 2001–8

Congress	House			Senate			Presidency		Pattern of Partisan Control
	Majority Party/ seat plurality	Majority and minority party popular vote in prior election	Majority Party Unity	Majority Party/ seat plurality	Majority Party Unity (%)	Party	Majority and minority party popular vote in prior election		
107th (January–June 2001)	*Republicans—9*	48–48	91%	*Republicans—0*	86	*Republican*	48–48		Unified Republican
(June 2001–December 2002)	*Republicans—9*			*Democrats—2*	86	*Republican*			Split
108th (2003–2004)	*Republicans—24*	51–49	90%	*Republicans—2*	92	*Republican*			Unified Republican
109th (2005–2006)	*Republicans—30*	50–47	89%	*Republicans—10*	87	*Republican*	51–48		Unified Republican
110th (2007–2008)	*Democrats—37*	53–45	86%	*Democrats—0**	86	*Republican*			Split

Source: CQ.com.
* Two independents usually vote with the Democrats.

his was a clear and decisive, albeit intuitive rather than evidence-based, executive style that demanded action, "forging on, rarely looking back, scoffing at—even ridiculing—doubt and anything less than 100 percent commitment."[30] "I am the commander, see," Bush told one interviewer, "I don't need to explain…why I say things. That's the interesting thing about being the President. Maybe somebody needs to explain to me why they say something, but I don't feel like I owe anybody an explanation."[31] Throughout his presidency, he exhibited an intense stubbornness, persistence, and obstinacy, as well as a pervasive loathing for bargaining and compromise, traditionally seen as essential to effective policymaking in Washington.

The legislative element of Bush's highly partisan governing strategy relied on a limited number of major agenda items, notably tax reduction, education reform, the war on terror, faith initiatives, social security, and immigration; a refusal to compromise until absolutely necessary; reliance on the majoritarian, Republican-controlled House to enact the most conservative legislation possible, aided by an ideologically compact Republican majority; and close coordination between the White House and Republican congressional leaders in both chambers of Congress. Despite Bush's still questionable legitimacy, sagging poll ratings, and diminishing approval from Democrats and independents, American-style party government prevailed in Washington in the period of single-party GOP control of government between the elections of 2002 and 2006.[32]

To overcome the strategic disadvantages that he faced, Bush emulated his predecessors in opting for a strategy of campaigning to govern—namely "going public" through the "permanent campaign."[33] In doing so, he looked to win support for his policies by focusing on certain symbolic, often, emotional, issues that were likely to grab media and public attention and thus enable the White House to influence, even control, the news cycle. Bush's so-called war on terror—with its purposeful heightening of fears among susceptible Americans about the risks of further terrorist attacks on U.S. soil, its moral idealism and symbolism, and soaring rhetoric—was replete with examples of this. The White House Iraq Group, created by Chief of Staff Andrew Card and chaired by Deputy Chief of Staff Karl Rove, coordinated administration efforts to depict Iraq as a threat.[34] Its ploy of asking for a new congressional use-of-force resolution two months before the 2002 midterm elections enabled the GOP to campaign on a major security issue and reinforced its image of being strong on defense. A similar strategy was pursued on domestic policy: enactment of tax reduction and Medicare/prescription drugs legislation honored 2000 campaign pledges but without serious consideration of their real cost and other implications. Yet, had Bush and his chief adviser, Karl Rove, examined similar efforts by previous presidents,[35] they might have concluded that this strategy could ultimately not reverse declining approval ratings when the substance of policy alienated most Democrats and independents, and latterly even Republicans. Just 31 percent of Democrats and 50 percent of independents compared to 88 percent of Republicans supported Bush in the 28 Gallup and CBS/*New York Times* polls taken before 9/11.[36] Bush proved increasingly divisive as his presidency progressed: Republican and Democratic identifiers became more sharply divided than over any other president since polling began. At the time of the 2006 and 2008 elections, only 7 percent and 5 percent of Democrats respectively approved of Bush's performance, compared with 81 percent and 61 percent of Republicans.[37]

Bush's Legislative Legacy

Notwithstanding the aggressively partisan nature of Bush's legislative strategy and the limitations of his permanent campaign, the magnitude and significance of his legislative achievements were not in doubt. Extending his earlier work, political scientist David Mayhew counted as many as fifty-four "major" pieces of legislation enacted by the 107th through 110th Congresses (2001–8). This total compares favorably with other two-term presidents (Clinton, 40; Reagan, 37; Eisenhower, 31), but not with the combined records of Nixon-Ford (73) or Kennedy-Johnson (65). In his first two years in office, Bush led the Congress in passing more major laws than any other new president since 1945.[38] Many of these—including the 2001 Use of Force Resolution, Patriot Act, airline bailout, and airline security legislation, the $40 billion emergency spending for New York City, and the creation of the Homeland Security Department—were enacted in a political climate favorable to national security legislation. The hugely expansive 2001 use-of-force resolution, approved by a Republican House and Democratic Senate, effectively gave Bush a carte blanche to pursue a presidentially declared war on terror with few congressional or judicial restrictions. The Patriot Act gave the Justice Department and other executive agencies draconian surveillance powers over citizens and noncitizens in the United States. Moreover, the 2003 reorganization of twenty-two federal agencies into a new Department of Homeland Security generated "the largest reorganization of government since the end of World War II."[39] Subsequently, Bush gained congressional approval for the Intelligence Reform and Terrorism Prevention of 2004, the Military Commissions Act of 2006, and the Foreign Intelligence Surveillance Amendment Act of 2008 Amendment. Furthermore, he generally obtained the funding he requested for military and reconstruction operations in Afghanistan and Iraq and other war on terror projects in every appropriations round from 2001 through 2008. Typically, this was granted in response to supplemental and/or emergency requests outside his annual budget request and provided maximum flexibility as to how the money was spent.[40]

According to Mayhew's computation, nearly a third (sixteen in total) of Bush's major enactments related to the war on terror. Another seven were domestic measures, including tax cuts, the educational reform, and new fast-track trade authority. Whatever their policy domain, many of these initiatives produced highly disruptive/nonincremental changes in public policy.[41] The ten-year $1.35 trillion tax cuts of 2001 and the $350 billion tax cuts of 2003, the largest since Reagan's tax reduction in 1981, deprived the federal government of significant amounts of discretionary revenue. The No Child Left Behind Act of 2001 disrupted traditional political coalitions between teachers' unions, state governments, and the Democratic Party in an effort to raise educational standards in schools. The landmark 2003 Medicare Reform allowed for substantial expansion of private health plans and huge windfall profits for the pharmaceutical industry. In 2007, Bush also gave Congress an object lesson in thwarting the Democratic majority's efforts to force him to bring home U.S. troops from Iraq. Despite appearing to be the lamest of lame ducks as his presidency drew to an end, he still persuaded the Democratic Congress with the help of Treasury Secretary Henry Paulson to pony up $700 billion, the largest appropriation in US history, to bail out a banking system that was on the verge of meltdown, without allowing the legislature much say on how the money would be spent.[42]

By any measure, these legislative achievements are considerable, the more so given the partisan strategic context. Yet, there were also important failures, some pertaining to core elements of the presidential agenda. There was no significant legislation to advance his faith-based initiatives, intended to fund the charitable operations of churches and religious groups. While the Republican-controlled House quickly approved Bush's proposals more or less intact in 2001, the Democratic Senate omitted key elements of the plan. In response, Bush used his unilateral powers to implement proposals that he could not get Congress to enact.[43] Even war on terror legislation in the immediate aftermath of 9/11 did not always sail through. In 2001, the Senate (and ultimately the House) forced a presidential climb-down on whether or not 30,000 newly created airport security jobs would be in the private sector or federal employees in the newly established Transportation Security Administration.[44]

Days after his relatively narrow reelection, Bush boasted that he had earned "political capital, and now I intend to spend it." Confident of avoiding the "second-term curse" that afflicted modern presidents, he opted for a bold agenda, undeterred by the deteriorating situation in Iraq, declining approval ratings, growing economic problems, and his "lame duck" status. There were even hints in public and private White House statements that Bush would emulate the New Deal's magnitude in domestic policy.[45] It soon became evident that he had seriously overestimated his mandate for change. Bush had announced in 2004 that his second-term legislative priority would be an ambitious plan to reform Social Security, the largest federal program costing almost $500 billions annually. Ronald Reagan and Bill Clinton had both failed in their efforts to reform a program dubbed the "third rail of politics" because of popular sensitivity regarding its maintenance. In light of this, Bush's plan to introduce controversial "personal retirement accounts" bordered on hubris. A vigorous sixty-day, sixty-city public relations campaign failed to generate either public support or congressional approval. Indeed, this attempt at "governing by campaigning" aroused such intense congressional opposition—even from Republicans—that the president never submitted detailed legislation to Congress. All he could do was to announce yet another blue-ribbon commission to "offer bipartisan solutions."[46]

A GOP-controlled Congress also refused to support Bush's immigration reform proposals, which would have legalized the status of over ten million undocumented (mainly Latino) immigrants by offering them a "path to citizenship." Owing to deep philosophical divisions among Republicans, Bush's plan got nowhere in either chamber.[47] The president was similarly unable to persuade Congress to make permanent the 2001 tax cuts scheduled to expire in 2011.[48] He also came up short in his efforts to get a Democrat-controlled Congress to approve an auto industry bailout in 2008. A stark warning, reportedly from Cheney, that failure to enact the measure would result in "Herbert Hoover time" had little effect on Senate Republicans.[49]

Despite such rebuffs, it should not be concluded that there was an *overall* balance-of-power between the White House and Congress in the Bush years. More typically, Bush's aggressively partisan strategy yielded impressive legislative results. It can, therefore, be concluded that he would not have achieved as much through a more accommodating approach. Of course, the president's assertiveness depended on strong political support from a highly disciplined, united Republican party in the House and close coordination with its leadership. The lower chamber generally gave Bush most of what he wanted, enabling him to negotiate from a position of strength with the Senate and make only limited compromises late in the legislative process.

One indication of this strategy's effectiveness was that Bush vetoed only one bill prior to the Democratic capture of Congress in the 2006 elections. In contrast, he issued well over a hundred veto threats in this time, usually to indicate his priorities and/or provide congressional Republican leaders with additional leverage over recalcitrant backbenchers. Bush's veto score rose to twelve after dealing with a Democratic Congress, but he suffered only three overrides (in 2007 on the Water Resources Development Act and in 2008 on the Food, Conservation, and Energy Act and Medicare Improvements Act). Although most Democrats voted to overturn these vetoes, bipartisan support to do so was rare.

Moreover, a sizable minority of Democrats often supported Bush on major legislation, especially in the Senate. One in four Senate Democrats supported Bush's 2001 tax cuts (compared with one in seven House Democrats). Three out of five Senate Democrats voted in favor of the 2002 Iraq use-of-force resolution while two out of three House Democrats voted against it. Similar divisions emerged on other major legislation, including the 2003 Prescription Drug and Medicare Improvement Act, the Patriot Act reauthorization, and warrantless wiretapping, detainee abuse and torture. Nor were the Democrats sufficiently united in votes to deliver their 2006 campaign pledge to withdraw troops from Iraq or reduce their number.

Notwithstanding its successes, Bush's partisan legislative strategy was far from being cost-free. It so offended centrist Senator James Jeffords (R-VT) that he assumed Independent status in May 2001, causing the GOP to lose control of the upper chamber. This was the first time in history that partisan control of the Senate had changed hands during the course of a congressional session. The Republicans controlled both chambers in the 108th and 109th Congress but experienced huge electoral losses in 2006 and 2008 as public support for Bush and his party declined sharply. Moreover, much of Bush's major legislation remained highly contentious, particularly among Democrats and the public. Even measures won with bipartisan support—on the war on terror, education, and Medicare—divided

Democrats and Republicans, further reinforcing hostile relations between supporters of the major parties inside and outside Congress.

Unilateral Policymaking and the Congress

Legislation is not the sole instrument of presidential policymaking, of course. Ever since John Adams engaged the United States in an undeclared war with France in 1798–1800, presidents have claimed unilateral powers to expand executive authority, especially in times of war and emergency.[50] Typically, they have justified their actions on grounds of necessity and in the twentieth century by using the techniques of the "personal" or "plebiscitary" presidency to invoke the demands of "the American people and their expectations."[51]

Presidents have been able to act as unilateral policymakers through exploitation of the notorious vagueness and ambiguities of the vesting clauses in Article II of the Constitution, precedents created by their predecessors, and imaginative use of evolving legal doctrine. They have done this through executive orders or executive agreements, presidential proclamations or national security directives, executive memoranda, and, more recently, issuing "findings," some of which may be secret. These instruments have been used for strategic purposes, including crisis management that requires swift and decisive action, and on occasions when congressional approval for their actions was unlikely.[52] Regardless of subsequent congressional authorization or its absence, these unilateral actions have the force of law. In taking such initiatives, presidents effectively challenge the Congress (and the courts) to overturn them. Typically, Congress does not—for the simple reason that it cannot muster a majority for such purpose—even less so a two-thirds majority in both chambers, if the president uses his veto.

Bush's aggressive claims of inherent presidential powers to take actions not explicitly authorized in the Constitution drew on "unitary executive" doctrine developed by conservative constitutionalists in the 1980s and 1990s.[53] Its leading exponents in the administration were Dick Cheney, his chief of staff, David Addington, Secretary of Defense Donald Rumsfeld, and other "old hands" from previous Republican administrations. According to one administration official critical of their viewpoint, "These men felt the same imperatives of responsibility that led Roosevelt and many other presidents to blow through 'legalistic' restrictions on presidential authority during times of crisis."[54]

Advocates of unitary power consider it all-embracing, indivisible, inherent, plenary, exclusive, and absolute. The doctrine holds that *all* executive powers are invested personally in the president and subject to his direct command. It effectively permits him to define policy in any area more or less unilaterally and regardless of congressional consent—by claiming and actually exercising unlimited and exclusive power based on inherent and implied discretionary, independent and formal powers derived from a very expansive interpretation of Article II and from congressional statutes. By definition, this theory of governance relegates almost to irrelevance the role of the Congress, the courts, and other institutional actors in seeking to insulate the president from the constitutional checks and balances in ways inconceivable to the founders. Any interference by these institutions with the president's exercise of executive authority is deemed to undermine the accountability that the Constitution gave to the president. Although the president may choose to accede to congressional demands, he is obligated neither to do so nor to submit to judicial review.

Bush's assertion of unitary powers were especially aggressive in response to the 9/11 attacks and the subsequent atmosphere of fear of renewed terrorist atrocities in the United States. He effectively exploited the strategic opportunities presented by the crisis and the ensuing war on terror to claim and use unilateral powers to advance a particular security agenda *and* to expand presidential and executive power through unilateral action—sometimes in secret—on the basis of dubious claims of "exclusive, independent and inherent" presidential powers. In the process, the administration successfully deterred—and often intimidated—Congress into *not* challenging the president or overturning the administration's unilateral actions. Indeed, most legislators were only too ready to give away or delegate their powers to enable the executive to deal with the crisis.

In the immediate aftermath of 9/11, Bush demanded and quickly obtained from Congress an all-embracing, loosely worded, use-of-force joint resolution, which ceded broad new discretionary powers to the executive. Although the resolution ostensibly placed presidential action under the auspices of the 1973 War Powers Act, legislators did not insist on replicating the original measure's provision for congressional accountability or scrutiny. Most significantly, as some lawmakers had predicted, the administration subsequently cited the resolution as the foundational legal authority for a presidentially initiated and presidentially defined "war" on terrorism unlimited by geography or time. In other words, it provided statutory justification for actions and policies that Congress did not explicitly authorize and became the legal basis for Bush claiming and using special wartime presidential powers.[55] When asked to justify electronic surveillance of U.S. citizens within the United States, use of torture and prisoner abuse, suspension of habeas corpus rights, extraordinary rendition, and so forth, administration officials invariably quoted the 2001 resolution or other foundational legislation, including the 2002 Homeland Security Act, the 2004 Intelligence Reform and Terrorism Prevention Act, the 2005 Patriot Reauthorisation and Improvement Act, and the 2006 Military Commissions Act, as legal authority for their actions.

The administration issued numerous executive and military orders, sometimes without disclosing the details to Congress, on the basis of the 2001 use-of-force resolution, dubious claims of "inherent" Article II powers, and often secret and "flimsy legal opinions."[56] One of the most controversial was a secret military order in November 2001 that unilaterally deemed noncitizens captured in the war on terror as "unlawful" or "enemy combatants," rather than prisoners of war under the protection of the Third Geneva Convention, and empowered military tribunals to try them. Disclosure in 2009 of various classified legal opinions written by Bush's Office of Legal Counsel (OLC) indicated that Cheney, Addington, and other administration officials also contemplated curtailing civil liberties in the United States, including free speech, press rights, and privacy and search and seizure protections. Contrary to the Fourth Amendment, they also considered using the U.S. military to apprehend terrorist suspects within the United States.[57] Other secret OLC memoranda advised that the president had the authority to suspend application of the Geneva Conventions or choose not to apply them, that even the harshest tactics used by the CIA were not "cruel, inhuman or degrading," and that the National Security Agency had authority to conduct warrantless wiretapping of Americans.[58] The implication of all this was that the administration could ignore existing U.S. statutory and international treaty obligations and unilaterally reformulate U.S. torture policy, then or at any other time in the future, without recourse to the Congress.

Basing its case for presidential unilateralism on arcane and controversial legal doctrine, the Bush administration received carte blanche foundational authority from an acquiescent Congress. It was also dismissive of the legislature's limited efforts to constrain its unilateralism. Some lawmakers sought to prohibit warrantless wiretapping of Americans following disclosures in the *New York Times* that Bush had secretly authorized this illegal activity in 2001. In response, Cheney asserted: "[The president]'s willing to listen to ideas from the Congress...[But *w*] *e'd have to make a decision as an administration whether or not we think* it would help and would enhance *our* capabilities...I don't think it would necessarily be in the interest of the country [for the Congress to become involved and write new legislation]."[59] Questioned by the Senate Judiciary Committee on presidential obligations to consult Congress about the scope of the war on terror, OLC Deputy Chief John Yoo insisted that Bush already enjoyed broad unilateral authority to use force against a mobile and elusive enemy "with or without specific congressional authorization.... Extensive congressional discussion will often be a luxury we cannot afford."[60] Public statements of this ilk by administration officials were based on classified memoranda. Attorney General Alberto Gonzales had penned one asserting that the president's "inherent" powers gave him authority to suspend the application of the Third Geneva Conventions since "a new kind of war...renders obsolete Geneva's strict limitations on questioning of enemy prisoners and renders quaint some of its provisions."[61] The notorious (and subsequently rescinded) "torture memo" written by Jay Bybee, Assistant Attorney General in the OLC, went even further. It proclaimed, *"Any* effort by Congress to regulate the interrogation of battlefield combatants would violate the Constitution's sole vesting of the Commander-in-Chief authority in the President."[62]

The administration's aggressive and exclusionary approach to Congress also featured a strong *penchant* for secrecy, based on claims of executive privilege and need to "preserve executive discretion in the operations of the government."[63] Administration officials and agencies frequently denied information to House and Senate lawmakers, whether Republican or Democrat. The first time Bush cited executive privilege in this regard was in 2001 to block a subpoena by GOP legislators seeking to investigate the Clinton administration. Even on matters of greatest public concern, such as intelligence on the 9/11 attacks, congressional committees frequently complained about the administration's withholding of information. When Senator Bob Graham (D-FL) requested declassification of part of the Joint House-Senate Intelligence Committee's report, twenty-eight pages that reputedly include details of Saudi Arabia's involvement in the plot were redacted.[64] Similarly, during the 9/11 Commission's investigations, the administration repeatedly cited executive privilege in refusing it permission to scrutinize relevant documents and question administration officials.[65] Moreover, following *New York Times'* revelations about the NSA's electronic surveillance program, it rebuffed Senate Judiciary Committee requests for classified departmental legal opinions questioning the legality of this undertaking.[66]

Nor were denials of information confined to war-on-terror issues. Executive agencies issued literally hundreds of new rules or regulations—on the environmental, food safety, workplace safety and conditions, and other issues—without informing Congress.[67] White House e-mails mysteriously disappeared following congressional requests for information. In 2008 Bush also threatened to veto a House-approved bill requiring the National Archives to issue stronger standards for preserving administration e-mails and "aggressively inspect" compliance.

In his seminal *Presidential Power*, Richard Neustadt made the important point that the power exercised and enjoyed by presidents is about much more than the exercise of their authority. A president's "power is the product of his vantage points in government, *together with his reputation in the Washington community and his prestige outside* [my emphasis]."[68] Lincoln in the Civil War, Wilson in World War I, and Franklin Roosevelt in the Great Depression and World War II had all attached considerable importance to achieving or maintaining political legitimacy, reputation, prestige, trust, and public approval, through consultation, deliberation, the appearance at least of deference to the Congress, and credible expressions of public concern for constitutional values, *at the same time* as they expanded presidential power significantly by unilateral claims.[69] In contrast, even as the unpopularity of his Iraq policy depressed his poll ratings, Bush and his aides disregarded the importance of what Jack Goldsmith dubbed "the soft factors of legitimation" in their drive to expand presidential power.[70]

Congressional Acquiescence

Lawmakers did little to challenge the president or rescind authority previously granted. This is of central importance to understand how Bush was able to assert his expansionary vision of presidential power. Regardless of partisan control, Congress mostly bent its knee to cede its policymaking prerogatives. Frequent oversight hearings, loud complaints, and the occasional challenge did not add up to a significant assertion of its power. Indeed the legislature emerged from the Bush era even more bereft of popular legitimacy than the president, with polls recording a 75 percent disapproval level of its performance in 2008.[71]

The hitherto contentious issue of executive privilege exemplified congressional deference. This was a grey area of constitutionality that the courts had never definitively resolved.[72] Other than Richard Nixon, Bush's predecessors had avoided confrontation over the issue and the legislature had previously shown its teeth in defending its prerogatives. Between 1975 and 2000, congressional committees cited ten cabinet-level or senior executive officials for contempt of Congress in failing to produce documents subpoenaed by a subcommittee or a full committee. In each case, the White House completely or substantially complied before criminal proceedings began.[73]

During the Bush administration's first six years, however, Congress showed a marked reluctance to issue subpoena challenges to executive secrecy. It displayed somewhat greater resolution after the Democrats took control. In July 2008, Senator Barbara Boxer (D-CA), chair of the Senate Environmental and Public Works Committee, threatened to subpoena an Environmental Protection Agency report containing a proposal to regulate greenhouse gases under the Clean Air Act. Having previously denied the existence of this document, the White House beat a partial retreat. It allowed the committee to borrow the report, while also insisting that senators could take "reasonable notes" only on the contents rather than photocopy them.[74] Moreover, in March 2007, in response to the discovery that some U.S. attorneys had been dismissed for political reasons, the House Judiciary Committee had actually authorized subpoenas against several high officials in the Bush administration. In May 2008, the same panel twice subpoenaed Bush's assistant, Karl Rove, to discuss his involvement in the Justice Department's decision to prosecute a former Democratic Governor of Alabama, who was likely to be a strong candidate against the Republican incumbent.

For the most part, however, Congress generally avoided confrontation with Bush, even when his disregard for its prerogatives was most blatant. During the debate over the Patriot Reauthorisation and Improvement Act in 2006, for example, the White House withheld information as a tactic to win immunity from prosecution for telecommunications companies that had complied with the administration's illegal wiretapping program. When it ignored committee subpoenas, Senate Majority Leader Harry Reid (D-NV) and House Speaker Nancy Pelosi (D-CA) consistently refused to bring legally enforceable contempt of Congress citations to floor votes for fear of not getting them approved. It was also remarkable how little investigatory action the Democrat-controlled Congress undertook in response to Bush's aggressive claims of unilateral power. This was in marked contrast to its Vietnam and Watergate era predecessors.

Nor was the Congress willing to flex its muscles through the power of the purse, notably with regard to the war on terror and Iraq. After approving the 2001 and 2002 use-of-force resolutions, legislators not only let Bush set the agenda and make the crucial decisions, with no enforceable requirements for congressional review, no expiration date, and no constraints on U.S. military engagement, but also complied with virtually every one of his appropriation requests. By late 2008, total war on terror appropriations totaled over $864 billions,[75] approximately $650 billions of which was earmarked for Iraq, compared with an initial administration estimate of $50–$60 billions.[76] Rather than proposing tax increases or encouraging substantive debate over financing the "war" or prioritizing budgetary demands, the Congress—under Republican and Democratic majorities—allowed the administration to spend willynilly and to run up huge budget deficits. More than this, legislators consistently allowed the administration to exploit a provision in the 1985 Gramm-Rudman-Hollings Balanced Budget and Emergency Deficit Control Act that permits the president to submit piecemeal supplemental spending requests additional to his annual budget. Since Bush usually submitted requests in mid–fiscal year, congressional appropriations committees had little time to scrutinize them properly.

Congress also failed to insist on detailed and credible "costs" or to ensure that outlays were used for the purposes authorized. On the few occasions it did impose conditions, the president signed the measure but refused to abide by its terms.[77] Even after appropriators prohibited future supplemental requests and in their FY 2007 defense authorization bill insisted that the president include all war funding requests within his annual budget with a "detailed justification" for each spending request, the administration responded by increasing its initial FY2008 request by one-third (subsequently reduced by the new Democratic majorities) and, then, continued submitting new supplementary requests to its FY2009 request.[78] Once in control of Congress, the Democrats sought to impose a timetable for withdrawal from Iraq through cut off funding for military operations, but lacked sufficient votes in the Senate. Bush then outmaneuvred his opponents to secure additional appropriations for the "surge" strategy of expanding U.S. troop levels in Iraq. This outcome was final proof, were any needed, of Congress's failure to defend its prerogatives in the war on terror, a record that contrasted with its assertiveness during the Korean, Vietnam, and Bosnian wars.

The Legacy

Bush's ambitious and unsubstantiated claims of vast unilateral executive authority and immunity from congressional (and judicial) oversight were assaults on Madisonian interpretations of the separated system, which require that presidential exercises of power derive directly from the U.S. Constitution or from a statute constitutionally enacted by the Congress. What Peter Shane has recently called "Madison's nightmare"[79] occurs when the president fails to comply with these constitutionally legitimizing requirements and the Congress compounds this failure by not insisting on his constitutional observance. Bush's approach to presidential-congressional relations was presidentialist, and to an unprecedented degree, most evidently when applied to national and homeland security issues. Informed by "unitary executive" theory, the president's responsibilities—according to the likes of Bush, Cheney, Addington, and Yoo—extended beyond Hamilton's advocacy in *Federalist 69* of "energy in the executive" to claim powers akin to the royal prerogative in Britain. Yet they were not alone in corrupting and destabilizing Madison's constitutional bargain. The Republican and Democratic Congresses were also culpable of failure to check Bush.

There can be no question but that Bush—as "defender of the homeland"—led the Congress on national and domestic security,[80] and that Congress followed his lead regardless of party control. Nonetheless, the growth of presidential power in these spheres did not begin with Bush. However tempting it is to assume that the drive to expand presidential power at the expense of the Congress enjoyed comparable success in domestic policy, the political realities facing the Bush administration made that impossible. Moreover, Bush's presidentialist success in the national and homeland security did not generate the political legitimacy necessary to safeguard his legacy in these domains from repudiation by the congressional Democrats in 2006 and 2008 and Democratic presidential candidate Barack Obama in 2008.

As we have seen, Bush assumed office in 2001 in questionable circumstances and lacking a mandate. This combination of factors raised major issues about the legitimacy of his presidency. The strategic context of his relations with Congress also appeared to disadvantage him. Nevertheless, Bush's response to 9/11 gave him unprecedented legitimacy, and by pursuing an aggressively partisan legislative strategy on a limited number of priorities, he won some major legislative achievements, and not exclusively on domestic and national security issues. However, this partisan strategy also yielded some huge legislative failures—notably on faith initiatives, immigration, social security reform, and making his 2001 tax cuts permanent. After the 2006 elections, moreover, the Democrats were in a position to pursue their own agenda—at least on domestic policy—in opposition to Bush, and did so to some effect with a significant payoff in the 2008 elections.

As this chapter has shown, however, the most significant aspects of presidential-congressional relations had to do with (1) Bush's aggressive and audacious assertions of unilateral executive powers, either based on "inherent" constitutional prerogatives or foundational congressional authorization, particularly in pursuit of the so-called war on terror and (2) the corollary congressional acquiescence or subsequent legitimization of his unilateral actions, including those that were illegal. On occasions Congress collectively challenged the forty-third president but overall it deferred to him.

Aggressive presidential use of unilateral powers did not begin with Bush, but he significantly extended them. His assertive and confrontational presidentialism in the post-9/11 environment may provide the impetus for the evolution of America's constitutional order from one equilibrium to another. According to Walter Dean Burnham, "constitutional moments" or transformations occur "toward the end of a protracted set of 'flipover' dynamics." If these dynamics were set in train by Bush's predecessors, war on terror initiatives could be the "change-forcers" necessary to stimulate evolution from one relatively stable equilibrium to the next.[81] The actions of his successor support this thesis. Barack Obama has certainly borrowed from the Bush toolbox, most notably in the continuing campaign against international terrorism.

Mention of Obama once again raises the crucial question of congressional response to increased presidential unilateralism, whether on domestic or national security or other issues. As Justice Jackson noted in the 1952 Steel Seizure case (*Youngstown Sheet and Tube v. Sawyer*), if presidents regularly assert a prerogative systematically, with the knowledge of the Congress, and "congressional inertia, indifference or quiescence" results in that action never being questioned, that practice subsequently becomes a constitutional power that cannot be infringed upon by the Congress or the courts. The war on terror and, to some extent, congressional and presidential responses to the 2008 banking crisis demonstrate that, beyond the rhetoric of congressional leaders, there was a good deal of Justice Jackson's congressional "inertia, indifference or quiescence." Presidential power, it is important to remind ourselves, is not only the power to persuade.

It is also a question of what a president seeks to get away with—and the leeway that the Congress and the courts allow him.

Notes

I am grateful to Jim Thurber of the Center for Congressional and Presidential Studies at the American University for providing me with office accommodation and a congenial base for my fieldwork in Washington DC.

1. James Bryce, *The American Commonwealth*, vol. 1 (New York: Macmillan, 1910), 58.
2. Fred I. Greenstein, "Change and Continuity in the Modern Presidency," in Anthony King, ed., *The New American Political System* (Washington DC: American Enterprise Institute, 1978), 45–86.
3. Charles O. Jones, *The Presidency in a Separated System*, 2nd ed. (Washington DC: Brookings Institution Press, 2005), 3; Michael Foley and John E. Owens, *Congress and the Presidency. Institutional Politics in a Separated System* (Manchester and New York: Manchester University Press, 1996), 6.
4. Stephen Skowronek, *Presidential Leadership in Political Time: Reprise and Reappraisal* (Lawrence: University Press of Kansas, 2008), 117–49.
5. James MacGregor Burns, *Leadership* (New York: Harper and Row, 1978), 344–45, 363; Erwin C. Hargrove, *The President as Leader. Appealing to the Better Angels of Our Nature* (Lawrence: University Press of Kansas, 1999), 30–32; Stephen Skowronek, *The Politics Presidents Make: Leadership from John Adams to Bill Clinton* (Cambridge MA: Belknap Press, 1997). For good analysis of transactional leadership, see Barbara Kellerman, *The Political Presidency: Practice of Leadership from Kennedy through Reagan* (New York: Oxford University Press, 1984), 18–21.
6. Lawrence H. Chamberlain, *The President, Congress and Legislation* (New York: Columbia University Press, 1946); Ronald C. Moe and Steven C. Teel, "Congress as Policymaker: A Necessary Reappraisal," *Political Science Quarterly*, 85, 2, 1970, 443–70; Mark A. Peterson, *Legislating Together: The White House and Capitol Hill from Eisenhower to Reagan* (Cambridge MA: Harvard University Press, 1990); Nelson W. Polsby, "Some Landmarks in Modern Presidential-Congressional Relations," in Anthony King, ed., *Both Ends of the Avenue. The Presidency, the Executive Branch, and the Congress in the 1980s* (Washington DC: American Enterprise Institute, 1983), 1–25; Jones, *The Presidency in a Separated System*.
7. Richard E. Neustadt, *Presidential Power* (New York: Wiley, 1960), 11.
8. Jones, *The Presidency in a Separated System*; Foley and Owens, *Congress and the Presidency*.
9. *Gallup Poll*, January 15–16, 2001.

10. *Gallup Poll*, September 7–10, 2001.
11. *Gallup Poll*, July 18–20, and July 25–27, 2003.
12. Al Gore won 540,000 votes more than Bush in the 2000 presidential contest. However, Bush won more votes than Gore in 240 House districts, running behind him in only 195. The lower efficiency of the geographic distribution of the Democratic vote is explained by the concentration of minority and other urban voters in districts with heavy Democratic majorities, and by the effectiveness of Republican gerrymandering in states such as Florida, Michigan, Ohio, Pennsylvania, and Texas. See Gary C. Jacobson, "Polarized Politics and the 2004 Congressional and Presidential Elections," *Political Science Quarterly*, 120, 2, 2005, 199–218; and Gary C. Jacobson, "Referendum: The 2006 Midterm Congressional Elections," *Political Science Quarterly*, 122, 1, 2007, 2.
13. *Gallup Poll*, October 10–12, 2008.
14. Gary C. Jacobson, "The Effects of the Bush Administration on Partisan Attitudes," *Presidential Studies Quarterly*, 39, 2, 2009, 172–209.
15. Gary C. Jacobson, "The 2008 Presidential and Congressional Elections: Anti-Bush Referendum and Prospects for the Democratic Majority," *Political Science Quarterly*, 124, 1, 2009, 8.
16. Nolan McCarty, Keith Pool, and Howard Rosenthal, *Polarized America: The Dance of Ideology and Unequal Riches* (Cambridge MA: MIT Press, 2006); Andrew Gelman, *Red State, Blue State, Rich State, Poor State: Why Americans Vote the Way They Do* (Princeton: Princeton University Press, 2008); Morris P. Fiorina, *Culture War? The Myth of a Polarized America* (New York: Longman 2004); Larry M. Bartels, *Unequal Democracy: The Political Economy of the New Gilded Age* (Princeton: Princeton University Press, 2008).
17. Jacobson, "Referendum," 3.
18. John E. Owens, "Challenging (and Acting for) the President: Congressional Leadership in an Era of Partisan Polarization," in George C. Edwards and Phillip John Davies, eds., *New Challenges for the American Presidency* (New York: Longman, 2003), 124.
19. DW-NOMINATE scores are based on roll call voting records, and range roughly from –1 to 1, where –1 is a very liberal score and 1 is a very conservative score. I am grateful to Keith Poole, Howard Rosenthal, and Nolan McCarty for the use of their DW-NOMINATE data at http://voteview.ucsd.edu/
20. Data compiled by the author show that in the period from the 99th to the 109th House (1985–2006), the percentage of rules that was restrictive (primarily limiting floor amendments) rose from 21.5 to 69, reflecting the tighter grip imposed by successive House majorities on the floor agenda. Senate cloture data are available at http://www.senate.gov/pagelayout/reference/cloture_motions/clotureCounts.htm
21. See Barbara Sinclair, *Party Wars: Polarization and the Politics of National Policymaking* (Norman: University of Oklahoma Press, 2006) for these effects in respect of major legislation.

22. Charles Tiefer, "Congressional Oversight of the Clinton Administration and Congressional Procedure," *Administrative Law Review*, 50, 1, 1998, 199–216; Linda Fowler and Seth Hill, "Guarding the Guardians: Senate Oversight Activity in Foreign Affairs, 1947–2004," paper presented at the annual meeting of the American Political Science Association, August 31, 2006.
23. Gary C. Jacobson, *A Divider Not a Uniter: George W. Bush and the American People* (New York: Pearson Longman, 2006); John E. Owens, "Presidential *Aggrandizement* and Congressional Acquiescence in the 'War on Terror': A New Constitutional Equilibrium?" in John E. Owens and John W. Dumbrell, eds., *America's "War On Terrorism": New Dimensions in United States Government and National Security* (Lanham MD: Lexington Books, 2008), 25–76; John E. Owens, "Congressional Acquiescence to Presidentialism in the US 'War on Terror,'" *Journal of Legislative Studies*, 15, June/September 2009, 147–90.
24. Ronald B. Brownstein, *The Second Civil War* (New York: Penguin: 2007), 230.
25. Quoted in Bob Woodward, *Plan of Attack* (New York: Simon and Schuster, 2004), 28.
26. Charles O. Jones, "The US Congress and Chief Executive George W. Bush," in George C. Edwards and Desmond S. King, eds., *The Polarized Presidency of George W. Bush* (New York: Oxford University Press, 2007), 401.
27. Richard B. Cheney, *Protecting the President's Power.* Memo to James A. Baker, November 19, 1980, http://blog washingtonpost.com/cheney/sidebars/cheney_on_presidential_power/index.html (Accessed June 25, 2009)
28. Alexis Simendinger, "Andy Card on Power and Privilege," *National Journal*, April 17, 2004, 1173; Alexis Simendinger, "Power Plays," *National Journal*, April 17, 2004, 1168.
29. Jones, "The US Congress and Chief Executive George W. Bush," 399.
30. Bob Woodward, *Bush at War* (New York: Simon and Schuster, 2002), 256.
31. Quoted in ibid., 144–45.
32. John E. Owens, "American-Style Party Government: Delivering Bush's Agenda, Delivering the Congress' Agenda?" in Iwan Morgan and Philip Davies, eds., *Right On? Political Change and Continuity in George Bush's America* (London: Institute for the Study of the Americas, 2006), 140.
33. George C. Edwards, *Governing by Campaigning. The Politics of the Bush Presidency* (New York: Pearson Longman, 2007), 215–80.
34. Barton Gellman and Walter Pincus, "Depiction of Threat Outgrew Supporting Evidence," *Washington Post*, August 10, 2003, A1.
35. George C. Edwards, *On Deaf Ears: The Limits of the Bully Pulpit* (New Haven CT: Yale University Press 2003), 24–78; Lawrence R. Jacobs and

Robert Y. Shapiro, *Politicians Don't Pander* (Chicago: University of Chicago Press, 2000).
36. Gary C. Jacobson, "The Bush Presidency and the American Electorate," *Presidential Studies Quarterly*, 33, 4, 2003, 701–29; Jacobson, "Polarized Politics and the 2004 Congressional and Presidential Elections," 199–218; Jacobson, "Referendum," 3.
37. *Gallup Poll*, November 2–5, 2006, and October 10–12, 2008.
38. I am grateful to David Mayhew for these data. See http://pantheon.yale.edu/~dmayhew/data3.html (Accessed July 3, 2009).
39. Richard S. Conley, "Reform, Reorganization, and the Renaissance of the Managerial Presidency: The Impact of 9/11 on the Executive Establishment," in Owens and Dumbrell, *America's "War On Terrorism*," 79.
40. Owens, "Presidential *Aggrandizement* and Congressional Acquiescence in the 'War on Terror,'" 165–68.
41. The term is drawn from Skowronek's works, *Presidential Leadership in Political Time* and *The Politics Presidents Make*.
42. John E. Owens, "Congress and Crisis: Will the 111th Congress Be Any Different?" *Extensions*, Spring 2009, 7–8.
43. Amy E. Black, Douglas L. Koopman, and David K. Ryden, *Of Little Faith: The Politics of George W. Bush's Faith-Based Initiatives* (Washington DC: Georgetown University Press, 2004); Bill Swindell, "Faith-Based Offices an End Run Around Languishing Legislation," *CQ Weekly*, November 2, 2002, 2861–63.
44. Dana Milbank, "Bush Expected to Back Federalized Screening at Airports; President 'Not Looking to Veto an Airline Security Bill' That Includes the Measure, Chief of Staff Says," *Washington Post*, October 29, 2001, A1.
45. Owens, "American Style Party Government," 156.
46. Adriel Bettelheim, "Bush's Rough Choice on Social Security: Backtrack or Take Flak," *CQ Weekly*, March 7, 2005, 550–51; Terry Weiner, "Touching the Third Rail: Explaining the Failure of Bush's Social Security Initiative," *Politics & Policy*, 35, 4, 2007, 872–97; Edwards, *Governing by Campaigning*, 215–80. Subsequently, without public fanfare, Bush also included privatization proposals amounting to $712 billions over seven years in his FY2007 budget proposals. See Allan Sloan, "Bush's Social Security Sleight of Hand," *Washington Post*, February 8, 2006, D2.
47. Alex Wayne, "GOP's Deep Divide on Immigration Frustrates Hill Efforts at Overhaul," *CQ Weekly*, October 23, 2004, 2525–26.
48. Richard A. Oppel, "Senate Raises Bar to Enact New Tax Cuts; Rebuff to Bush," *New York Times*, March 11, 2004, A1.
49. Stephen Labaton and David M. Herszenhorn, "White House Ready to Aid Auto Industry," *New York Times*, December 12, 2008, A1.
50. Edward Corwin, *Total War and the Constitution* (New York: Ayer, 1947); Louis W. Koenig, *The Chief Executive*, 5th ed. (New York: Harcourt,

Brace, Jovanovich, 1986), 235–37; Louis Fisher, *Presidential War Power*, 2nd rev. ed. (Lawrence: University Press of Kansas, 2004).
51. Theodore J. Lowi, *The Personal President: Power Invested, Promised Unfulfilled* (Ithaca NY: Cornell University Press, 1986), xi–xii, 180.
52. Kenneth R. Mayer, "Executive Orders and Presidential Power," *Journal of Politics*, 62, 2, 1999, 445–66.
53. Christopher Yoo, Steven G. Calabresi, and Anthony J. Colangelo, "The Unitary Executive in the Modern Era, 1945–2004," *Iowa Law Review*, 90, 2005, 690–729; John C. Yoo, *The Powers of War and Peace: The Constitution and Foreign Affairs after 9/11* (Chicago: University of Chicago Press, 2005).
54. Jack L. Goldsmith, *The Terror Presidency: Law and Judgment Inside the Bush Administration* (New York: W. W. Norton, 2007), 79.
55. John C. Yoo, *The President's Constitutional Authority to Conduct Military Operations against Terrorists and Nations Supporting Them*. Memorandum to Alberto Gonzalez, The White House, Washington DC.: US. Department of Justice. Office of Legal Counsel, September 25, 2001, http://www.usdoj.gov/olc/warpowers925.htm (Accessed June 4, 2006); John C. Yoo, *The President's Constitutional Authority to Conduct Military Operations against Terrorists and Nations Supporting Them*. Memorandum to Timothy Flanigan, the Deputy Counsel to the President. Washington DC: US. Department of Justice. Office of Legal Counsel, September 25, 2001, http://www.usdoj.gov/olc/warpowers925.htm (Accessed June 5, 2006). See Owens, "Presidential *Aggrandizement* and Congressional Acquiescence" for further discussion.
56. Goldsmith, *The Terror Presidency*, 181.
57. John C. Yoo and Robert J. Delahunty, *Re. Authority for Use of Military Force to Combat Terrorist Activities within the United States*. Memorandum to Alberto Gonzales, Counsel to the President and William J. Haynes, General Counsel, Department of Defense. Washington DC: US. Department of Justice. Office of Legal Counsel, October 23, 2001, http://www.usdoj.gov/opa/documents/olc-memos.htm (Accessed March 3, 2009). See also Mark Mazzetti and David Johnston, "Bush Weighed Using Military in Arrests," *New York Times*, July 25, 2009.
58. Alberto Gonzales, Memorandum for the President. *Decision Re Application of the Geneva Convention on Prisoners of War to the Conflict with Al Qaeda and the Taliban*. January 25, 2002, http://wid.ap.org/documents/doj/gonzales.pdf (Accessed January 25, 2007); Jay Bybee, "Standards of Conduct for Interrogation under 18 USC. 230–2340A." *Memorandum to White House Alberto Gonzales*, August 1, 2002. http://news.findlaw.com/hdocs/docs/doj/bybee80102ltr.html (Accessed June 25, 2009); David Johnston and Scott Shane, "Debate Erupts on Techniques Used by CIA," *New York Times*, October 5, 2007, A1.
59. Dick Cheney, "News Hour: Newsmaker: Vice President Dick Cheney," *Interview with Jim Lehrer, PBS Television*, http://www.pbs.org/

newshour/bb/white_house/jan-june06/cheney_02–07.html (February 7, 2006).
60. U.S. Congress Senate. Committee on the Judiciary. Subcommittee on the Constitution, Civil Rights and Property Rights. Hearings. *Applying the War Powers Resolution to the War on Terrorism*, 107th Congress, Second Session, April 17, 2002, http://judiciary.senate.gov/testimony.cfm?id=225&wit_id=437 and http://judiciary.senate.gov/hearing.cfm?id=1727 (Accessed July 26, 2009)
61. Alberto Gonzales, Memorandum for the President. *Decision Re Application of the Geneva Convention on Prisoners of War to the Conflict with Al Qaeda and the Taliban.* January 25, 2002. http://wid.ap.org/documents/doj/gonzales.pdf (Accessed December 28, 2006).
62. Bybee, "Standards of Conduct for Interrogation," 38.
63. Simendinger, "Power Plays," 1168
64. "Investigating the Investigators" (editorial), *New York Times*, August 10, 2002, A14.
65. Philip Shenon, "Bush to Limit Testimony before 9/11 Panel," *New York Times*, February 26, 2004, A1.
66. Eric Lichtblau, "Senate Panel Rebuffed on Documents on U.S. Spying," *New York Times*, February 2, 2006, A1.
67. Juliet Eilperin, "EPA E-Mail Concluded Global Warming Endangers Public Health, Senator Says," *Washington Post*, July 25, 2008, A19; Public Citizen's Global Trade Watch and Critical Mass Energy and Environment Program, *The WTO Comes to Dinner. US Implementation of Trade Rules Bypasses Food Safety Requirements* (Washington DC: Public Citizen, 2003); Carol D. Leonnig, "U.S. Rushes to Change Workplace Toxin Rules," *Washington Post*, July 23, 2008, A1.
68. Neustadt, *Presidential Power*, 150.
69. Arthur M. Schlesinger, *The Imperial Presidency* (Boston: Houghton Mifflin, 1973), 106, 109; Goldsmith, *The Terror Presidency*, 79, 202–3.
70. Goldsmith, *The Terror Presidency*, 79, 202–3, 215.
71. *Gallup Poll*, July 10–13, 2008. It should be noted, of course, that congressional approval has rarely been high.
72. Louis Fisher, *The Politics of Executive Privilege* (Durham NC: Carolina Academic Press, 2004).
73. Louis Fisher, *Congressional Investigations: Subpoenas and Contempt Power*, Congressional Research Service Report for Congress [CRSRC], RL31836, April 2, 2003, 18–39.
74. Eilperin, "EPA E-Mail Concluded Global Warming Endangers Public Health, Senator Says."
75. Amy Belasco, *The Cost of Iraq, Afghanistan, and Other Global War on Terror Operations since 9/11*, CRSRC, RL33110, October 15, 2008.
76. Elisabeth Bumiller, "Threats and Responses: The Cost; White House Cuts Estimate of Cost of War with Iraq," *New York Times*, December 31, 2002, A1.

77. Dana Milbank, "GOP Leader Challenges Bush Statements. House Republicans Sensitive to Criticism They Underfunded Homeland Security," *Washington Post*, March 8, 2003, A4.
78. Steven M. Kosiak, *Cost of the Wars in Iraq and Afghanistan and Other Military Operations through 2008 and Beyond* (Washington DC: Center for Strategic and Budgetary Assessments, 2008), 48–49; David Newman and Jason Wheelock, "Analysis of the Growth in Funding for Operations in Iraq, Afghanistan and Elsewhere in the War on Terrorism," Congressional Budget Office, February 11, 2008: 16, 19; Government Accountability Office, *Supplemental Appropriations. Opportunities Exist to Increase Transparency and Provide Additional Controls*. Report to the Ranking Member, Subcommittee on Oversight of Government Management, the Federal Workforce, and the District of Columbia, Committee on Homeland Security and Governmental Affairs, U.S. Senate. Report GAO-08-314. January 2008, http://www.gao.gov/new.items/d08314.pdf, 16, 29.
79. Peter Shane, *Madison's Nightmare: How Executive Power Threatens American Democracy* (Chicago: University of Chicago Press, 2009).
80. Owens, "Presidential *Aggrandizement* and Congressional Acquiescence," 65.
81. Walter Dean Burnham, "Constitutional Moments and Punctuated Equilibrium: A Political Scientist Confronts Bruce Ackerman's *We the People*," *Yale Law* Review, June 1999, 2238, 2240.

Chapter Four

Bush, the Judiciary, and the Conservative Constitutional Counterrevolution: Close but No Cigar

Robert J. McKeever

Measuring a president's judicial legacy is no easy task, particularly in the immediate aftermath of his tenure in office. When Franklin D. Roosevelt died in 1945, much could have been said about his judicial legacy, but the role that some of his Supreme Court nominees played in championing historically momentous advancements of civil rights and civil liberties over the next twenty-five years would not have been mentioned. With Supreme Court justices remaining in office many years after their appointing president has left the White House, it can take decades for the full and accurate picture of a judicial legacy to emerge. With only eighteen months having elapsed at time of writing since his presidency ended, assessment of George W. Bush's record on this score must be provisional and somewhat speculative.

Such caveats notwithstanding, some leading scholars and commentators have already seen enough evidence to discern the shape and direction of the forty-third president's impact upon the judiciary and related constitutional issues. According to one estimate, "George W. Bush left a judicial legacy that even his political opponents concede has had a major impact in the reshaping of the federal judiciary. Indeed…[it] may well be Bush's most enduring accomplishment."[1] One such opponent, Ronald Dworkin, similarly concluded, "The revolution that many commentators predicted when President Bush appointed two ultra-right-wing Supreme Court Justices is proceeding with breathtaking impatience."[2] In like vein, Barbara A. Perry noted, "Trading Sandra Day O'Connor's swing vote for [Samuel] Alito's predictably conservative stance has been crucial in shifting the Supreme Court to the right as George W. Bush and his supporters wished."[3] Finally, in his October 2008 speech to what he termed "the mighty Federalist Society," the president claimed to have fulfilled his promise to appoint more judges like Antonin Scalia and Clarence Thomas "who would faithfully interpret the Constitution and not use the courts to invent laws or dictate social policy." Very proud of his record in this regard, Bush affirmed, "And with your support, we have kept that pledge. I have appointed more than one-third of all the judges now sitting on the federal bench and these men and women are jurists of the highest calibre, with an abiding belief in the sanctity of our Constitution."[4]

These opinions reflect the prevailing consensus that Bush was extremely successful in his judicial strategy, both in terms of the quantity and quality of his appointees, and in the significant impact that these judges are already having and will continue to have for many years to come. This chapter contends, however, that the consensus is at best premature and at worst significantly overstated.

There are a number of criteria we can use to measure a president's success in bequeathing an important judicial legacy. For example, there are quantitative indicators, the number of successful judicial nominations he makes, to be specific. Closely related to this is the matter of the ideological characteristics of these successful nominees and the extent to which they share the president's views on constitutional issues and the role of the judiciary in American government. Another important measure is impact. Most obviously we can try to discern the cases where a president's nominees appear to have made a significant difference to the outcomes of cases, particularly those decided by the U.S. Supreme Court.

The highest level of presidential impact, however, is the extent to which he has achieved a change of historic proportions. This goes beyond the matter of whether the Supreme Court is deciding differently cases involving this or that constitutional issue. Rather it consists of making judicial appointments that change the strategic direction in which the Court is traveling, both in terms of the role it plays and the substance and jurisprudential underpinnings of the constitutional issues it resolves. Franklin D. Roosevelt consciously sought such a historic change, which he achieved after 1937, partly by putting political pressure on the existing Court and partly by appointing new Justices sympathetic to the regulatory and socioeconomic changes of the New Deal. Dwight D. Eisenhower unconsciously made an enormous contribution to the creation of Warren Court liberal activism by appointing Earl Warren and William Brennan.

For George W. Bush, the principal measure of his judicial success is whether he was the Republican president who at last fulfilled the conservative quest to halt and reverse the liberal activism of the Warren and early Burger Courts. For over thirty years, judicial scholars have engaged in a discourse focusing on the "conservative counterrevolution." In 1977, Richard Y. Funston asked whether Richard Nixon's Supreme Court appointees had achieved his goal of terminating Warren Court liberal activism and introducing a new era of judicial restraint. "The common knowledge," he observed, "has been that the differences have been very great, that the Nixon appointments have turned the Court around." In a portent for evaluating the Bush record, however, Funston's own detailed analysis yielded a different conclusion, namely that the continuities between the Warren Court and the Burger Court were far greater than the differences.[5] Similarly, Vincent Blasi's 1983 edited collection on the Burger Court announced its message in the title: *The Burger Court: The Counter-Revolution That Wasn't*.[6] In his own essay, Blasi concluded not only that there had been no counterrevolution to date, but also that "by almost any measure the Burger Court has been an activist court."[7]

It was Blasi's view that activism, rootless or otherwise, might have become a permanent feature of Supreme Court decision making. However, he was writing on the eve of the Reagan administration's most determined effort to change the direction of the Court's jurisprudence. In 1986, the fortieth president elevated William Rehnquist to the chief justiceship and placed the equally conservative Antonin Scalia on the Court. In 1987 came the ill-fated attempt to appoint Robert Bork, the intellectual doyen of conservative jurisprudence at the time. The failure to have him confirmed eventually led to the appointment of the moderate conservative Anthony Kennedy, something that was to impede the counterrevolution, as is discussed below. Nevertheless, President George H. W. Bush continued Reagan's approach to Supreme Court appointments, albeit cautiously given the Democrat majority in the Senate. Adopting a strategy of stealth, he appointed David Souter, whose lack of judicial record was deemed an advantage, but this supposed conservative turned out to be a moderate liberal. His next nominee, Clarence Thomas, coming straight out of the Rehnquist-Scalia mold, seemingly put the counterrevolution back on track. Unsurprisingly, Bill Clinton's appointees halted the conservative momentum but his successor took office intent on picking up where his father and Reagan had left off.

Given this historical and political context, if the impact of George W. Bush's judicial legacy is to be regarded as being of great significance—and more so than that of other modern presidents—it must be shown that he completed or greatly advanced the conservative constitutional counterrevolution.

The quantitative evidence suggests that Bush was successful in the number of federal judges he appointed, but not unusually so when compared to other modern presidents. Indeed his record is remarkably similar to that of Bill Clinton. Moreover, analysis of the most important Supreme Court cases since the arrival of Chief Justice Roberts and Associate Justice Samuel Alito does not support the conclusion that Bush's appointees so far have significantly changed judicial policy in any major way. Finally, despite his successes, Bush did not achieve or greatly advance the judicial counterrevolution. At the end of the 2008–9 Supreme Court term, it was still "a Kennedy Court" and not "a Roberts Court." The forty-third president certainly shored up the conservative bloc on the Court, but he did not achieve the ultimate goal for which his Republican predecessors Nixon, Reagan, and George H. Bush, had prepared the way.

Bush's Judicial Appointments

District Courts

Presidents nominate judges to federal district courts, circuit courts of appeal, and, most importantly, to the U.S. Supreme Court. District courts are essentially the trial courts of the federal judicial system and, as such, are not viewed as having a significant policymaking role. As a result, nominations to the district courts are rarely contentious and when they are, it is usually due to home state politics. The data on George W. Bush's appointments to the district courts place him squarely within the parameters established by other modern presidents.[8]

Bush made somewhat fewer nominations (286) (through October 20, 2008) to the district courts than other post-1977 two-term presidents, Reagan (306) and Clinton (350). On the other hand, his percentage of nominees confirmed (91.3) was higher than that of Bush Sr. (77.5) and Clinton (87.1), albeit below that of Carter (92.7) and Reagan (94.8). Despite Bush's pride in having appointed more than a third of all federal judges sitting at the end of his presidency, this too is not unusual or particularly noteworthy. In confirmation of this, Bush's tally of having appointed 38.1 percent of district court judges sitting on January 1, 2009 was equal only to the Clinton-appointed judges still sitting (38 percent).[9]

Circuit Courts of Appeal

The courts of appeal are viewed as significant players in judicial policymaking. While their decisions are subject to review by the Supreme Court, they can attempt to influence the law through their application of it to the facts established in the district courts. They can introduce new legal arguments in the hope of persuading the Supreme Court to adopt their line of thinking and may also seek to narrow or broaden the scope of precedents. Equally important, service on a circuit court is often seen as a prerequisite for appointment to the Supreme Court. Unsurprisingly, it is at the circuit court level that the struggle between the political parties, interest groups, and governmental institutions to control the appointment process can become intense.

At this level, however, George W. Bush actually had a worse statistical record than any of his four predecessors.[10] Bush nominated fewer appeal court judges (85) (through October 20, 2008) than fellow two-term presidents Reagan (94) and Clinton (90). He also had the lowest confirmation rate of all five presidents—71.8 percent compared with 72.2 percent for Clinton, 79.2 percent for Bush 41, 88.3 percent for Reagan, and 93.3 percent for Carter. Once again, his profile is very similar to that of Bill Clinton, reflecting the fact that both presidents faced stiff opposition and delaying tactics in the Senate. By the end of George W. Bush's presidency, his record on appointees to the courts of appeal was very similar to that for the district courts. His tally amounted to 32.9 percent of sitting judges, but Clinton's appointees effectively matched this (32.3 percent). In essence, therefore, the forty-third and forty-second presidents had a similar level of influence at this judicial level.[11]

The U.S. Supreme Court

Far more important than the lower federal courts is the Supreme Court. While opportunities to appoint Supreme Court justices are very few, the potential to influence public policy is considerable. This is particularly true when the Court is finely balanced between different voting blocs, as has been the case since at least the early 1980s. The chance to appoint a Supreme Court justice is largely a matter of luck, since it depends upon a sitting justice's death or retirement. George W. Bush had about average luck in this respect. He had the same number of vacancies to fill as Bill Clinton (two each), though one less than the other two-term president, Ronald Reagan. His father had also had two vacancies to fill in his single term, but Jimmy Carter had none.

In contrast to Clinton, however, George W. Bush had a significant and embarrassing error of judgment on his judicial record, namely his nomination of White House Counsel Harriet Miers. Conservative activists, fearful that she lacked ideological conviction and intellectual stature, considered her unequal to the position. Her subsequent withdrawal in the face of criticism from the very people whom he had hoped to please with her selection made the president look inept. Nevertheless, Bush's two successful nominees, Chief Justice John Roberts and Associate Justice Samuel Alito, are both intelligent and accomplished conservative jurists. His preferences were reflected in their judicial decision making, much as Clinton's has been in that of his two appointees, Ruth Bader Ginsburg and Stephen Breyer.

As far as the numerical evidence on appointments is concerned, Bush's record is not in the least exceptional or unusually successful when compared to that of other modern presidents. If a convincing claim is to be made that he bequeathed an unusually impressive legacy, therefore, it must be demonstrated by the quality, rather than the quantity, of the judges he has appointed. Most importantly, it must be shown not only that he succeeded in appointing judges who would reflect his own views, but that they changed the law in accordance with those views.

Bush's Judicial Nominees

It is clear beyond doubt that the forty-third president set out to appoint conservative judges to the federal bench. This was true even of his nominees to the district courts, where judicial philosophy is least likely to have an impact. One study of these district court appointees suggests that the Bush judges are significantly more conservative than Clinton's judges and somewhat more conservative than either Reagan's or George H. W. Bush's judges.[12] At the courts of appeal level, it was the uncompromising conservatism of some of his nominees that led to the near breakdown of the confirmation process. As for the Supreme Court, the president made it clear from the start that he intended to appoint justices in the mould of Antonin Scalia and Clarence Thomas, the two most conservative members of the Court. Even more indicative of his intent, however, was that he continued the use of the Judicial Selection Committee, pioneered by the Reagan administration and sustained by his father's, to identify nominees of the right conservative pedigree. In addition, Bush recruited Edwin Meese and C. Boyden Gray, respectively leading figures in the judicial selection process of the Reagan and Bush 41 administrations, to fulfill the same role in his. Finally, conservative interest groups were central to the Bush 43 judicial selection process, particularly the Federalist Society and the American Centre for Law and Justice.

The Impact of John Roberts and Samuel Alito

The claim that Bush has significantly advanced the judicial counterrevolution depends most heavily on his appointment of John Roberts and Samuel Alito to the Supreme Court as replacements respectively for Chief Justice William Rehnquist and Associate Justice Sandra Day O'Connor. The like-for-like replacement of the staunchly conservative Rehnquist may reasonably be expected to make little difference to the outcomes of Supreme Court cases. Greater potential for change and, therefore, impact lies in the replacement of the moderate conservative O'Connor with the more deeply conservative Alito.

Before analyzing the O'Connor-Alito differences, it is important to note that the contemporary composition of the Court places considerable constraints upon the progress of the conservative counterrevolution. Seven of the justices sitting at the end of Bush's presidency were appointed by Republican presidents, but the outcome has not been a reliable conservative majority. Justice John Paul Stevens (appointed by Gerald Ford) was consistently liberal in his voting behavior prior to his retirement in mid-2010; Justice Anthony Kennedy (appointed by Ronald Reagan) is a swing voter who moves between the conservative and liberal blocs; Justice Souter (appointed by Bush 41) usually supported the liberal bloc (and retired in 2009 to be replaced by Barack Obama's liberal appointee, Sonia Sotomayor). In addition to the Bush 43 appointees, the only reliable conservatives were Justice Antonin Scalia (appointed by Reagan) and Justice Clarence Thomas (appointed by Bush 41). At best then, George W. Bush's judicial picks only firmed up the conservative bloc, rather than create a consistent five-justice conservative majority.

We come now to the question of how much more conservative Justice Alito is than Justice O'Connor. If we take agreement rates with the Court's two most conservative justices, Scalia and Thomas, we find a significant difference. In her last three years on the Court, Justice O'Connor voted with them less than half the time in nonunanimous cases (46 percent with Scalia, 45.5 percent with Thomas). By contrast, in his first three years on the Court, Alito voted with them almost two-thirds of the time (65.2 percent with Scalia, 64.8 percent with Thomas).[13] It is intriguing to note, however, that Alito was in even closer judicial commune with Kennedy in this period, voting with him in 70.6 percent of nonunanimous cases.

Alito has certainly proved himself a more reliable conservative than O'Connor, but he has not altered the fundamental fact of life that has governed the Supreme Court for over twenty years: victory in the most contentious cases depends on obtaining the vote of a moderate justice such as Lewis Powell, Sandra Day O'Connor, or Anthony Kennedy. If we look at the occurrence of "classic" five-justice conservative majorities in recent years, we find that they are far from the norm: five in the 2002–3 term, nine in 2003–4, four in 2004–5, four in 2005–6, fourteen in 2006–7, and four in 2007–8.[14] It is Justice Kennedy who now has the pivotal role in four–five decisions. In the 2007–8 Term, for example, there were eight decisions in which the Court split along classic conservative-liberal lines. The liberal-moderate bloc prevailed in four of them and the conservative-moderate bloc prevailed in the other four. Kennedy was in the majority in all eight cases.

Early analysis of the data from the 2008–9 Term suggests that Kennedy continues to be the pivotal vote. He was in the majority in all sixteen cases decided on five–four splits, joining the liberals in five and the conservatives in eleven. Whether Kennedy's increased alignment with the conservative bloc in the 2008 Term reflects a long-term trend or simply the facts of these particular cases remains to be seen. However, one reporter was surely right to conclude from this judicial pattern, "The Constitution, it turns out, means what Justice Kennedy says it means."[15]

The Counterrevolution Delayed—Again

The statistical evidence presented above refutes the claim that the legacy of George W. Bush can already be considered a triumphant one. Certainly he accomplished much of what he set out to do in this area, as did other presidents of the modern period. But that may not be enough for history to say that the forty-third president had a decisive impact on the course of constitutional law. Analysis of the major Supreme Court cases since Roberts and Alito took their seats tends to point to the same conclusion.

Race and Affirmative Action

In *Parents Involved v. Seattle* and *Meredith v. Jefferson County*,[16] both 2007, the Court struck down two school pupil assignment schemes that made use of racial classifications. In both schemes, the goal was to achieve a specific minimum ratio of racial balance. If this minimum was not achieved by initial student choice, students would be assigned according to race until the desired balance was achieved. The four solid conservative justices were joined by Justice Kennedy and the two cases were cited by some as evidence that the two Bush appointees had swung the Court to the right. In Barbara A. Perry's assessment, "Justice O'Connor undoubtedly would have provided a fifth vote to swing the result to the opposite side. Alito's replacement of the Court's moderate swing voter was indeed having the effect the conservatives desired."[17] Moreover, these were among the cases that persuaded Ronald Dworkin that a new aggressive phase of conservative jurisprudence was on the march.[18] These assertions are far from convincing, however. In the first place, they misread the decision, especially the controlling opinion of Justice Kennedy. Second, they make assumptions about how Justice O'Connor would have voted had she remained on the Court that are not necessarily correct.

In *Parents Involved* Kennedy cast the deciding vote that condemned the pupil assignment plans. However, his concurring opinion made clear that his approach to race-conscious remedies was very different from that of the four conservatives who gathered behind Chief Justice Roberts' opinion. What Kennedy found impermissible was the explicit and decisive use of racial classifications to assign pupils in some instances.[19] Though contending that neither plan was "narrowly tailored" to achieve the goal of racial diversity, he criticized the conservatives' approach to issues arising from de facto racial segregation. Chief Justice Roberts adopted the familiar "color-blindness" formula of judicial conservatives in advising, "The way to stop discrimination on the basis of race is to stop discriminating on the basis of race."[20] In a passage worth quoting at length, Kennedy puts considerable distance between himself and the conservative bloc in rejecting this argument:

> [P]arts of the opinion by *The Chief Justice* imply an all-too-unyielding insistence that race cannot be a factor in instances when, in my view, it may be taken into account. The plurality is too dismissive of the legitimate interest government has in ensuring all people have an equal opportunity regardless of race.

> The plurality's postulate that 'the best way to stop discrimination on the basis of race is to stop discriminating on the basis of race' is not sufficient to decide these cases. Fifty years of experience since *Brown v. Board of Education* should teach us that the problem before us defies so easy a solution. School districts can seek to reach *Brown's* objective of equal educational opportunity... To the extent the plurality opinion suggest the Constitution mandates that state and local school authorities must accept the status quo of racial isolation in schools, it is, in my view, profoundly mistaken.[21]

Such a ringing endorsement of the state's legitimate interest in achieving racial diversity and balance in schools clearly dispels any notion that *Parents Involved* and *Meredith* constitute a major triumph for the conservative cause. Indeed, as Heather K. Gerken points out in the *Harvard Law Review*, Kennedy's opinion marks a move toward a more liberal position for him: "In the schools context, Justice Kennedy has moved from lauding a colorblind approach to brainstorming about the most useful race-conscious strategies the state can use to construct the educational space in which students can learn about race."[22] Moreover, she notes that Kennedy seems to have taken up the swing role once occupied by Lewis Powell and Sandra Day O'Connor, albeit on a different jurisprudential basis.[23]

In short, the constitutional position on race-conscious remedies to promote racial diversity in schools remains much the same as before. As J. Harvie Wilkinson wrote of the passions aroused in *Parents Involved*, "Yet this battle brought no peace or even truce, and indeed left only the impression that the Court's own decisions on the use of race in education remain in tension and that the profound differences that persist within the Court and throughout the country on these questions will be argued just as heatedly on another day."[24]

In view of Kennedy's move to the center in *Parents Involved*, the question of how O'Connor would have voted is less important, but still somewhat intriguing. Given her pragmatic, case-by-case approach to these issues, it is conceivable that she would have joined Kennedy's opinion about the unconstitutionality of the schemes under review. It is also possible that she would have joined his opinion in some part but voted with the four dissenters to uphold the schemes. Probably the best clues to her hypothetical vote in *Parents Involved* lie in the 2003 decisions in *Gratz v. Bollinger*[25] and *Grutter v. Bollinger*,[26] the last major affirmative action cases with which she was involved. In *Gratz*, O'Connor joined four other justices to strike down a University of Michigan student admissions scheme that automatically allocated twenty points to all minority applicants. In *Grutter*, however, she joined the four *Gratz* dissenters to uphold the University of Michigan Law School's admissions scheme that counted minority status as a plus factor, to be considered along with numerous other criteria when making admission decisions. In both cases, O'Connor agreed that achieving a diverse student body was a compelling state interest. The difference between the two cases in her view was that the Law School scheme was narrowly tailored to achieve that goal, whereas the university's scheme was not.

Hypothesizing how O'Connor might have voted in *Parents Involved* requires an understanding of her concept of narrow tailoring and her application of it to the facts of the case. She followed Justice Lewis Powell's controlling opinion in *Regents of the University of California v. Bakke* (1978) that if an admissions scheme involved a quota or an automatically applied race criteria without individualized consideration of the applicant, it fell foul of the Equal Protection clause of the Fourteenth Amendment. In *Grutter*, Justice O'Connor wrote:

> We find the Law School's admission program bears the hallmarks of a narrowly tailored plan. As Justice Powell made clear in *Bakke*, truly individualized consideration demands that race be used in flexible, nonmechanical way. It follows from this mandate that universities cannot establish quotas for members of certain racial groups or put members of those groups on separate admissions tracks...Universities can, however, consider race or ethnicity more flexibly as a "plus" factor in the context of individualized consideration of each and every applicant.[27]

As we saw above, the use of racial classifications in *Parents Involved* was automatic and not individualized. It was mechanical, even if it was employed only as a secondary factor. It is, therefore, perfectly possible that Justice O'Connor would have joined Justice Kennedy in striking down the admissions schemes in *Parents Involved* and *Meredith*, while still upholding racial diversity as a legitimate and compelling state interest in education. It is far from certain, then, that her replacement by Justice Alito had any material effect on the decision or, indeed, upon future decisions in this field of constitutional law.

Abortion

One case in which Alito's replacement of O'Connor certainly made a significant difference is *Gonzales v. Carhart* (2007).[28] This upheld the federal Partial Birth Abortion Ban Act of 2003 prohibiting the use of the partial birth abortion technique, the only exception being when necessary to save the mother's life. Its significance lies in the fact that in a recent precedent, *Stenberg v. Carhart* (2000),[29] the Court struck down a similar Nebraska statute on the grounds that it provided no exception for when the mother's health, in addition to life, would be endangered. Both cases were decided by five–four majorities. In *Stenberg*, O'Connor voted to strike down the legislation, whereas in *Gonzales*, Alito voted to uphold it.

That said, despite the enormous publicity and interest group campaigning that surrounded *Gonzales v. Carhart,* its importance within the broader battle over abortion rights is not very great. The basic right to abortion proclaimed in *Roe v. Wade* (1973) and reconfirmed albeit in modified form in *Planned Parenthood v. Casey* (1992)[30] is not threatened by O'Connor's replacement with Alito. The key vote, as in so many controversial issues on the contemporary Court, is that of Justice Kennedy.

Many had expected *Casey* to result in the demise of *Roe v. Wade*. The Reagan–Bush 41 appointments—Justices O'Connor, Scalia, Kennedy, Souter and Thomas—appeared to have moved the Supreme Court's center of gravity rightward. Indeed, when *Casey* was discussed in conference, Kennedy indicated that he was ready to uphold the Pennsylvania statute. As a result, Chief Justice Rehnquist assigned himself the Court's opinion and drafted one that declared *Roe v. Wade* to be an error. Not wanting to go so far, Souter and O'Connor persuaded Kennedy to join them in writing an opinion that upheld *Roe's* fundamental right to abortion. As Jeffrey Toobin noted, Kennedy's "was the most dramatic switch of the three."[31] Jan Crawford Greenburg similarly commented, "More than O'Connor and Souter, two other Republican appointees who let them down, Kennedy has been accused by conservatives of buckling under pressure from the cultural and media elite."[32]

Kennedy had moved to a position of believing that the Constitution protected a fundamental right to an abortion. This did not prevent him from differing with O'Connor and Souter over application of the *Casey* principles in particular cases. One such case arose out of the controversy over the partial birth abortion technique, a rarely used procedure that nevertheless achieved notoriety because of its gruesome nature. Congress had twice banned it, but President Clinton vetoed both bills because they did not contain an exception when the mother's health was endangered. In *Stenberg*, O'Connor and Souter were part of the five–four majority that struck down a Nebraska statute that lacked a health exception, but Kennedy wrote a strongly worded dissent. When the issue came up for renewed consideration in *Gonzales v. Carhart*, Kennedy once again voted to uphold the ban, but this time as part of the majority because of Alito's replacement of O'Connor.

The *Gonzales v. Carhart* decision was hardly a bolt from the blue, but it represented a propaganda victory for the prolife movement rather than a threat to the constitutional right to abortion affirmed in *Casey*. While it is undeniable that Alito made a difference to policy on the partial birth abortion technique, on the evidence to date, it made little difference to policy on abortion rights. Despite dissenting in *Stenberg*, Kennedy reiterated his adherence to *Casey* in stating, "Nebraska must obey the legal regime which has declared the right of the woman to have an abortion before viability."[33] In *Gonzalez v. Carhart*, he reaffirmed that the Court's opinion rested upon that principle.[34] As such this judgment does not support claims that Bush moved the Court sharply to the right.

The Death Penalty

In the areas of affirmative action and abortion, the impact of Bush appointees to the Supreme Court has, at best, been marginal. In the area of capital punishment, they have made no difference at all. The relevant case is *Kennedy v. Louisiana* (2008), which involved another highly emotive legal controversy, that of child rape.[35] Patrick Kennedy had been convicted of raping his eight-year-old stepdaughter. Under Louisiana law, the rape of a child below the age of twelve could be punished by death. Kennedy's prosecutor sought and obtained the death penalty and, on appeal, this was upheld by the Louisiana Supreme Court.

The U.S. Supreme Court, however, concluded by a vote of five–four that imposing the death penalty for child rape violated the Eighth Amendment to the Constitution, which forbids "cruel and unusual punishments." Kennedy wrote the majority opinion, while Alito wrote for the dissenters.[36] The former reaffirmed the controversial approach to death penalty cases he had adopted in the Court's 2005 decision in *Roper v. Simmons*, which involved the execution of juveniles.[37] In that case, Kennedy disagreed with his conservative colleagues over the relative weight to be given to objective indices of contemporary views on the death penalty—most importantly, state legislation—on the one hand, and the justices' own views of the proportionality of the imposition of the death penalty for different categories of crime and criminal, on the other.³⁸ In *Kennedy v. Louisiana*, Kennedy again spoke for the liberal bloc to hold that in crimes against individuals, the death penalty must be reserved for those when the victim's life is taken.³⁹

Once again, it is possible to speculate on how Justice O'Connor might have voted in this case but it is difficult to provide a convincing answer. In *Roper*, she dissented from Kennedy's opinion largely because she did not share his view that all seventeen-year-olds were insufficiently mature to be held fully culpable of the crime of murder. It is perfectly plausible, therefore, that she would have agreed with Justice Alito in *Kennedy v. Louisiana* that child rape can be punished by death because sometimes the moral depravity involved therein is greater than that involved in some murders.⁴⁰

Whether or not O'Connor would have held child rapists eligible for the death penalty makes no difference, however. Assuming that Justice Sonia Sotomayor, President Barack Obama's first Supreme Court appointee, adopts the same position as former justice Souter, there is a five-justice majority on the Court holding the opinion that in crimes against the individual the death penalty must be confined to murder—just as there was immediately prior to the appointments of Chief Justice Roberts and Associate Justice Alito. Equally important, there is a five-justice majority that believes their own proportionality review in death penalty cases is more dispositive than the prevalence of state legislation, the behavior of prosecutors or public opinion.⁴¹

Habeas Corpus and the Rights of Guantanamo Bay Detainees

The Bush administration, with the support of the Republican-controlled Congress, fought a long-running legal battle with the Supreme Court over the rights of so-called enemy combatants imprisoned at Guantanamo Bay. To its dismay, the judiciary consistently refused to grant the president the plenary power that he claimed in this area. This was true before the appointments of Roberts and Alito and it remains true after their accession to the Supreme Court, as demonstrated in *Boumediene v. Bush* (2008).⁴²

The issues in *Boumediene* had their origins in the Court's earlier decision in *Rasul v. Bush* (2004).⁴³ In that case, it rejected the administration's claim that the Guantanamo detainees had no habeas corpus rights that government was obliged to respect. The administration had argued that because the United States did not possess sovereignty over the Guantanamo Bay base in Cuba, the federal courts had no jurisdiction over any foreign national being held there. A six–three majority of the justices disagreed. Justice Stevens wrote the Court's opinion, joined by Justices O'Connor, Souter, Ginsburg, and Breyer. Justice Kennedy concurred in the judgment, but not the Court's opinion. The essence of the Court's decision was that because the United States exercised "plenary and exclusive jurisdiction" over Guantanamo Bay, its lack of formal sovereignty did not prevent the federal courts from intervening.

Far from accepting this decision, the Bush administration and its congressional allies promoted enactment of the Detainee Treatment Act of 2005, which stripped the federal courts of jurisdiction in cases involving Guantanamo Bay detainees. In *Hamdan v. Rumsfeld*,[44] however, the Court ruled by five votes to three that Congress had not intended to strip the Court of jurisdiction in cases already pending at the time of the Act's passage. Once again Kennedy voted with the majority without fully joining the controlling opinion.[45] Congress responded by passing the Military Commissions Act of 2006. This stripped the Court not only of all habeas corpus jurisdiction over Guantanamo Bay detainees but also over any aspect of their detention, trial, or treatment.

The message from Congress and the White House to the Court could not have been clearer. Nevertheless, in *Boumediene*, these provisions of the Military Commissions Act were held to be unconstitutional. Although Alito's presence boosted the dissenters to four in number, Kennedy's vote ensured that the liberal bloc prevailed. Moreover, having not fully joined the majority's reasoning in *Rasul* and *Hamdan*, in *Boumediene*, he wrote the Court's opinion. While this strove to avoid the appearance of judicial activism, it vindicated and entrenched all the Court's previous cases denying the Bush administration's claim of unrestricted power to deal with noncitizen enemy combatants as it saw fit. As Kennedy's opinion affirmed, "Within the Constitution's separation-of-powers structure, few exercises of judicial power are as legitimate or as necessary as the responsibility to hear challenges to the authority of the Executive to imprison a person."[46]

The 2008 Supreme Court Term

The headlines that greeted the end of the 2008–9 Term conveyed the distinct impression that the conservative counterrevolution was making progress.[47] However, analysis of the leading cases provides little evidence of significant change and mainly confirms Justice Kennedy's pivotal significance. One case that attracted considerable attention was *Ricci v. DeStefano*,[48] which involved a clash between the disparate treatment and disparate impact elements of federal civil rights legislation. The City of New Haven, Connecticut, had used objective tests to identify firefighters for promotion. The test results indicated that all those promoted would be white or Hispanic. Fearing that African-American firefighters would bring a disparate impact suit, the City scrapped the results, at which point the white firefighters brought a disparate treatment suit instead. The Supreme Court ruled five–four in favor of the white firefighters, but Justice Kennedy's majority opinion made it clear that this did not spell the demise of disparate impact claims, as many conservatives wished. He explicitly rejected the white firefighters' argument that fear of a disparate impact suit could never justify disparate treatment action and emphasized that the Civil Rights Acts of 1964 and 1991 protected against both forms discrimination.[49] Moreover, in searching for a standard by which to balance the competing claims of disparate treatment and disparate impact, Kennedy reached back to Justice Lewis Powell's opinion in *Wygant v. Jackson Board of Education* (1986).[50] In that case, the moderate Powell required that race-conscious remedies for alleged past racial discrimination would need "a strong basis in evidence" in order to survive judicial scrutiny.[51] Kennedy now held that the City of New Haven had failed to meet that standard of proof in arguing that a good-faith fear of a disparate impact suit was all that was necessary to justify its abandonment of the results of the promotion tests. In sum, the decision in *Ricci* was not a particularly conservative one, nor did it break new ground.

Conclusion

To say that George W. Bush failed to achieve the long-sought conservative counterrevolution is not to criticize his administration's efforts as inadequate in this regard. It is rather to recognize that the opportunity to appoint two solid conservatives to the Supreme Court proved insufficient to transform the situation he inherited. It is also to recognize the difficulty in defining any one president's historic legacy, since transformation of the Supreme Court is a collective exercise achieved by several presidents over a considerable number of years. As illustrated above, Bush shored up the conservative faction on the Court. Whether that proves to be a major contribution to a quest that will be achieved by a future Republican president, or an unavailing effort frustrated by appointments made by Barack Obama and other Democratic presidents remains to be seen. For the conservative counterrevolution, it is still all to play for.

Notes

1. Sheldon Goldman, Sara Schiavoni, and Elliot Slotnick, "W. Bush's Judicial Legacy: Mission Accomplished," *Judicature*, 92, May–June 2009, 258–88 (quotation p. 258).
2. Ronald Dworkin, "The Supreme Court Phalanx," *New York Review of Books*, September 27, 2007, 92–101 (quotation p. 92).
3. Barbara A. Perry, "The 'Bush Twins'? Roberts, Alito and the Conservative Agenda," *Judicature*, 92, May–June 2009, 302–11 (quotation p. 311).
4. President George W. Bush, Remarks on Judicial Accomplishments and Philosophy, Hilton Cincinnati, Ohio, October 6, 2008, http://www.usembassy.org.uk.bush863.html.
5. Richard Y. Funston, *Constitutional Counter-revolution? The Warren Court and the Burger Court: Judicial Policymaking in Modern America* (Cambridge MA: Schenkman, 1977), 328, 338.
6. Vincent Blasi, ed., *The Burger Court: The Counter-revolution That Wasn't* (New Haven CT: Yale University Press, 1983).
7. Vincent Blasi, "The Rootless Activism of the Burger Court," in Blasi, *The Burger Court*, 198–217, 198.
8. Denis S. Rutkus and Maureen Bearden, "Nominations to Article III Lower Courts by President George W. Bush During the 110th Congress," *Congressional Research Service Report for Congress*, RL33953, October 20, 2008, 19.
9. Goldman et al., "W. Bush's Judicial Legacy," n1, 283.
10. Rutkus and Bearden, "Nominations to Article III Lower Courts," n5, 19.
11. Goldman et al., "W. Bush's Judicial Legacy," n1, 283.
12. Robert A. Carp, Kenneth L. Manning, and Ronald Stidham, "Right On: The Decision-Making Behaviour of George W. Bush's Judicial Appointees," *Judicature*, 92, May–June 2009, 312–19.
13. All Voting Alignment data is taken from the *Harvard Law Review* annual review of the relevant Supreme Court Term, unless otherwise stated.
14. A "classic" 5–4 conservative majority is one including Scalia and Thomas, plus Rehnquist or Roberts, and two of Alito, O'Connor, or Kennedy.
15. Adam Liptak, "Roberts Court Shifts Right, Tipped by Kennedy," *New York Times*, July 1, 2009. See too, Carp, Manning, and Stidham, "Right On: The Decision-Making Behaviour of George W. Bush's Judicial Appointees."

16. *Parents Involved in Community Schools v. Seattle School District No. 1 et al.* and *Crystal D. Meredith v. Jefferson County Board of Education et al.*, 551 US 701, 127 S Ct 2738, 168 L.Ed. 2d, 508 (2007).
17. Perry, "The 'Bush Twins'?" 310.
18. Dworkin, "The Supreme Court Phalanx."
19. In both pupil assignment schemes, the aim was to achieve a minimum level of racial balance in the public schools. If that balance was not achieved by initial student choice, the race of pupils could be taken into account.
20. 551 US 701, 127 S Ct 2738, 168 L.Ed. 2d 508, 541.
21. Ibid., 565–66.
22. Heather K. Gerken, "Justice Kennedy and the Domains of Equal Protection," *Harvard Law Review,* 121, November 2007, 104–30, 106.
23. Ibid., n21,.104–5.
24. J. Harvie Wilkinson, "The Seattle and Louisville School Cases: There Is No Other Way," *Harvard Law Review*, 121, November 2007, 158–83, 158.
25. 539 US 244 (2003).
26. 539 US 306 (2003).
27. 539 US 306, 334 (2003).
28. 550 US 124 (2007).
29. 530 US 914 (2000).
30. 505 US 833 (1992).
31. Jeffrey Toobin, *The Nine: Inside the Secret World of the Supreme Court* (New York: Anchor Books, 2008), 63.
32. Jan Crawford Greenburg, *Supreme Conflict: The Inside Story of the Struggle for Control of the United States Supreme Court* (New York: Penguin Books, 2008), 161.
33. 530 US 914, 963–64 (2000).
34. 550 US 124, 147.
35. 554 US-, 128, S Ct-, 171 L.Ed. 525 (2008).
36. Joining the Court's opinion were Justices Stevens, Souter, Ginsburg, and Breyer. Joining Alito's dissent were Chief Justice Roberts and Justices Scalia and Thomas.
37. *Roper v. Simmons*, 543 US 551 (2005).
38. Justice Kennedy first switched his position on this in *Atkins v. Virginia*, 536 US 304 (2002) and his Opinion for the Court in *Simmons* serves as the strongest possible indication that the switch is permanent.
39. 554 US-, 128 S Ct-, 171 L.Ed. 525, 549 (2008).
40. 554 US-, 128 S Ct-, 171 L.Ed 525, 567 (2008). Justice Alito points out that an unarmed robber who does not envisage the use of violence can nevertheless receive the death penalty if his accomplice commits murder. He compares the level of depravity in this case with that of a convicted child rapist who kidnaps a child and repeatedly rapes her.

41. For a fuller discussion of this, see Robert J. McKeever, "Executing Juveniles in the United States: The Supreme Court Changes Course," *King's College Law Journal*, 17, 2006, 136–43.
42. 553 US-, 128 S Ct-, 171 L.Ed. 2d 41 (2008).
43. 542 US 466 (2004).
44. 584 US 557 (2006).
45. Chief Justice Roberts took no part in the case, as it had come before him when he served on the Court of Appeals.
46. 553 US-, 128 S Ct-, 171 L. Ed. 2d 41, 97 (2008).
47. Robert Barnes, "Term Saw High Court Move to the Right: Roberts-Led March Likely to Continue," *Washington Post*, July 1, 2009; Liptak, "Roberts Court Shifts Right, Tipped by Kennedy."
48. 557 US (2009). Docket no. 07–1428.
49. *Ricci v. DeStefano*, Slip Opinion of Justice Kennedy, 20–21.
50. 476 US 261 (1986).
51. *Ricci v. DeStefano*, Slip Opinion of Justice Kennedy, 2.

Chapter Five

The Ethical Record of the Bush Presidency

Clodagh Harrington

> He that would make his own liberty secure must guard even his enemy from oppression; for if he violates this duty he establishes a precedent that will reach to himself.[1]
>
> —Thomas Paine

Once a rarity, accusations of presidential ethical impropriety have become relatively commonplace since the downfall of Richard Nixon. In the case of Watergate, the evidence of wrongdoing was incontrovertible. Most instances are not so black-and-white, however. In the Iran-Contra scandal that beset Ronald Reagan, accusations of well-meaning naivety tempered more serious constitutional concerns regarding the privatization of foreign policy. In an era of moral relativism, defining ethics is fraught with difficulty. At its most basic, however, if ethics are understood as constituting a system of moral principles, this translates in the case of presidents to observance of the Constitution and the laws, to speak the truth, and to display integrity with regard to financial affairs and personal conduct. In contrast to Bill Clinton, George W. Bush was never accused of inappropriately seeking financial gain, marital infidelity, or sexual misconduct during his time in political office. Nevertheless, he came under greater attack for ethical shortcomings regarding the Constitution and the laws than any president since Nixon. Indeed, his critics accused him of advancing the imperial presidency to a level beyond anything contemplated by Nixon.

With one exception—the so-called Plamegate affair, none of Bush's constitutionally questionable actions attracted the "gate" suffix that had coded presidential wrongdoing since Nixon. Instead, they were manifest in myriad ways that added up in incremental fashion in the eyes of critics to a serious abuse of power rather than being exposed in a single dramatic episode. These included the erosion of civil liberties following enactment of the Patriot Act of 2001; the expansion of presidential power through unprecedented use of signing statements; the torture and abuse of enemy combatants in the War on Terror; the questionable justification for the invasion of Iraq in 2003; and the aforementioned "Plamegate" affair.

Some of Bush's supporters excused his conduct as the inevitable consequence of increased national and homeland security requirements in the face of the threat posed by terrorists after the 9/11 attacks on New York and Washington. While accepting that the president exaggerated the WMD threat posed by Iraqi leader Saddam Hussein and had little capacity for self-doubt, a sympathetic commentator like onetime neoconservative Francis Fukuyama remarked that benevolent hegemony in the circumstances of the post-9/11 world could not be expected to be flawless.[2] Liberal commentators were not so indulgent. Their criticisms ranged from accusations of a criminal conspiracy within the administration to engineer the invasion of Iraq to claims that the president was a "pathological liar."[3] Basing his analysis on psychologist Lawrence Kohlberg's stages of moral development, ethicist Peter Singer described Bush as an "ethical adolescent." According to him, the president's incapacity for reflective thinking, which usually comes with maturity, led him to make ethical judgments in the manner of an adolescent male.[4]

Quite clearly, analysis of Bush's ethics in office is fundamental to any evaluation of his presidency and its legacy. Historical assessment of Ulysses S. Grant, Warren G. Harding, and—most notably—Richard Nixon has conventionally laid great stress on the ethical transgressions associated with their administrations. Accordingly, this chapter offers a review of the main issues concerning Bush's ethical record to evaluate whether his presidency posed a threat to constitutional democracy.

Abuse of Executive Power

Faith and Imperialism

Historian Arthur Schlesinger Jr. popularized the term "Imperial Presidency" to signify the culmination under Richard Nixon of presidential tendency since the 1940s to act beyond the limits of the Constitution. In his assessment, the American political system was threatened during the Nixon presidency by "a conception of presidential power so spacious and peremptory as to imply a radical transformation of the traditional polity."[5] Prior to the Bush era, the thirty-seventh president was considered the embodiment of such imperial pretensions. During the forty-third president's first term, however, Schlesinger told John Dean, the former Nixon White House Counsel and Watergate conspirator now turned columnist, that he would "certainly say that this is an imperial presidency" and adjudged Bush as being "more grandiose than Nixon."[6]

Bush's faith and certainty in God were matched by the faith and certainty that he displayed in himself. During a November 2001 press conference on the war on terror, he declared, "you are either with us or against us."[7] This encapsulated his entire approach to leadership as part of the faith-based presidency. Fact-based open dialogue was not encouraged in his White House. If each administration is shaped by its president, in the post-9/11 years Bush operated, in the words of his onetime Treasury Secretary Paul O'Neill, as "a blind man in a room full of deaf people."[8] When journalist Ron Suskind put O'Neill's comment in print, he received a barrage of calls from Democrats and Republicans alike, all offering further testimony to the president's disengagement and un-inquisitive style in meetings.[9]

After the 9/11 terror attacks dramatically raised the stakes of government action, the president's faith-based approach took on a far more significant meaning. Speaking of a "new kind of evil" in a September 2001 press conference, he avowed that "the American people are beginning to understand. This crusade, this war on terrorism, is going to take a while."[10] This was a profoundly unfortunate choice of phrase and, though aides were quick to suggest it was an impromptu comment, it spoke volumes about the mindset of the president and his administration. An unnamed senior Bush adviser further manifested this outlook in conversation with Ron Suskind. Deriding the journalist for living in a "reality-based community," whose members "believe that solutions emerge from your judicious study of discernible reality," the aide explained that the world no longer worked this way. "We're an empire now, and when we act, we create our own reality. And while you're studying that reality—judiciously, as you will—we'll act again, creating other new realities, which you can study too....[W]e're history's actors...and you, all of you, will be left to just study what we do."[11] Such self-confidence would ultimately run into the constraints of reality but it suggested that the Bush White House would not let its hands be tied by the Constitution or the laws.

Significant Players

President Bush was hardly alone in his assertion of executive branch privilege. He interacted with a compliant Congress, at least for his first six years in office, and staffers who strongly believed in enhanced presidential power. The "new" imperial presidency was, in the view of critics, largely constructed and implemented by Dick Cheney and his chief legal advisor, David Addington. The former was a key proponent of the imperial presidency and a vice president with unprecedented powers. Chosen as Bush's running-mate for his depth of experience in government, Cheney was responsible for the transition to the new administration and oversaw much of its early organizational and policy planning. Though Addington kept a low profile, White House officials affirmed that he played an integral role in shaping the administration's legal strategy in response to 9/11. Secretary of State Colin Powell was heard to remark that he "doesn't care about the constitution."[12]

Other administration officials also held an expansive view of presidential power. Conservative legal scholar and Deputy Assistant Attorney General John Yoo, who would face calls for bar investigations into his conduct after Bush left office, produced the first confidential memoranda regarding the president's war powers in the period directly after 9/11. While classified, his writings were not subject to critical scrutiny within or outside the White House. Moreover, holding what was in theory a low level post, Yoo had not been required to receive Senate confirmation. Nevertheless, he was endowed with the immense authority of "signing power"—in other words, his opinion could become law simply as a result of him signing a memo.[13] Yoo's many critics claimed that he ignored and overrode the Bill of Rights, notably in his insistence that the Fourth Amendment, which prohibits unreasonable searches and seizures, did not apply to domestic military operations relating to the war on terror.[14] In its condemnation of him, the House Committee Report on the Imperial Presidency of George Bush charged that the administration "had been characterised by the determined effort to arrogate for the president vast uncheckable power in large spheres of government action, coupled with the equally determined willingness to do battle with the courts and Congress for the president's right to maintain these prerogatives."[15]

In combination with Yoo, David Addington viewed any consultation with Congress as a form of "giv[ing] away the president's power."[16] Despite being under Republican control during Bush's first six years in office (excepting a nineteen-month period when the

Senate was in Democratic hands in 2001–2), the legislative branch was still considered a hindrance. Summing up his belief that the president should act unilaterally, Cheney's legal adviser avowed that "we're going to push and push and push until some larger force makes us stop."[17] In line with this, the administration seized the moment of national unity in the wake of the 9/11 terrorist attacks to engage in massive aggrandizement of executive power. In response to Bush's request on September 12, Congress provided formal authorization six days later for the use of military force against those responsible for the atrocities, but placed certain limitations on the president's scope of action. A John Yoo memorandum, written on September 24, promptly freed the White House of any such shackles. Entitled "The President's Constitutional Authority to Conduct Military Operations against Terrorists and Nations Supporting Them," it asserted that the president had more or less unlimited power regarding how to respond to 9/11 and could disregard congressional opinion.[18]

Patriot Act

By 2002, Democrats and Republicans were in agreement that President Bush had created one of the most powerful White Houses in at least a generation. Conservative pundit William J. Bennett commented that "there's now a unified theory of the White House in this town: it is strong, it is confident, it is all going in the same direction and it doesn't leak."[19] In the assessment of Robert Strauss, former Democratic Party chair and presidential advisor, "George Bush and several talented people around him have made the White House a power center in ways that I haven't seen in a long, long time, all the way back to Lyndon Johnson. That is a big statement."[20]

Forty-five days after the September 11 attacks, the Patriot Act received approval by overwhelming majorities in both houses of Congress. Its provisions broadened the definition of who could be considered a terrorist, particularly in a domestic sense, and increased the attorney general's scope to deal with them. The measure also made significant changes to the legal structure within which the law enforcement and intelligence communities operated. It relaxed limits on surveillance and endowed the president with sole authority to decide who constituted an enemy combatant without recourse to the other branches of government.[21] Another controversial provision increased the authority, scope, and preconditions for National Security Letters (NSL) requests, written directives from the FBI seeking information regarding an individual's telephone, Internet, library, financial, and credit details. These had been in regular use long before 9/11 to monitor the activities of individuals and groups suspected of criminal or subversive activity without having to obtain a warrant. However, their issuance increased dramatically in the wake of the Patriot Act.[22] According to a Justice Department Inspector General's Report, the FBI sent out approximately 200,000 NSLs between 2003 and 2006. The same report also found that it perpetrated serious abuses of the NSL power. As a consequence, the ACLU contested the authorizing statute in court on three occasions.[23] In addition, a November 2005 *Washington Post* article, which reported a hundredfold increase in the NSL usage since 9/11, accused the FBI of spying on ordinary Americans and abusing the Patriot Act provision.[24] These findings prompted congressional enactment of the Patriot Improvement and Reauthorization Act of 2006 that authorized examination of NSL use to check for possible abuse. However, Bush subsequently issued a signing statement to the effect that he was empowered to disregard the requirement for him to report to Congress on how he was implementing the Act's provisions.[25]

Signing Statements

When a president signs a bill into law, he will sometimes issue a signing statement expressing his view on the bill. Dating back to James Monroe, this device was initially intended to function as part of the checks and balances between the separate branches of government. It was primarily a rhetorical instrument to demonstrate presidential support or reservations about a bill or its parts. The creative use of signing statements as a tactic for evading particular provisions of legislation was started in earnest by Richard Nixon and carried on by Ronald Reagan, George H. W. Bush, and Bill Clinton.[26] However, George W. Bush massively expanded the practice in both frequency and scope—in many instances employing signing statements as a de facto line-item veto, whose formal issuance the Supreme Court had previously ruled unconstitutional.[27]

Initially, the American public remained largely ignorant of Bush's excessive use of signing statements because they related to complex or obscure issues of legislation. However, their increasing focus on more controversial issues such as the Patriot Act, use of torture, and illegally gathered intelligence generated greater awareness. Investigating the practice, an American Bar Association task force found that "from the inception of the Republic until 2000, Presidents produced signing statements containing fewer than 600 challenges to the bills they signed. According to the most recent update, in his one and a half terms so far, President George Bush (Bush II) has produced more than 800." The task force concluded that the forty-third president's signing statements undermined the separation of powers.[28]

The House Committee on the Judiciary also set up a panel to investigate whether and to what extent the Bush administration had abused its executive power in its use of signing statements. The language of its subsequent report left no doubt about its conclusions. Quoting Arthur Schlesinger that America was faced with "the imperial presidency *redux*," Chair John Conyers (D-MI) declared the Bush administration's pretensions on this score a threat to the constitutional checks and balances, but took some reassurance from the eminent scholar's confidence in "democracy's singular virtue—its capacity for self-correction."[29]

At the Judiciary Committee's hearings in January 2007, there was strong bipartisan opposition to Bush's use of signing statements.[30] In his testimony, Harvard law professor Charles Ogletree asserted that their issuance entailed refusal not only to implement parts of some legislation but also to identify the provisions disregarded in practice, thus violating the law and the Constitution. Bush's frequent signing statements contrasted vividly with the lack of any veto from his pen in his first six years in office. Like other critics, Ogletree surmised that the former had made the latter unnecessary.[31]

Torture and Extraordinary Rendition

Guantanamo

In December 2001, the Bush administration announced its intention to detain captives at Guantanamo Bay, Cuba. This decision was based on a private legal conclusion that "a district court cannot properly entertain an application for a writ of *habeas corpus* by an enemy alien" detained there.[32] At an oversight hearing on detention-related issues held by the Congressional Subcommittee on the Constitution, Lieutenant Commander Charles Swift asserted, "To me, Guantanamo Bay, as a recruiting magnet and a cloak for those who would abuse human rights the world over, does far more damage than any one person who might be let go following the rule of law."[33] Guantanamo was not sovereign U.S. territory as it nominally belonged to Cuba.

The U.S. base there was outside U.S. court jurisdiction and yet not on soil that was under any other court system. Its status as a law-free zone made it a prime location for establishment of a prison to hold terrorist suspects.[34] In his memoir, John Yoo stated that "one thing we all agreed on was that any detention facility should be located outside the United States."[35]

Initially, Guantanamo detainees were treated "by the book" of the Geneva Convention. Under the command of Military Police General Rick Baccus, copies of the Qur'an were issued, Ramadan meal requirements were observed, and rights of prisoners were displayed in writing. His replacement by a military intelligence officer in 2002 was a significant change that brought with it a "72 point matrix for stress and duress."[36] In the fall of that year, CIA and military interrogators began asking how far they were permitted to go in questioning detainees presumed to be withholding information.[37] On the basis of Bush's declaration that detainees were "not protected by the Geneva Conventions," Lieutenant Colonel Diane Beaver of the Army's Judge Advocate General Corps authored an opinion in October 2002 that all desired interrogation methods were appropriate because "no international body of law directly applies."[38] Shortly afterward, the Haynes Memorandum—written by Pentagon General Counsel William Haynes—requested approval for specific coercive techniques that went far beyond conventional military practice. This was signed into law by Donald Rumsfeld in December. According to law professor Philippe Sands, its issuance formally abandoned adherence to the initial presidential requirement that detainees be treated "humanely."[39]

Navy General Counsel Alberto Mora informed an Army general investigating detainee abuses of his opinion that the Rumsfeld-approved interrogation techniques were "unlawful and unworthy of the military service." These included waterboarding, exposure to temperature extremes, and creating detainee fear of imminent death or severe injury. Though a Bush administration political appointee, Mora avowed that such techniques "constituted, at a minimum, cruel and unusual treatment, and at worst, torture."[40]

A 2006 *Lancet* report by over 260 doctors discussed the abuse of force-feeding prisoners (with feeding pipes inserted into their nasal passages), in Guantanamo. Despite employing techniques condemned by Amnesty International, a number of Guantanamo doctors received medals for "inspiring leadership and exemplary performance."[41] In 2007, some medical health professionals accused the American Medical Association (AMA) of being complicit in the Guantanamo abuse by not taking steps to penalize an AMA doctor for participating in such abuse. To date, no doctor has been disciplined for misconduct in the war on terror. Current international medical ethical guidelines, after the post–World War II Nuremburg Trials, are undermined as long as organizations such as the AMA do not act to ensure its members' full adherence to them.[42]

Extraordinary Rendition

On January 27, 2005, President Bush told the *New York Times* that "torture is never acceptable, nor do we hand over people to countries that do torture."[43] In his testimony to the House and Senate Intelligence Committees in September 2002, however, CIA counterterrorism operative Cofer Black declared, "After 9/11, the gloves came off."[44] For example, the McCain Torture Ban (as the Detainee Treatment Act of 2005 became known) was one of the many laws that Bush circumvented through a signing statement.[45] The president also claimed the power to bypass laws stipulating that he inform Congress before diverting funding from authorized programs to other projects, including new "black sites" where the CIA could operate prisons outside of U.S. territory and legal jurisdiction.[46]

Extraordinary rendition is the CIA's term for its practice of sending captured suspected terrorists to other countries for interrogation. This was a subject of great controversy during the Bush presidency, not least because it was widely assumed that suspects were sent to countries where torture was not unusual. Professional intelligence officers tend to agree that torture does not result in the provision of reliable information. The point, however, should surely be more about morality than reliability. According to American and Arab intelligence chiefs, the advantage of extraordinary rendition is emotional leverage. In other words, when a suspect is taken to his home country and perhaps faced with a family member, he may be far more likely to offer information than if he were sent to Guantanamo, for example. A former CIA official posed a hypothetical scenario to *Washington Post* journalist David Ignatius on the subject of torture. Had the FBI captured 9/11 terrorist leader Mohammad Atta prior to the attacks on New York and Washington, the agency would probably not have been allowed to hold or interrogate him in the United States. Would it, therefore, have been justifiable to render him to another country where interrogation techniques might have extracted information on the planned attacks?[47] Such moral conundrums complicated congressional and public views on the issue of torture, which did not seem so distasteful if conducted in secret, faraway locations to save American lives.

In a speech delivered in Panama in November 2005, Bush defended the use of extraordinary rendition, declaring "you bet, we'll aggressively pursue them [terrorists], but we'll do so under the law." He also affirmed that "we do not do torture."[48] In reality, the United States did do torture in the Bush years, but outsourced it. In his confirmation hearings, Attorney General Alberto Gonzalez justified the use of extraordinary rendition on grounds that the UN Convention against Torture's ban on "cruel, inhuman and degrading treatment" of terrorist suspects did not apply when Americans were interrogating foreigners overseas.[49] Extraordinary rendition was one of many instances where the administration adhered to the letter of the law—albeit barely—if not the spirit.

Though it was not responsible for inventing extraordinary rendition, the Bush administration took this practice to unprecedented heights. One aspect of extraordinary rendition that became a particular cause for concern was what to do with those subject to it once they were deemed no longer of use. Former CIA counterterrorism expert Michael Scheurer, an architect of Bush-era extraordinary rendition, later acknowledged the problems related to it. Having turned to the practice "in desperation," policymakers had not thought beyond the initial extraordinary rendition and interrogation. Once a detainee's rights had been violated, Scheurer observed, he could "neither be reinstated into the court system nor killed." In his assessment, "all we've done is create a nightmare."[50] In contrast, former FBI agent Dan Coleman argued that the whole point of the extraordinary rendition process was that suspects could "disappear off the books and never be heard of again" and this was exactly what appealed to the CIA.[51]

Abu Ghraib

When the U.S. Army took over Abu Ghraib, it converted one of Saddam's most notorious prisons into a U.S. military incarceration facility. When abuse of detainees within its walls became public knowledge, the administration was quick to criticize the "few bad apples" responsible for it.[52] The reality was more complex. An internal Department of Defense report stated that in August 2003 Major General Geoffrey Miller, then commander of Guantanamo, had arrived in Iraq with policy guidelines used for Guantanamo. He reportedly gave these to the Combined Joint Task Force as a potential model, noting that the Geneva Conventions did apply in Iraq in contrast to Guantanamo.[53]

In 2008, *ABC News* reported that a White House "Principals Group," comprising Dick Cheney, Condoleezza Rice, Donald Rumsfeld, Colin Powell, CIA director George Tenet, and Attorney General John Ashcroft, had approved the use of "combined" interrogation techniques, entailing more than one method at a time, at Abu Ghraib. Controversy already raged over the abuse of detainees, but this was the first disclosure that high-level administration officials had discussed and approved it.[54] It was further revealed that Ashcroft, who considered the tactics legal, was "troubled" that the details were being discussed at such high level.[55]

Abu Ghraib was already a stain on the Iraqi psyche after tens of thousands had been tortured and killed during Saddam's regime. In view of this, American treatment of detainees in this prison contradicted U.S. claims of having liberated the Iraqi people from oppression. The 2004 Taguba Report found that in late 2003, "numerous incidents of sadistic, blatant, and wanton criminal abuses were inflicted on several detainees." The incidents it listed included "breaking chemical lights and pouring the phosphoric liquid on detainees...threatening male detainees with rape.... sodomizing a male detainee with a chemical light.... using military working dogs to frighten and intimidate detainees..."[56] Images of naked, hooded, humiliated prisoners, along with corpses, caused widespread outrage and debate regarding where the buck of authorization stopped. Was the president to blame? Perhaps not personally, but the torture had occurred on his watch, so moral responsibility ultimately lay with him. Legally, however, it did not. A Department of Defense memorandum stated that the prohibition of torture should be considered "inapplicable to interrogations undertaken pursuant to his Commander in Chief authority."[57]

Hence, Bush escaped censure for the Abu Ghraib detainee abuse. The Taguba Report offered an "unsparing study of collective wrongdoing and the failure of Army wrongdoing at the highest levels."[58] It was deemed neither appropriate nor necessary to investigate how or why the commander-in-chief allowed such unacceptable behavior. In this case, the buck stopped with the Pentagon, but White House–inspired leaks to the *Washington Post* suggested that the president was unhappy with Rumsfeld's handling of the Abu Ghraib abuse. While the blame may have fallen far enough from the door of the Oval Office, the culture of secrecy and lack of accountability that were evident in the administration's way of doing business further damaged its already battered public image.

Plamegate

In his 2003 State of the Union address, Bush asserted that "the British government has learned that Saddam Hussein recently sought significant quantities of uranium from Africa. Our intelligence sources tell us that he has attempted to purchase high-strength aluminum tubes for nuclear weapons production."[59] In addition, the president claimed that Saddam had flouted the UN weapons inspections. In contrast, chief UN weapons inspector Hans Blix had declared the previous day that Iraq "has on the whole cooperated rather well so far" with the weapons inspectors, even if it had yet to provide the required documentation.[60]

The extent to which Bush sold the Iraq War to the U.S. public via questionable intelligence is the most contested issue of his presidency. Instead of subjecting the deeply flawed intelligence they received to critical scrutiny, the president and his aides seized on it as gospel. It is clear that they considered Saddam and his weapons program a serious threat that justified his military overthrow. While the idea of invading a country controlled by a ruthless tyrant may seem legitimate on a moral level, the inevitable question that follows is, why only Iraq when there were many equally brutal regimes elsewhere in the world? In addition, the White House's modus operandi to secure approval of its policy raised serious ethical questions.

The administration saw itself as upholding what Robert Kagan and William Kristol had praised as the "straight and admirable path" of the Bush Doctrine.[61] As far back as 1997, these two neoconservatives had called for war against Iraq, proposing that it was time to start "thinking the unthinkable" to prevent Saddam developing his chemical and biological capabilities.[62] According to some commentators, their advocacy planted the seeds for the second Gulf War.[63] Bush would later claim a moral purpose for his foreign policy in his 2005 declaration that "it is the policy of the United States to seek and support the growth of democratic movements and institutions in every nation and culture, with the ultimate goal of ending tyranny in our world." Describing this mission effectively in religious terms, he said it was "the calling of our time."[64]

Francis Fukuyama regarded the Bush Doctrine, in the context of Iraq, as a way of using preventive war against nuclear proliferation by certain states. However, as he acknowledged, the outcome was the opposite to administration intent. The more likely a country is to cross the nuclear threshold, the less likely an American conventional attack is to be effective.[65] Clearly, focusing on the perceived WMD threat offered a more concrete reason for going to war than the somewhat abstract concept of the global public good. If the American public felt threatened by a possible direct attack from Iraq, they would be more inclined to support a unilateral preventive war. And so, the administration went about promoting the idea that the U.S. homeland was actually in peril because of Saddam.

In the aftermath of 9/11, according to journalists Michael Isikoff and David Corn, the CIA had devised an extensive covert operation plan, DB/Anabasis, to destabilize and ultimately oust Saddam. Bush was perfectly clear in his intentions toward the Iraqi dictator, telling aides that he would "kick his sorry motherfucking ass all over the Middle East."[66] The CIA project aimed to do just that. A two-year plan, costing $400 million, was drawn up to infiltrate Saddam's regime and provoke a response that ostensibly justified a U.S. attack. Bush approved the plan in February 2002, but later decided against it on the advice of General Tommy Franks, military chief of U.S. Central Command in the Middle East.[67]

Around this time, the CIA's Counterproliferation Division (CPD) of the Director of Operations had its Joint Task Force on Iraq working on uncovering possible WMDs with Valerie Plame as the Chief Operations Officer.[68] It was the uncovering, intentional or otherwise, of Plame's CIA identity by journalist Robert Novak that sparked what became known as the Plamegate scandal. On September 26, 2003, a criminal investigation was launched to ascertain who had leaked Plame's identity to reporters. In December, a special counsel, Patrick Fitzgerald, was appointed to head the investigation and a grand jury began in January 2004 to investigate the possibility of violations of federal criminal laws.[69] The Plame identity scandal, serious in itself, was representative of a more profound issue pertaining to the Bush administration's casus belli with Iraq.

In February 2002, Plame's husband, former U.S. ambassador Joseph Wilson, had visited Niger to ascertain whether there was any truth to intelligence that Saddam had attempted to purchase uranium "yellowcake." Wilson's trip was discreet, his time was pro bono, and his expenses were paid by the CIA. In September 2002, Bush delivered a speech to world leaders at the UN warning them of the "grave and gathering danger" in Iraq. He clearly stated that the United States would act unilaterally if necessary.[70] In the same month, the British government published a white paper dealing with the perceived threat posed by Saddam and his weapons program, with specific mention of the Niger uranium connection and the possibility of Iraq being capable of a biological or chemical attack within a forty-five–minute period.[71]

Shortly after the Iraq invasion was launched on March 20, 2003, Donald Rumsfeld affirmed in an *ABC News* interview, "[W]e know where they [Saddam's WMD's] are. They're in the area around Tikrit and Baghdad and east, west, south and north somewhat."[72] On May 29, Bush declared, "We have found the weapons of mass destruction." The president's supporters embraced this claim as a vindication of his decision to go to war, but it was untrue.[73] In July 2003, however, in a *New York Times* article, headed "What I Didn't Find in Africa," Wilson asserted that "some of the intelligence relating to Iraq's nuclear weapons program was twisted to exaggerate the Iraqi threat."[74] Dick Cheney moved swiftly to undermine his credibility. Two days after publication of Wilson's article, the vice president's chief of staff, Lewis Libby, met with Judith Miller of the *New York Times* to show her excerpts from classified documents pertaining to the prewar intelligence community consensus on going to war with Iraq. During this conversation, Libby also apparently mentioned the identity of CIA operative Valerie Plame, which was further leaked in anonymous briefings by White House staff in the coming weeks.[75] Later, CIA director George Tenet took the blame for the inclusion of the uranium reference in President Bush's speech, saying that he was "responsible for the approval process in my agency."[76]

According to reporters Isikoff and Corn, there was bad blood between the Bush administration and the CIA. Cheney, Rumsfeld, and other officials had little faith in what they considered its consistent underestimation of threats facing the United States. In turn, the CIA believed that the Bush administration was cherry-picking intelligence to suits its requirements and possibly even excluding the agency from the screening of raw data.[77] Deputy director John McLaughlin had indicated that the CIA did not believe that Saddam was likely to attack America with conventional, biological, or chemical weapons. What it did fear was that Saddam might assist terrorists in attacking the American homeland if the United States attacked him.[78]

This was the context in which the Robert Novak article on Wilson's Niger trip, published in the *Washington Post* on July 14, 2003, made mention of his wife. In it, the columnist wrote, "Wilson never worked for the CIA, but his wife, Valerie Plame, is an agency operative on weapons of mass destruction." In addition, he claimed that Wilson went to Niger at the behest of his wife.[79] In accordance with the 1982 Intelligence Identities Protection Act, revealing the identity of an undercover CIA agent was a federal crime, punishable by up to ten years in prison.[80] In the minds of partisans, Wilson became either a hero or villain. Among many Democrats, left-wing commentators, and bloggers, there was a feeling of "gotcha" politics in the widespread desire to demonstrate that Bush and his aides had "lied."[81] As usual, the partisans tended to focus their argument on who was good and bad rather than on what actually occurred and how.

On October 28, 2005, Lewis Libby was indicted on five counts: obstruction of justice and two counts each of false statements and two counts of perjury. In January 2007, the vice president's chief of staff went on trial in what was arguably the biggest political court case since the Watergate era. He was convicted on charges of perjury and obstruction of justice but not indicted for having leaked classified intelligence documents on Iraq.[82] Libby was fined $250,000 and sentenced to thirty months in jail. In June 2007, Congress denied his request to remain out of jail during his appeal against the convictions. The same day, without consulting the Justice Department, Bush commuted the sentence, which he characterized as "excessive," thereby saving Libby from prison without actually pardoning him. Administration supporters defended this as appropriate since Libby had not been charged with leaking Plame's identity and had, in their opinion, been made a scapegoat by those opposing the war. In contrast, critics like Senate Majority Harry Reid (D-NV) asserted that the conviction "was the one faint glimmer of accountability for the White House efforts to manipulate intelligence."[83] Special prosecutor Patrick Fitzgerald also condemned the decision to overturn the sentence delivered by a Bush-appointed district judge in accordance with federal sentencing guidelines. House Speaker Nancy Pelosi (D-CA) bluntly declared the president's action a "betrayal of trust" in putting his administration above the rule of law.[84]

Conclusion

The 9/11 attacks raised an age-old conundrum. The question of how the state should react to a legitimate and significant threat without endangering the Constitution was not new, but in many ways the situation was unprecedented. The military, financial, and technological prowess of the United States was second to none and the main constraints on its actions were legal. If such boundaries were ignored or circumvented, the limits on how the executive could act were few. The Bush administration evidently acted outside and sometimes against the law in pursuit of its national security policy. Its conduct unnerved those more concerned with maintaining the constitutional order and the rule of law. Claims that the president must act unilaterally in times of crisis can and have always been justified to an extent but the nation is exposed to other perils when diminished constraints on presidential action become the norm. In the post-9/11 period, the other branches of government and the media had a heavy responsibility to ensure that necessary checks and balances were maintained, whatever the external threat. In this instance, all concerned fell short of their duties.

Bush's tenure changed the presidency in ways that raised significant ethical issues. To perceive it positively, he acted in the best interests of the country and through sometimes unconventional and unprecedented use of executive power prevented further attacks on U.S. soil. If the civil liberties of a few were temporarily threatened as a result, that was unfortunate but unavoidable. To see it negatively, Bush did untold damage to the reputation and standing of the presidency and international respect for the United States. He may not have had the dysfunctional psyche of Nixon or the self-destructive qualities of some of his predecessors, but the questionable legitimacy of the Iraq invasion, the moral obloquy of detainee abuse, and the undermining of the constitutional separation of the powers testified to leadership that was unbound by ethical constraints.

According to Robert Kagan, America did not change after the events of September 11, 2001, but rather "only became more itself."[85] Previous administrations had certainly engaged in ethically questionable, if not downright immoral, conduct. In this regard, however, the Bush presidency surpassed such precedents in both qualitative and quantitative terms. It was truly the imperial presidency redux but on a bigger scale than ever previously envisaged by advocates of a powerful executive. Ethical transgressions associated with this development ranged from suspect to shocking, legal to categorically illegal.

Arguably, the single gravest offense was invading Iraq under false pretences. In addition to its dubious legality, this legitimized a "wartime" approach to human rights and constitutional adherence. Nevertheless, actions undertaken in the war on terror had foreshadowed the administration's intent to work through the "dark side" using "any means at our disposal," as Dick Cheney told NBC's *Meet the Press*.[86] The human rights violations that occurred in Iraq had a seamless connection to the Guantanamo abuses and extraordinary rendition. Taken together, therefore, there is a case to be made that these collectively constituted ethical transgressions at least comparable in scale to the morally questionable decision to invade Iraq. The use of torture, detaining prisoners without trial and dismissal of the Geneva Conventions sullied America's status as a liberal democracy and did immense damage to its standing abroad. The scale of these ethical transgressions posed the question of where the buck of responsibility stopped. Casting blame on a few overenthusiastic subordinates, as was the case with Abu Ghraib, is not the answer. In reality the finger of guilt points to the upper echelons of the Bush administration that provided the essential authorization for the morally questionable actions undertaken in the name of national security.

The administration's promotion of the Patriot Act that sanctioned restraint of civil liberties at home and presidential signing statements that circumvented the law may appear to constitute a secondary tier of ethical transgressions because their immediate consequences were not as damaging to life and human rights as those cited above. Nevertheless, the long-term effect may prove more portentous because of their precedent for the expansion of executive power in the name of national security. In this regard, the outing of CIA agent Valerie Plame, something of a delicious scandal for the media, also had serious overtones about the wartime suppression of democratic dissent. In contrast to the fate of the Watergate burglars and conspirators, Bush's commutation of Lewis Libby's prison sentence sent out a signal that those who broke the law in service of the executive need not suffer the full legal consequences if their wrongdoing was uncovered.

In the 1990s, America was the only remaining superpower with a global reputation as robust as its economy. Giving voice to the national sense of confidence, which some might call arrogance, Secretary of State Madeline Albright declared, "[W]e are the indispensable nation. We stand tall. We see further into the future."[87] Within a decade, however, America's global reputation and moral authority were on a downward spiral. If the country's democratic values are indeed the greatest source of its strength, this was profoundly undermined during the Bush years. However, America's historically proven capacity for self-renewal suggests that the damage can be put right. Alexis de Tocqueville optimistically commented that America's greatness "lies not in being more enlightened than any other nation, but rather in her ability to repair her faults."[88] It remains to be seen whether the post-Bush United States will prove this.

Notes

1. Thomas Paine, *The Writings of Thomas Paine*, vol. 3 (Boston: Adamant Media, 2001), 277.
2. Francis Fukuyama, *After the Neocons: America at the Crossroads* (New Haven CT: Yale University Press, 2007), 93.
3. Mary Jacoby, "The Dunce," *Salon.com*, September 16, 2004.
4. Katherine C Reilly, "The Ethics of George W Bush: A Conversation with Peter Singer," *Nation*, September 28, 2004.
5. John Nichols, "Arthur Schlesinger v. the Imperial Presidency," *Nation*, March 1, 2007.
6. Ibid.
7. "Bush Says It Is Time for Action," *CNN*, November 6, 2001.
8. "O'Neill Lashes 'Blind Man' Bush," *BBC News Channel*, January 10, 2004.
9. Ron Suskind, "Faith, Certainty and the Presidency of George W Bush," *New York Times*, October 17, 2004.
10. "Bush Vows to Rid the World of Evil Doers," *CNN*, September 16, 2001.
11. Suskind, "Faith, Certainty and the Presidency of George W Bush."
12. Barton Gellman, *Angler: The Cheney Vice-Presidency* (New York: Penguin, 2008); Jane Mayer, "The Hidden Power: The Legal Mind Behind the White House's War on Terror," *New Yorker*, July 3, 2006.
13. Charlie Savage, *Takeover: The Return of the Imperial Presidency and the Subversion of American Democracy* (Boston: Little, Brown, 2007), 79.
14. Gary Kamiya, "John Yoo Is Sorry for Nothing," *Salon.com*, March 10, 2009.
15. House Committee on the Judiciary Majority Staff Report to Chairman John C. Conyers Jr., *Reining in the Imperial Presidency: Lessons and Recommendations Relating to the Presidency of George W. Bush* (Washington DC: Government Printing Office, 2009), 24.
16. Jack Goldsmith, *The Terror Presidency: Law and Judgement in the Bush Administration* (New York: W. W. Norton, 2009), 124–26.
17. Ibid.
18. John Yoo, "The President's Constitutional Authority to Conduct Military Operations against Terrorists and Nations Supporting Them," September 25, 2001.
19. Adam Nagourney, "Divisive Words: The President. Shift of Power to the White House Reshapes Political Landscape," *New York Times*, December 22, 2002.
20. Ibid.
21. Andrew Rudalevige, *The New Imperial Presidency: Renewing Presidential Power after Watergate* (Ann Arbor: University of Michigan Press, 2006), 12.

22. House Committee on the Judiciary Majority Staff Report to Chairman John C. Conyers Jr., 166.
23. American Civil Liberties Union Report, *National Security Letters*, October 11, 2007, www.aclu.org/national-security-technology-and-liberty/national-security-letters
24. Barton Gellman, "The FBI's Secret Scrutiny: In Hunt for Terrorists, Bureau Examines Records of Ordinary Americans," *Washington Post*, November 6, 2005.
25. House Committee on the Judiciary Majority Staff Report to Chairman John C. Conyers Jr., 166, 188.
26. James Pfiffner, *The Modern Presidency*, 5th ed. (Belmont CA: Thompson Wadsworth, 2008), 157.
27. Charlie Savage, "Examples of the President's Signing Statements," *Boston Globe*, April 30, 2006; Charlie Savage, "Bush Challenges Hundreds of Laws," *Boston Globe*, April 30, 2006.
28. American Bar Association, "Task Force on Presidential Signing Statements and the Separation of Powers Doctrine," July 24, 2006.
29. House Committee on the Judiciary Majority Staff Report to Chairman John C. Conyers Jr., 9.
30. Ibid., 189.
31. Charles J. Ogletree Jr. testimony before U.S. Senate Committee on the Judiciary, June 27, 2006.
32. John Yoo and Patrick F. Philbin, Memorandum to William J. Haynes, "Re: Possible Haebus Jurisdiction over Aliens, Held in Guantanamo Bay," December 28, 2001.
33. Lt. Commander Charles Swift testimony at the Subcommittee on the Constitution, Civil Rights. and Civil Liberties, June 26, 2007, cited in House Committee on the Judiciary Majority Staff Report to the Chairman John C. Conyers Jr, 349.
34. Savage, *Takeover*.
35. John Yoo, *War by Other Means: An Insider's Account of the War on Terror* (Boston: Atlantic Monthly Press, 2006), 142.
36. James Pfiffner, *Power Play: The Bush Presidency and the Constitution* (Washington DC: Brookings Institution Press, 2008), 141; John Barry, Michael Isikoff, and Michael Hirsh, "The Roots of Torture," *Newsweek*, May 24, 2004.
37. Savage, *Takeover*, 177.
38. Karen J. Greenberg and Joshua L. Dratel, eds., *The Torture Papers: The Road to Abu Ghraib* (New York: Cambridge University Press, 2005), 227.
39. Philippe Sands, *Torture Team: Uncovering War Crimes in the Land of the Free* (London: Penguin, 2009), 3–4.
40. Statement for the Record: Office of General Counsel Involvement in Detainee Legal Issues, July 7, 2004, quoted in Jane Mayer, "The Memo: How an Internal Effort to Ban the Abuse and Torture of Detainees was Thwarted," *New Yorker*, February 27, 2006.

41. David Nicholl, Department of Neurology, City Hospital, Birmingham, *Guardian*, Letters, September 8, 2009, 37.
42. Ibid.
43. Jane Mayer, "Outsourcing Torture: The Secret History of America's 'Extraordinary Rendition' Program," *New Yorker,* February 14, 2005.
44. Ibid.
45. Savage, *Takeover,* 237.
46. Ibid.
47. David Ignatius, "Extraordinary Rendition Realities," *Washington Post,* March 9, 2005.
48. Michael Fletcher, "Bush Defends CIA's Clandestine Prisons," *Washington Post,* November 8, 2005.
49. Alberto Gonzales response to questions from Senator Dianne Feinstein, quoted in American Civil Liberties Union Report, "The Failure of the United States to Comply with the Convention Against Torture."
50. Michael Schauer, quoted in Mayer, "Outsourcing Torture."
51. Ibid.
52. Paul Wolfowitz interview, Pentagon Channel television broadcast, May 4, 2004.
53. James R. Schlesinger, Final Report to the Independent Panel to Review Department of Defense Operations, August 24, 2004.
54. Jan Crawford-Greenburg, Howard Rosenberg, and Ariane de Vogue, "Sources: Top Bush Advisors Approved Enhanced Interrogation," *ABC News*, April 9, 2008.
55. Jan Crawford-Greenberg, Howard Rosenberg, Ariane de Vogue, "Sources: Principals Ok'd Harsh Tactics," *ABC News,* April 10, 2008.
56. Tabuga Report, Articles 15–16 investigation of the 800th Military Police Brigade, 2004.
57. Dana Priest and Jeffrey Smith, "Memo Offered Justification for Use of Torture," *Washington Post,* June 8, 2004.
58. Seymour Hersh, "Annals of National Security: Torture at Abu Ghraib," *New Yorker,* May 10, 2004.
59. George Bush, State of the Union Address, January 28, 2003.
60. Hans Blix Report to the UN on the State of Weapons Inspections in Iraq, January 27, 2003.
61. Robert Kagan and William Kristol, "Remember the Bush Doctrine," *Weekly Standard,* April 22, 2002.
62. Robert Kagan and William Kristol, "Saddam Must Go," *Weekly Standard,* November 17, 1997.
63. Craig Aaron, "Standard Issues," *In These Times,* October 6, 2005.
64. Dick Meyer, "The Bush Doctrine: Bush Vows to Change the World but Never Mentions Iraq," *CBS News,* January 20, 2005.
65. Fukuyama, *After the Neocons,* xii.
66. Michael Isikoff and David Corn, *Hubris: The Inside Story of Spin, Scandal and the Selling of the Iraq War* (New York: Random House, 2007), 20.

67. Ibid., 7–11.
68. Valerie Plame-Wilson, *Fair Game: My Life as a Spy, My Betrayal by the White House* (New York: Simon and Schuster, 2007), 60–61.
69. "Timeline of the Leak," *New York Times,* www.nytimes.com/ref/washington/2006_LEAKTIMELINE_GRAPHIC.html
70. George Bush, "Address to the United Nations General Assembly Delegations in New York," *The American Presidency* Project, www.pres.uscb.edu
71. "Iraq's Weapons of Mass Destruction: The Assessment of the British Government," Government Dossier on Weapons of Mass Destruction, September 24, 2002.
72. Donald Rumsfeld interview with George Stephanopolous, *ABC News,* March 30, 2003.
73. Joby Warrick, "Lacking Biolabs, Trailers Carried Case for War," *Washington Post,* April 12, 2006.
74. Joe Wilson, "What I Didn't Find in Iraq," *New York Times,* July 6, 2003.
75. Savage, *Takeover,* 164–65.
76. "Tenet Admits Error in Approving Bush Speech," *CNN,* December 25, 2003.
77. Vicky Ward, "Double Exposure," *Vanity Fair,* January 1, 2004.
78. Isikoff and Corn, *Hubris,* 141.
79. Robert Novak, "Mission to Niger," *Washington Post,* July 14, 2003.
80. National Security Act, Title VI—Protection of Certain National Security Information.
81. Lanny David, *Scandal: How Gotcha Politics Is Destroying America* (New York: Palgrave, 2006), 10.
82. Savage, *Takeover,* 165.
83. Daniel Politi, "Prison Break," Slate.com, July 3, 2007.
84. Savage, *Takeover,* 326–27.
85. Andrew Bacevich, *The Limits of Power: The End of American Exceptionalism* (New York: Metropolitan, 2009), 10.
86. House Committee on the Judiciary Majority Staff Report to Chairman John C. Conyers Jr., 75–76.
87. Sandra Mackey, *The Reckoning: Iraq and the Legacy of Saddam Hussein* (New York: W. W. Norton, 2002), 358.
88. Lexington, "Two Cheers for America," *Economist,* September 19, 2009.

Chapter Six

Did Bush Pursue a Neoconservative Foreign Policy?

Timothy J. Lynch

Introduction

When Michelle Obama met Sarah Brown, the wife of the British prime minister, the First Lady gave, as a gift to Sarah's two sons, a $15 model of Marine One, the presidential helicopter. According to one commentator, better tokens of esteem would have been "Action man models of her husband smiting the evil forces of neoconservatism."[1] The advent of the Obama presidency in January 2009 was widely expected to be a repudiation of the foreign policy of his predecessor. There was widespread anticipation in America and abroad that Bush's failures, which were conventionally attributed to neoconservative influence, would be put right; the United States would "reset" relationships "crashed" by Bush's war on terror; multilateralism would replace unilateralism; international law would be taken seriously again; extraordinary rendition would end and Guantanamo Bay would be closed; climate change would be prioritized; and ideology and idealism in foreign policy would be swapped for realism and pragmatism. In sum the *deneoconization* of foreign policy would restore America's legitimacy as a force for good in the world.

Such projections assumed that neoconservatism had been both malign in effect and powerful in influence during the Bush years. According to this narrative, the forty-third president was either a willing agent in a neoconservative "revolution" or its pawn. This chapter is skeptical of such claims. It argues that George W. Bush, far from being a fervent neoconservative in his foreign policy, was insufficiently one in his response to 9/11, especially regarding Iraq. His war on terror actually represented far more historical continuity than discontinuity. Significantly, it is a conflict his successor has sustained and escalated rather than abandoned. Bush's foreign policy, neither an unqualified success nor a study in failure, was the largely predictable reply to global terrorism as manifested in September 2001. Aspects of that foreign policy were neoconservative—but its substance was not.

The chapter deals first with the problem of definition; to measure the neoconservatism of recent foreign policy requires a working definition of what that word means. The body of the chapter then tests the attribution of neoconservatism to Bush's foreign policy at two levels of analysis—personnel and grand strategy. At neither level is neoconservatism dominant. In the conclusion we will consider more appropriate labels for the foreign policy of the Bush administration.

Definitions

Neoconservatism is not self-defining. For most of its career, the word was an epithet, used by its detractors on both the political left and right. Those who accept the label for themselves define neoconservatism differently from those who wield it against them. We will take each group in turn.

Antineocon Definitions

Much of the literature critical of neoconservatism deals in denunciations rather than definitions. "No one," Joseph Heilbrunn observes, "has ever really succeeded in precisely defining neoconservatism."[2] Neocons are variously derided as "idiots," "protofascists," "militarists," "sexists," "racists," and even "liberal fundamentalist jihadists."[3] Such labeling is not the preserve of the political and academic left. One of the most widely read accounts of early Bush foreign policy is Stefan Halper and Jonathan Clarke's conservative-leaning *America Alone: The Neo-conservatives and the Global Order* (2004). Its dust jacket belies its thesis: Bush (with a demonic red-eye), his ear bending toward Rumsfeld's Iago-like whisper, with Condoleezza Rice manouvring in the background. Yet none of these is a self-identifying neocon.

Halper and Clarke offer several caricatures. "A neoconservative," they write, "is a contributor to the *Weekly Standard* who takes his intellectual cue from the American Enterprise Institute and agrees that the French are a 'strategic enemy.'"[4] Neocons, "in complete contrast to their patron saint, Ronald Reagan," are deeply pessimistic about the human condition:

> The here-and-now world in which neo-conservatives see themselves is a world of Hobbesian state-of-nature primitivism and conspiracy

where perpetual militarized competition for ascendancy is the norm, and moderation (even of the sort envisioned by Hobbes) by the community of nations is impossible, where the search for a social contract à la Locke or Rousseau is illusory, where trust (even Reagan's "trust but verify") among human beings is elusive, and where adversaries (defined as anyone who does not share the neo-conservative worldview) must be preemptively crushed lest they crush you.[5]

A more typical conservative depiction of neoconservatives is as leftist interlopers, part of a liberal Trojan horse that will ruin from within the pragmatism of Republican foreign policy. In contrast to Halper and Clarke, conservatives like James Bovard, Patrick Buchanan, and Philip Gold are suspicious of neocons, not for their pessimism but for their optimism.[6] Neocons, in their eyes, are radicals. Where conservatives accept the constancy of human nature, neocons believe in its malleability; as Aristotle and Plato taught, good cities produce good citizens. In this sense, conservatives have grounds for rejecting neocons on the basis of their Trotskyist lineage. Inspired by Trotsky in the 1930s, neoconservative luminaries like Irving Kristol saw regime type as the fundamental determining factor in how people lived. Men and women were political animals, whose behavior was ideologically determined. The ideology of a regime had a crucial bearing of the character of its citizens. It followed that one could change human nature—or at least human behavior—by changing the political system in which that nature expressed itself. "Lenin understood that very clearly," wrote Irving Kristol:

> What communists call the theoretical organs always end up through a filtering process influencing a lot of people who don't even know they're being influenced...We've had ideological politics for quite a while now. *In the end, ideas rule the world because even interests are defined by ideas.* The closer you get to the game of politics the less likely you are to see that.[7]

The conservative, and especially realist, disquiet with this ideological determinism—traditionally the preserve of the left—has produced on the right of the political spectrum an essentially pejorative definition of neoconservatism. Dangerous radicalism, a communist genesis, and a misplaced faith in the efficacy of government action make the neocons unwelcome guests in the conservative tent. "It's their ideas and their style," fumes Philip Gold, "the grandiose theories and intellectual arrogance of yet another crop of 'Best and Brightest' who have gotten us into yet another unnecessary war, that I find abhorrent."[8]

Like their opponents on the right, many liberals disdain the neocons, but get no closer to defining them. Anne Norton and Shadia Drury damn them as Straussians ("disciples" of Leo Strauss), whereas Tony Smith seeks to rescue the German theorist from neoconservative appropriation. Stephen Sniegoski contends that, together with Likudniks, the neocons form a "transparent cabal" making U.S. foreign policy to suit Israeli security interests.[9] Consequently, liberal critiques lack a unified theme. Neocons are either imperialists (or Zionists) (and, therefore, wicked) or liberal fanatics (and, therefore, naive). Much liberal analysis has become synonymous with realist approaches to neoconservatism. For example, liberal scholars see a faith in the democratization of the Middle East as misguided and unrealistic.[10] In line with realists, they believe that attempts to transform Arab autocracies into secular democracies will only incite an anti-American counterresponse. Much liberal analysis accepts the logic of balancing behavior, once the preserve of realist IR theory, and indicts neocon prescriptions accordingly.[11]

Neoconservative Definitions

Neoconservatives locate their persuasion within the tradition of American foreign policy—though even among neoconservatives there is little semantic consensus on what neoconservatism is. Charles Krauthammer calls his neoconservatism "democratic realism" and Robert Kagan's "democratic globalism."[12] Kagan himself, one of the most widely read of neoconservative thinkers, embraces a neocon label only with reluctance and his brother, Frederick, rejects it entirely.[13] Francis Fukuyama claims he is no longer a neocon but a "realistic Wilsonian."[14] In 1996, Norman Podhoretz, a central figure within the neocon movement for several decades, declared neoconservatism dead.[15] At the same time, Bill Kristol and Robert Kagan, its young Turks, redefined it as "neo-Reaganite" and very much alive.[16] This imprecision and debate led David Brooks to warn, "If you ever read a sentence that starts with 'Neocons believe,' there is a 99.44 per cent chance everything else in that sentence will be untrue."[17]

Even neoconservatism's genesis and evolution is subject to vigorous dispute.[18] Its rise was only partially rooted in foreign policy. Several neocons became prominent because of their response to domestic, not foreign, policy. The domestically orientated journal *Public Interest* (founded in 1965) predated the foreign policy emphasis of the *National Interest* (founded in 1985). The imbibing of much neocon public policy analysis by the broader conservative movement rendered the former increasingly indistinct. *Public Interest*, for four decades the in-house journal of neoconservative debate over domestic policy, folded in 2005. This was not the case in foreign policy, where neoconservative prescriptions have struggled to influence the broader conservative movement and have had an even more marginal impact on the realist school of international relations (that now characterizes the *National Interest*).

Part of the problem in defining neoconservatism so as to measure its foreign policy effect is the movement's fluidity. As Irving Kristol observed, "there is no set of neoconservative beliefs concerning foreign policy, only a set of attitudes derived from historical experience." He offered four "theses":

> First, patriotism is a natural and healthy sentiment and should be encouraged by both private and public institutions...
>
> Second, world government is a terrible idea since it can lead to world tyranny...
>
> Third, statesmen should, above all, have the ability to distinguish friends from enemies...
>
> Fourth...large nations, whose identity is ideological, like...the United States...inevitably have ideological interests...the United States will always feel obliged to defend, if possible, a democratic nation under attack from non-democratic forces...No complicated geopolitical calculations of national interest are necessary.[19]

However, these recur throughout the history of U.S. diplomacy and hardly represent a worldview mutually exclusive of other foreign policy traditions. We can imagine most American presidents embracing most of Kristol's theses.

Francis Fukuyama offers a narrower definition that seeks to reduce the "diversity" of neoconservative thought on foreign affairs to four "basic principles." These can be abbreviated and tabulated as follows:

1. The internal character of any given regime is the more reliable predictor of its external behavior. How a state treats its own people is indicative of how it will treat foreigners. It follows that there are good states and bad states.
2. American power should be used explicitly to protect the good states and challenge and retard the bad. This prescription applied in the fight against Hitler in World War II and against Slobodan Milosevic in the 1990s. Power counts in the pursuit of justice.

3. Big government programs, at home and abroad, are more likely to decrease than increase human liberties. Neocons are as disquieted by 1960s Great Society liberalism as by 1940s Soviet Stalinism in this regard.
4. International law and institutions, like the United Nations, can and should never be the arbiters of international morality. Individual rights are better protected though national, not international, frameworks. The U.S. Constitution is unlikely to be improved upon in this regard. International institutions that are built on a commonality of interests and facilitate the use of American power, like NATO, are acceptable, however.[20]

George W. Bush's foreign policy certainly embodied some of these principles, but even their proliferation across his administration would not bespeak a neocon ascendancy. The problem is that schools of thought defining themselves in antithesis to neoconservatism also embrace one or more of these principles. Realists and conservatives would accept much of no. 3 and some of no. 4. Many liberals would applaud no. 1 and clearly during the 1990s supported no. 2. In light of this, it is unsurprising that neoconservative Paul Wolfowitz, among others, has questioned the accuracy of the labels that have marked out debate about American foreign policy:

> Because I agreed with [Brent] Scowcroft about the Gulf War and agreed with [Zbigniew] Brzezinski in his support for NATO enlargement and intervention in Bosnia, I don't know whether that makes me a realist or makes them ideologues. But I do know that ignoring the nature of states is to ignore a fundamental reality that has a huge bearing on the U.S. national interest. To do so is not realistic. It is dogmatic or even ideological.... In Eastern Europe, the Iron Curtain no longer stands because true realists—"democratic realists"—confronted the true nature of the Soviet threat.[21]

Searching for neoconservative influence in Bush foreign policy is really a hunt for aspects of liberal, conservative, and realist design—because neoconservatism is in some ways an aggregation of all three. According to Wolfowitz, his approach is the more "realistic."[22] Indeed it is unclear whether a single foreign policy episode of the Bush era embraced each principle. Nor is there a self-evident neoconservative case study in Bush foreign policy. Even the 2003 Iraq invasion fails to meet all four principles, despite its reputation as "the neocon war."

Levels of Analysis

Measuring the amount of neoconservatism, as distinct from any number of competing and complementary approaches, in Bush's foreign policy is no easy task. The remainder of this chapter considers two levels of analysis and asks how far neoconservatism was evident within both.

Personnel

If Bush's foreign policy was neoconservative we would expect to see that reflected in the number and status of neocon officials making it. To some extent, we do see this. According to Gary Dorrien, "the neocons did stunningly well in the appointment derby" that marked Bush's truncated transition to power from December 2000 to January 2001.[23] By Dorrien's count, "more than twenty won high-ranking positions." This figure is achievable if the net is cast widely. By Dorrien's expansive definition, Dick Cheney, Donald Rumsfeld, and even Condoleezza Rice all count as neocons.[24] Dorrien insists that these "unipolarists" (his term) had so much in common with neoconservatives as to be essentially indistinguishable from them.

There are inherent problems with this accounting method. First, because several neocons held positions just below the principals' level, Dorrien assumes a pervasive neoconservatism that the record will not sustain. For example, the highest ranking official whose neocon credentials few would dispute, Deputy Secretary of Defense Paul Wolfowitz, "felt increasingly marginalized" by Donald Rumsfeld.[25] Rather than a key shaper of foreign policy, several accounts reveal a deputy often ignored by his immediate superior.[26] Wolfowitz's plans for postinvasion Iraq—which he called "realistic" when "compared with the alternatives of installing another dictator or prolonging the U.S. occupation"[27]—were rejected by Rumsfeld. The defense secretary's near-obsession with transforming the U.S. military into a rapier-like tool took precedence over nation-building, which relied on huge force deployments over the long term.

Second, assertions of an executive bureaucracy weighted toward a neoconservative worldview necessarily ignore the more powerful conservative and nationalist credentials and policy positions of the men and women who led it. As Douglas Murray reminds us, "The liberation of Iraq was supported, but not run, by neocons."[28] The political nurturing of Condoleezza Rice, Bush's first national security advisor, was undertaken by Brent Scowcroft, who became one of the most vociferous realist critics of the Bush strategy.[29] Vice President Dick Cheney, whilst an occasional backer of more stereotypical neocon concerns (his 2003 Christmas card bore Benjamin Franklin's words: "And if a sparrow cannot fall to the ground without His notice, is it likely that an empire can rise without His help?") is more accurately characterized as a "conservative nationalist" or even a "natcon" than a neocon, both before and after 9/11. He was hardly, as the latter term implies, a "new" conservative.[30] Rumsfeld, similarly, was a "mainline" conservative.[31] "In foreign and defense policy," notes a biographer, "this meant a certain geopolitical realism and a wariness of US military interventions," especially the Balkan ones that were backed by leading neoconservatives in the 1990s.[32]

As Steven Hurst has shown, both Cheney and Rumsfeld were minimalists when it came to the Afghan and Iraq wars.[33] They engineered a strategy that paid little attention to the character of the regimes that would replace the Taliban and the Baathists. Very much in line with his position regarding the first Gulf war (as defense secretary), in the second Cheney wanted U.S. troops out of harm's way sooner rather than later. The notion that American soldiers would remain in Baghdad to transform it into an Iraqi Houston was anathema to him—a position shared by Secretary of State Colin Powell. Saddam was removed to make the United States more secure. The democratization of Iraq and the Middle East might follow but these happy eventualities would be consequences of America's search for security, not its primary purpose, nor the central test of the war's legitimacy. For Bush's vice president and secretary of defense, regime character only mattered so long as that regime was not Osama bin Laden's landlord or run by Saddam Hussein. The costs of this minimalism to ordinary Afghans and Iraqis was enormous but was not a product of neoconservative design. As Hurst argues, if we continue to construe Bush foreign policy, especially in Afghanistan and Iraq, as neoconservative "then we do not understand it."[34]

Third, the bureaucracy of U.S. foreign policy is very difficult to hijack—by a branch of government or an ideological sect—in the fashion that Dorrien and others suggest. Richard Nixon's designation of the U.S. State Department as a liberal hegemony still holds. My own judgment, having worked with and interviewed serving U.S. diplomats, is that they have a far greater bias toward liberal relativism than toward conservatism; I have never met a foreign service officer who was also a neoconservative (and only very few card carrying Republicans). Studies have shown how career diplomats reflect biases and interests sufficiently different from their temporary political masters to make control of the former by the latter difficult to achieve.[35] This dynamic is magnified when any Republican president inherits the traditionally Democrat-leaning State Department.

The notion, fed by a popular misconception, that the president is more powerful than the apparatus and character of the world's oldest democracy, and that every four or eight years the foreign policy machinery of the U.S. government quickly and uniformly conforms to the worldview of the new president is at best an exaggeration. As Edward Corwin reminds us, the U.S. Constitution "is an invitation to struggle for the privilege of directing American foreign policy."[36] That struggle, far from being suspended or won by the White House, let alone by some "neocon cabal" within it, remained intense during the Bush years.

Fourth, because hijacking the foreign policy bureaucracy is actually very hard, presidents have sought to somehow get around the State Department, its largest component. Even Bill Clinton circumvented Foggy Bottom when its innate caution militated against his foreign policy adventurism—his Irish diplomacy was a case study in this.[37] Had Secretary of State Warren Christopher and his officials had their way, Clinton would never have issued Sinn Fein's Gerry Adams with his U.S. entry visa. A crucial first step on the long road to peace in Northern Ireland would have foundered on the rocks of State Department negation. Sometimes "cutting out" the State Department is necessary to move a foreign policy in a direction that careerists oppose. Clinton's NSC Staff Director, Nancy Soderberg, has argued this forcefully.[38] This is not to applaud all presidential activism nor to indict all careerist obfuscation but to recognize that when an irresistible political force meets an immovable bureaucratic object—irrespective of partisan affiliation—there will be contestation and, if the president is to win, circumvention. Several neoconservatives might have prized such a strategy during the Bush years; they did not invent it.

Finally, perhaps we are looking to blame various neocon personnel for the failures of Bush foreign policy when a better explanation lies in the intellectual-political climate that made their ideas seem timely. Francis Fukuyama's classic text, *The End of History and the Last Man* (1992), did more than any other single book to make the triumph of liberal democracy seem inevitable and even, like communism before it, scientifically sound. In that book, important for many neocons and, indeed, for the Clinton administration, elected in the year of its publication, Fukuyama suggested that, with the collapse of Soviet Communism, history, understood as the conflict between competing ideologies, had come to an end. Posthistory, the task of Western governance would be the fostering of neoliberalism and free market capitalism around the world. What, after all, he asked rhetorically, was the alternative? The thesis was enormously influential in fostering notions of a democratic peace, which dominated university research agendas in the 1990s. To paraphrase how Fukuyama was interpreted, rather than what he actually meant, the world was all American now, or on the verge of being so. All that was required was a foreign policy that gently accelerated the pace of democratization.

Given this context, argues Tony Smith, "it would be a serious mistake to exaggerate the importance of the neoconservatives."[39] Rather, it was the "pact" made with them by various "neolib scholars, scholar-activists, and activists" that generated the blinkered optimism of Middle East democratization generally and the Iraq war in particular. By this measure, neoconservative White House officials were decidedly marginal to the strategy and tone adopted after 9/11. Instead, the "intellectual underpinnings" were provided by thinkers such as Paul Berman, Ian Buruma, Larry Diamond, Thomas Friedman, Francis Fukuyama, Andrew Moravcsik, and John Rawls.

Smith overstates his case but the intellectual context he describes invites consideration of a final problem with identifying a neoconservative hold on the personnel of Bush foreign policy. It is one that lies in the character of Bush himself. As John Micklethwait and Adrian Wooldridge remind us, neocons "were not natural comrades of a president who judged people by the content of their hearts rather than the quality of their minds."[40] "The only Strauss whom Bush and Cheney had probably heard of," quipped Jacob Heilbrunn, "was the jeans maker Levi Strauss."[41] When former Missouri senator John C. Danforth, a prospective running-mate for Bush in 2000, was asked whether the Texan was a neoconservative, he said "I don't know what that word means and I'm sure Bush doesn't either."[42] William Kristol, son of Irving and Project for the New American Century [PNAC] chair, supported George W. Bush's opponent, John McCain, in the Republican primaries in 2000. Bush's campaign theme of "humility" abroad hardly caught the neoconservative imagination.[43]

Observers of a neocon bias within the White House are in part correct to emphasize the number of officials who migrated from neocon-sympathetic think tanks into the Bush administration. The list of signatories to the PNAC, a tiny think tank housed within the American Enterprise Institute in Washington DC, is often cited in evidence of this claim (despite Fukuyama's friendly dismissal of this organization as "Bill Kristol and his fax machine").[44] As table 6.1 indicates, of the twenty-four men and one woman signing PNAC's declaration of principles in 1997,[45] ten became part of the extended Bush team after 2000.

What this tabulation does not reveal is the extent of actual influence over, as opposed to formal access to, President Bush.[46] For all but two or three of the ten, both influence and access were limited. Emerging memoirs and the bestselling accounts by Bob Woodward fall some way short of proving Bush a pawn of his neoconservative advisors or that he paid much attention to theoretical justifications of his foreign policy.[47] As Don Abelson concludes, having studied the impact of think tanks on foreign policymaking, "the greatest influence on George W. Bush was George W. Bush."[48] "We'd love to take credit for the Bush doctrine," PNAC president Gary Schmitt told Abelson, "but in all honesty we can't."[49]

Poaching think tankers does not seem to have increased the depth of Bush's thinking about international relations. Cheney, Rumsfeld, and—especially—Rice exerted significant influence over

Table 6.1 PNAC Signatories Hired and Not Hired by the George W. Bush Administration

Hired	*Not Hired*
Elliott Abrams	Gary Bauer
Dick Cheney	William J. Bennett
Eliot A. Cohen	Jeb Bush
Paula Dobriansky	Midge Decter
Aaron Friedberg	Steve Forbes
Zalmay Khalilzad	Francis Fukuyama
Lewis Libby	Frank Gaffney
Peter W. Rodman	Fred C. Ikle
Donald Rumsfeld	Donald Kagan
Paul Wolfowitz	Norman Podhoretz
	Dan Quayle
	Stephen P. Rosen
	Henry S. Rowen
	Vin Weber
	George Weigel

Bush foreign policy but, as we have argued, the neocon label does not stick easily to them. Rice, the official with whom Bush spent more time than possibly any other, was not a PNAC signatory and had been mentored by realists not neocons. Indeed, conservative nationalists and foreign policy realists became more apparent as the administration aged, though they were present from the very beginning, not least in the persons of Cheney and Rice. Neocons, conversely, declined in rank (from a midlevel starting point) and we can assume in influence. Paul Wolfowitz went to the World Bank. Lewis "Scooter" Libby, Cheney's chief-of-staff, nearly went to jail (which he only avoided through presidential commutation of a prison sentence). Paula Dobriansky pursued no obvious neoconservative agenda as Bush's special envoy to Northern Ireland. Aaron Friedberg, Cheney's deputy national security adviser and noted China expert, did not succeed in crafting an ideological China policy because he had no such ambition—his academic work is far more realist than neoconservative.[50] Bush's China policy rarely conformed to a neoconservative prescription because, on the PRC especially, there is no obvious neocon prescription.

If PNAC did shape part of the Bush worldview, it also had some role shaping of his predecessor. As early as 1992, Clinton sought to woo neoconservatives disgruntled by what they saw as George H. W. Bush's sterile realism.[51] PNAC was born during the second Clinton administration and had arguably as much impact upon it as upon its Republican successor. Clinton's war against Serbia in 1999 was in several respects more synchronized with neoconservative principles than was Bush's against Saddam Hussein. In the Balkans, little public diplomacy was devoted to justifying the impending action on realist grounds; realists had, since the break-up of Yugoslavia, insisted America had no dog in that fight.[52] Rather, Clinton employed neoconservative rationalizations and enjoyed neoconservative support for his Kosovo war, waged without a UN resolution and in the face of an explicit refusal by the U.S. Congress to authorize it—the first such refusal in U.S. history. Similarly, it was during the Clinton administration that regime change in Iraq was made the official position of the U.S. government, as per the terms of the Iraq Liberation Act of 1998. Clinton deployed military force abroad on over eighty occasions and engaged in a significant intervention abroad about every eighteen months (Somalia, 1992–93; Haiti, 1994; Bosnia, 1995–96; Iraq, 1998; and Kosovo, 1999).[53] Several of the liberal hawks who backed these wars went onto join the Obama administration in 2009, including Joe Biden, Hillary Clinton, and Richard Holbrooke. It is not fanciful to suggest that the pace of foreign invasions had actually slowed—only two states were invaded, for explicitly national security reasons, and their rebuilding was insufficiently attended to—during the supposed neocon ascendancy of the Bush era.

Diplomacy and Grand Strategy

Several accounts place the Bush administration outside the mainstream American foreign policy tradition. There are at least three common parts to this argument. Let us examine each in turn.

Unilateralism

The Bush doctrine is often construed as an explicit repudiation of an appropriate multilateral approach basic to American foreign policy from World War II to the end of the Cold War. Bush's unilateralism, some have argued, was the defining feature of his neoconservative diplomacy. There is some substance to this. The National Security Strategy of September 2002 (NSS 2002) made clear that the supposed morality of multilateralism would not replace the potentially greater efficacy of unilateralism, or at least of ad hoc alliances formed outside of a UN framework. The document referred to these as "coalitions of the willing."[54] Critics disparaged this as "posse diplomacy." According to Robert Tucker and David Hendrickson, these flexible friendships were ruinous of an American approach that, until Bush, had acted in "conformity with the principles of the UN Charter and its rule forbidding aggression."[55] The question is how far this supposed Bush departure was informed by neoconservatism.

Certainly, neocons are inherently suspicious of claims that multilateralism is morally superior to its alternatives. As Robert Kagan has asked, "Is there a certain, magic number of supporting nations that bestows legitimacy? Or is it the quality of one's allies that matters more than the quantity when defining 'multilateralism'? Is France worth more than Spain?"[56] Throughout U.S. diplomatic history more attention has been paid to the efficacy of alliances than to their computation with international law. The US-USSR alliance in World War II seems a fair example of this trend. Indeed, during the Cold War, most American military interventions were waged in ad hoc alliances (with Australia in Vietnam or with Britain in Libya, for example) or alone (as in Grenada and Panama). The UN-sponsored Korean war was an exception that proved the rule—though even this was, like the Iraq war, an overwhelmingly U.S.-led affair. Even after the Cold

War, as we have already observed, presidents waged war in temporary coalitions. In Kosovo in 1999, Bill Clinton bombed Serbia in violation of the UN Charter's prohibition on internal state interference and without a UN Security Council resolution—even bombing the Chinese embassy in Belgrade by mistake.

The Bush wars conform to a similar pattern—but commanded a level of congressional approval denied to Clinton's Balkans' adventure. If Iraq was a neoconservative war, so was Kosovo. Both depended on alliances outside of a UN framework. Both violated the inviolability of each target state's sovereignty. Both failed to secure a UN resolution. Both alienated China and Russia. One might also contend that Operation Iraqi Freedom should have enjoyed a greater legitimacy because of its explicit grounding in a U.S. national security interest—the destruction of Iraq's WMD capacity—which Operation Allied Force in Kosovo lacked. The objections of assorted realists not withstanding, the Iraq war conforms to as many realist precepts as neoconservative ones. The method of its fighting (embracing any and all allies it could muster) and the poverty of ambition in its aftermath (where full-scale nation-building was not countenanced or planned for) reveal a minimalist approach to foreign policy at odds with the maximalist, hubristic, empire-building visions of neoconservatism.

Wars aside, the character of Bush diplomacy better fits a preexisting template. In North Korea, Bush relied on a multiparty approach (comprising six nations), pioneered under his predecessor. Beyond his designation of the regime as part of "an axis of evil" in 2002, there was very little of a neoconservative color in his policy toward Pyongyang. Since leaving the Bush administration, John Bolton has expended much intellectual energy reminding us of this fact.[57] The DPRK was recurrently appeased by both the Clinton and Bush administrations, an approach continued by Barack Obama. Multilateralism not unilateralism was and remains the order of the day. The 1938 Munich analogy, liberally deployed in much neoconservative writing, had no discernable impact on America's Korean policy.[58] In Iran, similarly, Bush relied on European multilateralism (the so-called EU-3 process, comprising British, French, and German diplomats) to check the Islamic Republic's nuclear ambitions—with limited success. Ironically, it was not the supposedly neocon Bush, Jr., but his realist father whose invocation of Munich in the buildup to the Gulf War in 1990 had a decisive mobilizing effect.[59]

Preemption

The doctrine of preemption figures prominently in accounts that seek to blame the Iraq fiasco on neoconservative influence. Preemption has become the defining feature of the Bush doctrine—largely despite itself. Its most famous expression was in NSS 2002:

> we will not hesitate to act alone, if necessary, to exercise our right of self-defense by acting preemptively against...terrorists [of global reach], to prevent them from doing harm against our people and our country.[60]

Much of this is commonsensical statecraft and not especially neoconservative. Franklin Roosevelt observed the lunacy of ignoring a rattle snake until after it had struck.[61] As Melvyn Leffler points out, "Preemptive strikes to eliminate threats are a strategy nearly as old as the United States."[62] In 1818, General Andrew Jackson invaded Spanish Florida to preserve order and thus preempt a potential threat to the United States. Preemption, properly understood and as construed in NSS 2002, is a tool of national security rather than a strategy or a doctrine in and of itself. If a catastrophic threat to a state can be averted by destroying the source, then any state has a duty to so act. How that threat is preempted—through an international legal authority or formal alliance—matters less than whether it is preempted.

The instrumentality and universality of preemption raises a question mark over its attribution to neoconservatives. In most respects, the preemption of Iraq's WMD capacity had nothing to do with a neocon agenda (indeed there is some debate over whether the Iraq war constituted preemption or prevention).[63] Rather, the decapitation of the Baathist regime met a number of old-fashioned realist standards. The action was justified primarily on the basis of the American security that would accrue from it. It cared very little about the regime that would follow Saddam. It is valid to speculate that a President Gore would have felt compelled to preempt Iraq's WMD threat. He had wanted to prevent its realization for over a decade. As president he would not have been afforded the opportunity to blame the previous administration for failing to deal with the gathering terrorist threat—he had been that administration's vice president. As president, Gore would have seen the same imperfect intelligence through the same prism of 9/11. Choosing to act on it would not have made him a neocon or a puppet of the neocons. Gore was hawkish on Iraq through the 1990s for reasons unconnected to neoconservative intellectuals. America began its long war against Saddam Hussein in 1991, the intensity of which was contingent on Saddam's behavior rather than neoconservative lobbying. Gore was one of only nine Senate Democrats to back the first Iraq war (in January 1991) and thus grant congressional approval to George H. W. Bush's Operation Desert Storm. Opposing Saddam Hussein, seeing his rule as a threat to U.S. security and interests, is not a litmus test for neoconservatism. If it were, Clinton, Gore, and any number of Democrats who called for regime change would be neocons.

Donald Rumsfeld did not credit the 2003 Iraq war to neoconservative machinations. "The coalition," he told Congress, "did not act in Iraq because we had discovered dramatic new evidence of Iraq's pursuit of WMD; we acted because we saw the existing evidence in a new light—through the prism of our experience on 9/11."[64] This rationale for the Iraq war, grounded in a blunt realism, was more powerful than neoconservative visions of what a liberated Iraq might look like. This provides one possible explanation as to why the planning for postinvasion Iraq was so poor—the primary intention was to preempt the threat rather than remake a nation once the threat was gone. Preemption, as Richard Perle and Ahmed Chalabi learned, had no ideological component.

This is not to deny that ideology had a role to play in Bush's foreign policy. However, appeals to democracy and freedom, which came to consume Bush's speeches in his first term and reached a climax in his second inaugural address, have been basic to presidential rhetoric since Jefferson. This is not to doubt their sincerity but to observe that such appeals are not the exclusive preserve of neoconservatives.

Democratization

If preemption was not a neoconservative invention, how far can we credit the wider Bush grand strategy to neoconservatism? Was the Forward Agenda of Freedom in the Middle East a neocon project? There is at least circumstantial evidence that it was. During his first eight months in office, the Middle East did not figure prominently in Bush's diplomacy. The contrast with the lengthy, if ultimately ineffectual, politicking of Bill Clinton in the Israel/Palestine peace process in the final weeks of his administration could not be more marked. When nineteen Arabs crashed four planes into New York, Pennsylvania, and Washington, however, the Middle East necessarily assumed a centrality in the Bush response. The president was swift in identifying not Islam but the nature of Arab governance as the enemy. He offered an explicit refutation of the political realism that had allowed Arab autocracies to stay in power: "For decades, American policy sought to achieve peace in the Middle East by promoting stability in the Middle East, yet these policies gave us neither."[65] The promotion of instability by fostering more liberal forms of Arab rule presented itself as an alternative to a decades-long failure.

It is at this juncture that several neoconservative predispositions and agendas assumed relevance. The swift demise of authoritarianism in Eastern Europe that began in 1989 prompted the neocons to paint the Middle East in similar shades. With appropriate support and cajolement from the West, Arab democrats would flourish, dictators would fall and thus the grievances on which terrorism fed would vanish. This optimistic manifesto was offered by David Frum and Richard Perle in *An End to Evil*.[66] In a twist on the Marxian dialectic, they contended that the recreation of an Arab middle class would spur reform and negate Islamist terrorism. Their analysis was shared by several fellow neoconservatives, such as Michael Novak and Natan Sharansky. Bush himself offered it rhetorical support: "[B]y advancing freedom in the greater Middle East, we help end a cycle of dictatorship and radicalism that brings millions of people to misery and brings danger to our own people."[67]

The argument that neoconservatism was tangential to Middle East strategy has two components. First, neocon prescriptions about the region were sufficiently diverse to make a linear cause and effect problematic. Certainly, some neocons were optimistic that the Middle East could be democratized along the lines of Germany and Japan after 1945 and Eastern Europe after 1989. But many were not so sure.[68] James Q. Wilson, for example, remained decidedly skeptical toward the notion that the Middle East and Islam were appropriate targets for democratization.[69] Daniel Pipes went further still in arguing that greater Arab freedom and wealth distribution would create more terrorists, rather than fewer: "Militant Islam (or Islamism) is not a response to poverty or impoverishment; not only are Bangladesh and Iraq [in 2002] not hotbeds of militant Islam, but militant Islam has often surged in countries experiencing rapid economic growth."[70] The policy prescriptions that might flow from such an analysis are difficult to imagine.

Second, Bush's grand strategy, despite some neoconservative flourishes, was a study in geopolitical realism that had at its core the security of the American state and people. As Robert Kagan argues, "the idea that the Bush administration engaged in a massive effort to promote democracy around the world is mostly myth."[71] Some neocon advice carried policy weight but only that which synchronized with the dominant realist analysis. China, Egypt, Pakistan, Russia, Saudi Arabia: none of these states was pressured by Bush to democratize, despite their importance to the war on terror. To appreciate how tangential neoconservatism was to Bush's grand strategy we need to recall that strategy's fundamental purpose after 9/11. Its aim was not to capture the world's oil supplies. Otherwise, a deal as opposed to a war with Saddam Hussein would have been a far cheaper means of achieving this. Nor was its purpose the happiness of the people of the Middle East. Rather, grand strategy after 9/11 was predicated upon the negation of WMD-terrorism. The thought of a second 9/11 paled in comparison to a nuclear attack. Grand strategy under Bush sought to make the American people secure from such an eventuality.

Achieving this objective meant a geopolitical strategy that targeted regimes that might produce and then transfer weapons of mass destruction to terrorist groups. Like the Cold War, the war on terror is better understood as a state-level campaign. It was neoconservative only by coincidence. By employing democratization as a means, the Bush administration was adopting a core neoconservative principle within its grand strategy. If America could change the nature of governance in the Middle East, it would, as per the terms of some neoconservative analysis, alter what that region exported. Democratization was first about making Americans safe; making Muslims free was secondary.

However, unlike the U.S.-led post–World War II democratization project that was for many neoconservatives a case study in effective grand strategy, American planning in the war on terror extended not much beyond the removal of two dangerous regimes. Meanwhile, two-thirds of the axis of evil survived Bush's war on terror. The democratization projects of neoconservative imagination were replaced by the decapitation methods of conservative realism. Iraq, by this measure, was an insufficiently neoconservative war that paid too little attention to the regime that would replace Saddam Hussein. Iraqis and Afghans paid a high price *not* for a neoconservative imperial will—but for its absence. When we recall the key actors making those wars—Cheney, Rumsfeld, Rice, and Bush himself—it is no surprise that neoconservatism featured far less than has previously been supposed. As Thomas Carothers has argued, "the place of democracy in Bush foreign policy, was no greater, and in some ways was less, than in the foreign policies of his predecessors."[72] The great failure of his administration, argues Carothers, was not in speaking of democracy promotion but of then subsequently neglecting it. Talking-the-talk but not walking-the-walk left democratization "badly tarnished" in the eyes of the people it was meant to help.[73]

Conclusion

This chapter has argued that neoconservatism was an important but not a decisive influence on the foreign policy of George W. Bush.

Despite aspects of policy that conformed to neoconservative tenets and the presence of neoconservatives in his administration, Bush's response to 9/11 was shaped by forces more enduring than those of neoconservative intellectuals. His bilateral relations were studies not in ideology but, as in the case of China, in ambivalence. Wanting Bush's foreign policy to be more neoconservative than it actually was does not make it so. For reasons of contrast with Barack Obama and the need to find a culprit for the Iraq debacle, neocons carry a burden greater than their actual role merits.

American foreign policy is the work of an orchestra, not a soloist. We should be wary of imbuing a single intellectual impulse with magical powers to revolutionize governmental behavior, especially one as rife with competing power loci as Washington. Very few presidential administrations, if any, have a singular ideological character. Most borrow approaches, realist and liberal, practical and theoretical, from a variety of sources. Bush's was no different in this regard. In his domestic policy, Bush was hardly a neoconservative, as his welfare spending and further nationalization of education policy are evidence. In his foreign policy, he accepted the worth of democratization to American security but failed, ultimately, to provide the means to achieve it. Michael Foley defines "classic" neoconservativism as one of "uninhibited ideological warfare" abroad.[74] By this measure, Bush was no neoconservative in his foreign policy.

Notes

1. Sarah Vine, "First Lady Shows Even She Has a Gift for the Gaffe," *Times*, March 5, 2009, 9.
2. Jacob Heilbrunn, *They Knew They Were Right: The Rise of the Neocons* (New York: Anchor Books, 2009).
3. Max Hastings, *Daily Telegraph*, February 21, 2009; Elizabeth Kelley, *Post-9/11 American Presidential Rhetoric: A Study of Protofascist Discourse* (Lanham: Lexington Books, 2007); Andrew J. Bacevich, *The New American Militarism: How Americans Are Seduced by War* (Oxford: Oxford University Press, 2006); Anne Norton, *Leo Strauss and the Politics of American Empire* (New Haven CT: Yale University Press, 2004), 188, 211; Stefan Halper and Jonathan Clarke, *America Alone: The Neo-Conservatives and the Global Order* (Cambridge: Cambridge University Press, 2004), 42; Tony Smith, *A Pact with the Devil: Washington's Bid for World Supremacy and the Betrayal of the American Promise* (London: Routledge, 2007), 195–235.
4. Halper and Clarke, *America Alone*, 43.
5. Ibid., 12.

6. James Bovard, *The Bush Betrayal* (New York: Palgrave Macmillan, 2004); Patrick Buchanan, *Where the Right Went Wrong: How Neoconservatives Subverted the Reagan Revolution and Hijacked the Bush Presidency* (New York: St. Martin's Press, 2004); Philip Gold, *Take Back the Right: How the Neo-Cons and the Religious Right Have Hijacked the Conservative Movement* (New York: Carroll and Graf, 2004).
7. Irving Kristol in Heilbrunn, *They Knew They Were Right*, 161. Emphasis added.
8. Gold, *Take Back the Right*, xxxvi.
9. See Norton, *Leo Strauss and the Politics of American Empire*; Shadia Drury, *Leo Strauss and the American Right* (New York: St. Martin's Press, 1997); Smith, *A Pact with the Devil*, 30–31; Stephen Sniegoski, *The Transparent Cabal: The Neoconservative Agenda, War in the Middle East, and the National Interest of Israel* (Norfolk VA: IHS Press, 2008).
10. See Smith, *A Pact with the Devil*, x and 154–59.
11. See Jonathan Freedland, "Bush's Amazing Achievement," *New York Review of Books*, June 14, 2007.
12. Krauthammer, *Democratic Realism* (Washington, DC: AEI Press, 2004).
13. Robert Kagan, "I Am Not a Straussian, At Least, I Don't Think I Am," *Weekly Standard*, February 6, 2006; Fred Kagan, remarks at Institute for International Strategic Studies (London), July 5, 2007 (attended by author).
14. Fukuyama, *After the Neocons: America at the Crossroads* (London: Profile Books, 2006), 9–10 and Fukuyama, "After Neoconservatism," *NYT Magazine*, February 19, 2006.
15. Norman Podhoretz, "Neoconservatism: A Eulogy," *Commentary*, March 1996.
16. See William Kristol and Robert Kagan, "Toward a Neo-Reaganite Foreign Policy," *Foreign Affairs*, July/August 1996.
17. David Brooks, "The Neocon Cabal and other fantasies," in Irwin Stelzer, ed., *Neoconservatism* (London: Atlantic Books, 2004), 42.
18. See John B Judis, "Trotskyism to Anachronism: The Neoconservative Revolution," *Foreign Affairs*, July/August 1995, a critical review of John Ehrman, *The Rise of Neoconservatism: Intellectuals and Foreign Affairs, 1945–1994* (New Haven CT: Yale University Press, 1995).
19. Irving Kristol, writing in 2003, in William Kristol, ed., *The Weekly Standard: A Reader, 1995–2005*, 2005, 167–68.
20. Adapted from Fukuyama, *After the Neocons*, 48–49.
21. Paul Wolfowitz, "Think Again: Realism," *Foreign Policy*, September/October, 2009.
22. Ibid.
23. Gary Dorrien, *Imperial Designs: Neoconservatism and the New Pax Americana* (New York: Routledge, 2004), 2.

24. Len Colodny and Tom Shachtman, *The Forty Years War: The Rise and Fall of the Neocons, from Nixon to Obama* (New York: HarperCollins, 2009) also casts the net widely to include numerous officials over several decades.
25. Bob Woodward, *State of Denial: Bush at War, Part III* (New York: Simon and Schuster, 2006), 310.
26. See Andrew Cockburn, *Rumsfeld: an American Disaster* (London: Verso, 2007); Alan Weisman, *Prince of Darkness: Richard Perle—The Kingdom, the Power, and the End of Empire in America* (New York: Union Square Press, 2007), 170; and Woodward, *State of Denial*, 309–10.
27. Wolfowitz, "Think Again: Realism."
28. Douglas Murray, "Mission Distorted," *Guardian*, October 31, 2006.
29. See Jeffrey Goldberg, "Breaking Ranks: What Turned Brent Scowcroft against the Bush Administration?" *New Yorker*, October 31, 2006.
30. See Barton Gelman, *Angler: The Cheney Vice Presidency* (New York: Penguin, 2008).
31. Bradley Graham, *By His Own Rules: The Ambitions, Successes, and Ultimate Failures of Donald Rumsfeld* (New York: PublicAffairs, 2009), 183.
32. Ibid.
33. Steven Hurst, "Myths of Neoconservatism: Bush's Neocon Foreign Policy Revisited," *International Politics*, 42, 2005, 75–96.
34. Ibid., 77.
35. See Leslie H Gelb, "Why Not the State Department?" in Charles W. Kegley, Jr. and Eugene R. Wittkopf, eds., *Perspectives on American Foreign Policy: Selected Readings* (New York: St. Martin's Press, 1983); and Duncan L. Clarke, "Why State Can't Lead," *Foreign Policy*, 66, Spring 1987, 128–42.
36. Edward S. Corwin, *The President: Office and Powers, 1787–1957*, 4th rev. ed. (New York: New York University Press, 1957), 171.
37. See Timothy J. Lynch, *Turf War: The Clinton Administration and Northern Ireland* (Basingstoke: Ashgate, 2004).
38. Ibid., 98.
39. Smith, *A Pact with the Devil*, 43.
40. Micklethwait and Wooldridge, *The Right Nation: Conservative Power in America* (New York: Penguin, 2004), 200.
41. Heilbrunn, *They Knew They Were Right*, 262.
42. Danforth in conversation with the author, London, October 22, 2009.
43. See, for example, Reuel Marc Gerecht's indictment of early Bush administration "timidity" in "A Cowering Superpower," *Weekly Standard*, July 31, 2001.
44. Derek Chollet and James Goldgeier, *American Between the Wars, 11/9 to 9/11: The Misunderstood Years between the Fall of the Berlin Wall and the Start of the War on Terror* (New York: PublicAffairs, 2008), 171.
45. See http://www.newamericancentury.org/statementofprinciples.htm.

46. This problem is considered by Aggie Hirst, "Intellectuals and US Foreign policy," in Inderjeet Parmar, Linda B. Miller, and Mark Ledwidge, eds., *New Directions in US Foreign Policy* (London: Routledge, 2009), 106–19.
47. See, for example, John Bolton, *Surrender Is Not an Option: Defending America at the United Nations* (New York: Threshold Editions, 2007); Douglas Feith, *War And Decision: Inside the Pentagon at the Dawn of the War on Terrorism* (New York: HarperCollins, 2008); and Peter W. Rodman, *Presidential Command: Power, Leadership, and the Making of Foreign Policy from Richard Nixon to George W. Bush* (New York: Knopf, 2009).
48. Donald E. Abelson *A Capitol Idea: Think Tanks and US Foreign Policy* (Montreal: MQUP, 2007), 219.
49. In ibid.
50. See, for example, Aaron L. Friedberg, "The Future of U.S.-China Relations: Is Conflict Inevitable?" *International Security*, 30, Fall 2005, 7–45.
51. See Chollet and Goldgeier, *America Between the Wars*, 35–37.
52. See, for example, Henry Kissinger, *Washington Post*, February 24, 1999.
53. George C. Herring counts eighty-four; see his *From Colony to Superpower: US Foreign Relations since 1776* (Oxford: Oxford University Press, 2008), 936. The eighteen-month figure is offered by Ivo H. Daalder and Robert Kagan, "America and the Use of Force: Sources of Legitimacy," Stanley Foundation, June 2007.
54. NSS 2002, introduction, http://georgewbush-whitehouse.archives.gov/nsc/nss/2002/.
55. Robert W. Tucker and David C. Hendrickson, "The Sources of American Legitimacy," *Foreign Affairs*, 83, 6, 2004, 18–32.
56. Robert Kagan, *Of Paradise and Power* (New York: Vintage Books, 2004), 146.
57. See John R. Bolton, "The Tragic End of Bush's North Korea Policy," *Wall Street Journal*, June 30, 2008.
58. See, for example, Paul Wolfowitz, "Statesmanship in the New Century," in Robert Kagan and William Kristol, eds., *Present Dangers: Crisis and Opportunity in American Foreign and Defense Policy* (San Francisco: Encounter Books, 2000), 307–36, 313.
59. See Steve A. Yetiv, *Explaining Foreign Policy: US Decision-Making and the Persian Gulf War* (Baltimore MD: Johns Hopkins University Press, 2004), 62–77.
60. *National Security Statement 2002*, 6.
61. See Melvyn P. Leffler, "Think Again: Bush's Foreign Policy," *Foreign Policy*, September/October, 2004, 22–28, 23.
62. Ibid., 22.
63. See Robert S. Litwak, *Regime Change: U.S. Strategy through the Prism of 9/11* (Baltimore MD: John Hopkins University Press, 2007).

64. Prepared Testimony by U.S. Secretary of Defense Donald H. Rumsfeld, Senate Armed Services Committee, July 9, 2003, www.au.af.mil/au/awc/awcgate/congress/rumsfeld_09july03.pdf
65. "The President's Radio Address, July 29, 2006," *American Presidency Project*, www.pres.usbc.edu
66. David Frum and Richard Perle, *An End to Evil: How to Win the War on Terror* (New York: Random House, 2003).
67. George W. Bush, "Remarks at Whitehall Palace in London, United Kingdom," November 19, 2003, *American Presidency Project*, www.pres.usbs.edu.
68. This neocon divide is considered in Timothy J. Lynch, "*Kristol Balls*: Neoconservative Visions of Islam and the Middle East," *International Politics*, 45, 2008, 182–211.
69. See James Q. Wilson, "Democracy for All?" *Commentary*, March 2000, 25–28; and Wilson, "Islam and Freedom," *Commentary*, December 2004, 23–28.
70. Daniel Pipes, "God and Mammon: Does Poverty Cause Militant Islam?" *National Interest*, 66, Winter 2001/02, 14–21.
71. Robert Kagan, "Foreign Policy Sequels," *Washington Post*, March 9, 2009.
72. Thomas Carothers, "Democracy Promotion under Obama: Finding a Way Forward," *Carnegie Policy Brief*, 77, February 2009, 4, www.carnegieendowment.org/files/democracy_promotion_obama.pdf.
73. Ibid., 1.
74. Michael Foley, *American Credo: The Place of Ideas in US Politics* (Oxford: Oxford University Press, 2007), 328.

Chapter Seven

Bush's Foreign Policy Legacy: Counting the Cost

John Dumbrell

Reputation, Legacy, and Opportunity

Writing at the end of the Clinton presidency, Colin Campbell and Bert A. Rockman rather unhelpfully noted that "legacies are a complicated business to deal with."[1] In the case both of recent and more remote presidencies, "legacy" is intimately bound up with "reputation." A president with a generally positive reputation will be presumed to have left a strong legacy. "Reputation" is, in turn, as Campbell and Rockman also noted, bound up with opportunity: "Crises *force* presidents to do things; big congressional majorities *allow* them to do things."[2] In the early months of Barack Obama's administration, one phrase—initially associated with Chief of Staff Rahm Emanuel, but reiterated by other White House insiders—encapsulated the forty-fourth president's need to escape from the confines of his predecessor's legacy: "never allow a crisis to go to waste." Let us briefly consider this triad of reputation, legacy, and opportunity.

Regarding reputation, many people (not least George W. Bush himself) have pointed out that several presidents, whose record appeared poor at the time of leaving office, have scored better in terms of the more mature judgment of history. The obvious example here is Harry Truman, whose poll ratings during the early stages of the Korean conflict were comparable to George W. Bush's at the end of his second term. By the same token, some presidential foreign policy reputations—Lyndon Johnson's is the obvious example—remain stubbornly in the doldrums. Both "reputation" and "legacy" have short-term and long-term dimensions. An outgoing president's short-term reputation is bound up with journalistic commentary, public opinion polling, and early academic evaluation. His long-term reputation will depend more on popular memory as it develops in succeeding years. Films, novels, and generational changes will all have an impact, as will the shifting judgment of professional historians. Also of significance will be the behavior of succeeding presidents. Did these presidents develop their predecessor's legacy, drawing on it as a positive point of reference? Did later presidents struggle to throw off the negative effects of their predecessor's policies and policy assumptions? Did later presidents more or less ignore the policy positions of their predecessor, or did they use the earlier presidency as something against which to define their own policy stances? Both reputation and legacy are linked to opportunity, though arguably less in foreign than in domestic policy, where the existence of congressional majorities is more consequential.

It is also the case that the concept of "legacy" begs the question of "legacy to whom?" In this book, we are concerned almost exclusively with the Bush legacy to Obama, or, more generally, to America and the world after January 2009. Foreign policy legacies, like presidential reputations, may, however, take a long time to become apparent. Only many years later will it be possible to judge which political leaders and administrations actually "changed the weather." Concepts formulated during the Truman years continued to affect U.S. foreign policy in the 1980s. Some foreign policy legacies, both material (the Louisiana Purchase comes to mind) and conceptual (such as the Monroe Doctrine) last even longer. Foreign policy legacies are also generally uneven and unpredictable in their impact. Unresolved international problems may explode in the face of a successor. Short-term commitments made by one president may create huge problems for his successor. Ronald Reagan bequeathed to George H. W. Bush not only new hope about the resolution of the Cold War but also dangerous uncertainty about the immediate future of the Soviet Union. The legacy that Bush passed on in turn featured Cold War victory—in the words of Michael Mandelbaum, "the greatest geopolitical windfall in the history of American foreign policy"[3]—an uncertain domestic base for the future of U.S. internationalism, and a problematic intervention in Somalia.

Such musings on reputation, legacy, and opportunity provoke some rather obvious observations about the case of George W. Bush. The foreign policy reputation of the forty-third president was certainly low when he left office. Commenting on his various exit interviews, the London *Times* editorialized, "[Bush] prided himself on taking decisions on gut instinct. Given the mismanagement of two wars, the obstinate refusal to tackle climate change, and the unraveling of the economy, the lesson of the Bush presidency is surely that the gut is for digestion, not for decision-making."[4] An interim academic verdict may be gleaned from two recent works of contemporary history. For Hal Brands, in *From Berlin to Baghdad*, the George W. Bush administration misconceived international politics after the 9/11 terror attacks: "In weaving a compelling narrative about the national purpose, the administration greatly oversimplified US aims and world realities... The world was not dichotomised between terror and freedom."[5] In *America between the Wars*, Derek Chollet and James Goldgeier saw Bush as carrying on both his father's 1992 Defense Planning Guidance "strategy to sustain American dominance" *and* Bill Clinton's commitment to the United States as the "indispensable nation." In their estimate, however, the effect of his foreign policy was to make American dominance "all the more difficult to achieve," while a "steady rise in discomfort with US power around the world" compromised the doctrine of "indispensable nation."[6]

The general verdict on Bush's foreign policy record on his departure from office was a negative one. This reflected a broadly held belief among analysts that he had bungled a historic opportunity to develop a viable new foreign policy for the United States. To some degree, of course, presidents create their own opportunities. Yet 9/11 was an event in American history only paralleled in modern times by Pearl Harbor. In 1962, President John Kennedy *chose* (rightly or wrongly) to elevate Russian missiles in Cuba to the status of first-level crisis. Franklin Roosevelt and George W. Bush had no such luxury. First-level crises do, however, create opportunities. They enable presidents to rethink and reconceptualize, to cut through bureaucratic politics, and to shape public and congressional opinion, possibly for generations to come. Arguably, Bush endured one first-level crisis in 9/11, only to bequeath yet another—the near-collapse of the global financial system in 2008—to President Obama.

This chapter offers a conceptual typology of Bush's foreign policy legacy. It considers leftover problems and immediate opportunities for the incoming administration, moving on to discussion of possible longer-term implications of the legacy—was there a "Bush revolution" in foreign affairs? It then assesses the status and nature of American international power at the end of the George W. Bush presidency. The chapter concludes with some brief reflections on the kind of domestic foreign policy consensus bequeathed by the forty-third president to his successor. First, however, the framework for assessing Bush foreign policy needs to be established.

Assessing Bush

Assessment of presidential foreign policy performance raises complex issues of structure and agency, and of levels of analysis in international relations. Perhaps the quickest way of disposing intelligently of such questions is to paraphrase and adapt Karl Marx: presidents make history, but not under conditions of their own choosing. Presidents do not have a free hand; they are bound by history, international structures of power, bureaucracies, and legislatures. Perceptions of free action may be generated by election victory, and by the kind of first-level crises (real or manufactured) discussed above. Yet foreign policy leaders remain, to a greater or lesser degree, stranded in webs of circumstantial and structural power. Accordingly, presidential performance is just one level of foreign policy analysis. Nevertheless, it is an extraordinarily important one. Let us consider a key decision from the Bush years—arguably *the* key decision: the decision to invade Iraq. Such a course of action was in no sense imposed by the international system. Indeed, adherents to theories of structural power were at something of a loss to explain it, with some taking uncharacteristic recourse to the citation of unusually powerful domestic forces.[7] The decision to choose war was the work of a small policymaking elite, headed by the president.[8] In light of this, assessing presidential performance, including the presidential legacy, is not a romantic abstraction from complex webs of causation, but a necessary function of responsible academic commentary.

How should we judge presidential foreign policy performance? The conventional way is to begin with an assessment of both the possibilities and limits of presidential freedom of action. According to the relevant literature, a good foreign policy president is one with a fine "contextual intelligence," namely the ability to assess the international and domestic constraints on action. He will aspire to rationality in decision making, but will be aware of the limits to pure rationality imposed by factors ranging from bureaucratic politics to time constraints, from incomplete knowledge to the impact of the American system of separated powers. A good foreign policy president will have an integrated purpose to his international policy, but will avoid dogmatism. He will have a sense of the intense complexity of international power relations, but will not succumb to paralyzing inaction in the face of such understanding. He will also understand the need, and will develop the ability, to sell his policy to domestic audiences and to allies abroad.[9]

When set against the above criteria, it is difficult to imagine how the reputation of Bush administration foreign policy can be revived. "Contextual intelligence" was not its strong suit. To quote a not entirely unsympathetic British journalist, "The proper indictment of

Mr Bush...is not the silly idea that he was some uniquely evil tyrant, seeking selfishly to enlarge the American Government's power around the world. It is that he was grotesquely, almost picturesquely, inept."[10] The Bush reputation will surely struggle to free itself from the charge of recklessness attaching to the decision to invade Iraq in 2003 and more broadly from accusations of narrow dogmatism. Memories of the global rise in anti-Americanism, woefully inept public diplomacy and alliance management, and the negative repercussions of Vice President Dick Cheney's "dark side"—especially his role in the sanctioning of torture—are also likely to deter favorable revision of Bush foreign policy for the foreseeable future.[11]

The mythology of the "toxic Texan" does, of course, require a degree of critical interrogation. It certainly is the case, for example, that the uniquely unilateralist thrust of the Bush foreign policy has been exaggerated. Bill Clinton's second-term foreign policy was already moving in a unilateralist direction—both as a result of pressure from the Republican Congress and as an expression of the reality of late 1990s global unipolarity. Showing its own capacity for adaptation, the Bush administration manifested new signs of "contextual intelligence" and an awareness of the limits to American power in its second term. This largely reflected the chastening effect of first-term mistakes. In other words, it was more a case of Ozymandias than Tamburlaine. As a consequence, real improvements took place in alliance management, as well as a long overdue effort (as in regard to North Korea) to move toward some genuine engagement with enemies. The shift in tactics in Iraq—apparently linked to the personal intervention by the president on the side of U.S. military figures such as Jack Keane and David Petraeus—also led to significant improvements in prospects there.[12]

These developments prompted David Frum to challenge the predominantly negative assessments of Bush's final legacy. Disputing the assumption that the Iraq invasion would ultimately be remembered as an unmitigated disaster, he anticipated that "it will come to be seen more like the frustrating Korean conflict, or the Philippine insurrection, rather than the debacle of Vietnam." In addition, Frum numbered among Bush's positive achievements the formation of a newly vigorous U.S.-India alliance, a new global convention on cybercrime, and "the wise decision to give [Venezuela President] Hugo Chavez enough rope to hang himself."[13] This revisionism may one day be seen as prophetic but in the short and medium terms it represents little more than a voice crying in the wilderness against the dominant orthodoxy.

Leftover Problems and Immediate Opportunities

One way of assessing immediate foreign policy legacies is to consider the briefings given by outgoing administrations to their successors. In testimony to the 9/11 Commission, Bill Clinton recalled telling George W. Bush at a December 2000 meeting: "I think you will find that by far your biggest threat is Bin Laden and the al Qaeda."[14] When J. Michael McConnell, Bush's director of national intelligence, prepared briefing reports for the candidates in the 2008 presidential elections, he identified no less than thirteen vulnerabilities. The proliferation of worries did not reflect much in the way of a diminution of the threat posed by Islamic terrorism. Indeed, McConnell reported a significant expansion and reorganization of al Qaeda in the Afghanistan-Pakistan border region. He also highlighted the Iranian and North Korean nuclear threats, apparently undiminished by Bush policies toward those countries; the military and economic implications of the rise of China; and the American exposure to cyber war. Following the election, Obama was also briefed for the first time directly on "special action programs"—ongoing U.S. covert operations in various countries, including "allies" such as Pakistan and "enemies" such as Iran.[15] All this took place, of course, within the context of what was being widely described as the biggest global economic crisis since the Great Depression.

The contrast between the Clinton and the McConnell briefings is slightly unfair to Bush. For one thing, the content of the outgoing Clinton administration briefings on terrorism has been challenged.[16] For another, all administrations leave a plethora of difficulties and, indeed, a legacy of "special" operations—in Clinton's case, this included a number of covert operations in Iraq. Nevertheless, it is very difficult to hold that Bush's legacy to Obama was in any sense superior to that bequeathed by Clinton in 2001. Obama faced an improving, if still very dangerous, situation in Iraq, and a deteriorating one in Afghanistan. Perhaps the clearest contrast with the Clinton legacy, however, lay in the area of global economics. First thoughts, of course, were with the global financial crisis of 2008–9, but other international economic problems also loomed large. Just as Clinton handed on a stalemated global trade agenda (following the collapse of the Seattle negotiations in 1999), Bush bequeathed the frozen (Doha) trade round. Like Clinton, Bush was essentially a free trader, but the problems with the Doha round were arguably linked to his administration's approval of a massively protectionist U.S. farm bill.[17]

Possibly the most damaging of all elements in Bush's global economic policy legacy in the long term related to climate change. Whereas Bill Clinton—and, of course, Vice President Al Gore—had gone some way down the road of at least raising awareness of global environmental issues, the Bush record on climate change policy was one of neglect and incomprehension.

Perhaps the greatest opportunity offered by the outgoing administration in 2009 derived precisely from its reputation for not listening, for insensitive dogmatism, and for cowboy diplomacy. The expectations surrounding any new president represent a potent resource for all incoming administrations. The trick is to feed off expectations for a new era, while postponing as far as possible the onset of disappointed hopes. Bush himself in 2001 followed the strategy of ABC—anything but Clinton—as a way of signaling hope and a distancing from the putatively irresolute and compromised outgoing administration. The hopes attending the election of the first African American president raised the bar of expectation-generated opportunity to new heights. Clearly aware of the dangers of expectation collapsing into disappointment, the Obama team in 2009 was keen to keep memories of the former presidency alive. Key speeches by senior figures in the new foreign policy team were littered with phrases that sought to encourage and sustain memories of the mistakes and coarse oversimplifications of Bush's first term. Vice President Joe Biden's speech to the Munich Conference on Security Policy (February 2009) may be taken as an example of the potent rhetorical opportunities offered by the Bush reputational legacy. The atmospherics attending the speech were significantly intensified by memories that Deputy Defense Secretary Paul Wolfowitz had informed the parallel gathering of European defense ministers in 2002 that Washington was looking to operate via "coalitions of the willing" as much as through traditional alliance structures.[18] In 2009, Biden vowed to "reject the zero sum mentalities and rigid ideologies, and to listen and learn from one another"; "we'll engage, we'll listen;" "our administration does not believe in a clash of civilizations."[19]

A Bush Revolution in Foreign Affairs?

Overtly and obliquely, Biden's Munich address sounded the theme of distance from the bad old days of Bush. This chimed with Obama's 2008 election mantra of "change." But there was also some continuity, even at the level of rhetoric. Biden explained the virtues of "a common commitment not only to listen...but to enforce the rules when they are...clearly violated."[20] Outlining a "comprehensive new strategy for Afghanistan and Pakistan" in March 2009, Obama indicated that his approach to relations with the Muslim world involved far more than an imprecation to unclench fists and an implicit move—already evident in the Bush approach after 2004—toward containing threat where it could not be eradicated. Obama now defined the goals of war as to "disrupt, dismantle and defeat al Qaeda and its safe havens." Disavowals of unilateralist intent ran up against clear expressions of core U.S. interest: "Pakistan must demonstrate its commitment to rooting out al Qaeda and the violent extremists within its borders. And we will insist that action be taken—one way or another—when we have intelligence about high-level terrorist targets."[21] Addressing the Turkish parliament in April 2009, Obama appeared to depart from the Bush administration script in extending a degree of legitimacy to the regime in Tehran: "the United States seeks engagement based on mutual interest and mutual respect... Iran is a great civilization." On the other hand, the new president signaled continuity with his predecessor's stand against Tehran's acquisition of nuclear weapons in remarking: "Iran's leaders must choose whether they will try to build a weapon or build a better future for their people."[22]

Was there a Bush revolution in foreign affairs? Or, to put the question another way, did the Bush administration "change the weather" in charting a new post-9/11 strategic course that future leaders would have to follow? There are various possible positions here. One is to argue that the Bush foreign policy was "revolutionary," both in the sense that it represented an aberration from the cooperative order-building of the post-1945 era and in the degree to which it concentrated power in the White House.[23] The implication in this line of argument is that future presidents are likely to revert to the cooperative, liberal world order tradition—but liberal-minded occupants of the Oval Office may prove reluctant to surrender power. An alternative approach is to argue that the Bush response to 9/11 was not aberrant at all in that it represented an interests-based authentication of traditional foreign policy priorities.[24] From this perspective, future presidents are likely to remain within the general strategic tramlines set by Bush, but will make choices *within* those tramlines. Even if more competent in policymaking than Bush, they will not themselves make a "revolutionary" break from his administration's priorities and strategic understanding.[25]

All this plunges us into deep and muddy definitional waters. What constitutes a "revolution" in foreign affairs? Can *any* president "change the weather" to such an extent that successors are trapped in the climatic conditions they inherit? A few, reasonably straightforward, points will help clear the waters and develop the argument.

First, it is the case that leading figures in the Bush administration embraced a view of international affairs, and of America's global role, which—though not novel—stood apart from the generally expressed and articulated views of U.S. foreign leaders since the middle of the twentieth century. Their perspective was to some degree the product of American global eminence—the reflection of confident primacy and global unipolarity. It was also the product of debates in the Republican Party following the end of the Cold War.[26] Equally important, Bush and his advisers drew on the Wilsonian democracy-promotion tradition in foreign policy, as well as the Jeffersonian view that there is no distinction between American ideals and American interests. All this added up to commitment to (more or less permanent and unremitting) American global military primacy; skepticism about the value of alliances; belief that American had the power to extinguish threats, rather than merely contain them; conviction that deterrence was best achieved through the demonstrative exercise of military power; lack of enthusiasm for activist diplomatic engagement, including the notion that, at least in the case of the Israeli-Palestine conflict (and also, for much of the Bush presidency, in relation to North Korea), haughty disengagement was a viable option; and insistence that a comprehensive settlement in the Middle East could be achieved by a liberationist invasion of Iraq. This outlook, constituting a kind of "advanced Bushism," drew on elements of neoconservatism, conservative nationalism, and offensive realism. Perhaps more than anything else, it held that containment was yesterday's doctrine.[27]

Such views were certainly not held by all senior members of Bush's administration, and greatly diminished in their strength during his second term. As his presidency entered its latter stage, it was particularly evident that the aim of eradicating rather than containing threats to U.S. security had foundered.[28] Nevertheless, ideas associated with "advanced Bushism" were expressed sufficiently often and had sufficient impact on actual policy to constitute a real departure—"revolution" is probably putting it too strongly—from prior foreign policy history. These beliefs were to some extent the product of geographical and generational shifts within the Republican Party, where they still hold considerable sway.[29] However, such thinking was aberrant in the context of modern U.S. history, especially in relation to the era of Cold War containment. Obama's rejection of it represented a real and substantive shift in the development of American internationalism.

My second point relates to the policies followed in the early months of the Obama presidency. In a sense these policies did respect the tramlines set by the preceding administration. The phrase "war on terror" was quietly dropped, but the shift in emphasis from Iraq to Afghanistan was broadly in line with the Bush inheritance, and indeed would very probably have been John McCain's chosen course had he been elected president in 2008. The changes effected by Obama, however, were certainly not trivial. His policy stances (both during the election campaign and in the early months in power) toward both Russia and Cuba represented major departures from the past, and also from what might have been expected if McCain were president. Both McCain and Obama, it is true, were committed to closing the Guantanamo detention center. Obama's closure announcement did not resolve the problem of what to do with potentially dangerous detainees, especially where evidence—plausibly obtained via torture—might be inadmissible in the regular court system. Meanwhile, the Obama team found it difficult entirely to dispose of the Bush-era commitment to military tribunals for the treatment of terrorist suspects.

Whatever their limitations, the Obama administration's initiatives, especially regarding the end of torture, not only had potent symbolism but also were indicative of a substantive policy shift. Former vice president Richard Cheney, arguably the main architect of the previous administration's "dark side" policies, certainly considered them a real departure from the Bush tramlines. From his perspective, they constituted a major, and extremely dangerous, break with the old order.[30] The relative emollience of Obama's initial reaction to the disputed Iranian election of June 2009 also drew a furious response from leading Republicans.

John Bolton, Bush's former ambassador to the United Nations, saw some continuity in detail between the foreign policy of his old boss and the new president but considered the differences in principle to be fundamental. In his view the second Bush administration had been very different from its first-term incarnation. As such Obama had in some cases "essentially ratified or continued Bush Administration policies," notably in Iraq and Afghanistan. Bolton even saluted him for moving beyond the Bush legacy to accord Pakistan's security a far higher priority than it had enjoyed before 2009. In his estimate, however, the forty-fourth president *was* different for he did not partake in the primacist worldview of his predecessor. "Obama is the first post-American President," asserted Bolton, "Central to his world-view is rejecting American exceptionalism and the consequences that flow therefrom."[31]

It is worth emphasizing that words and symbolism really do matter in foreign policy, which is as much the product of declaration as of legislation. In February 2009, Secretary of State Hillary Clinton addressed charges that President Obama's commitments to pragmatic engagement were mere words. What happened, she was asked, if America's foes did not *want* to engage? In response, Clinton insisted that "the message of our extended hand has impact." The simple promise of dialogue and engagement toward Iran, made in Obama's early speeches, set up new dynamics—within Iran itself, in the Gulf region, and among U.S. allies. If fists remain clenched, at least "we have a more understanding international community that'll say, well the Obama Administration was at least trying, unlike others who said no, we're never going to talk to these people."[32] The behavior of the Obama administration in early 2009 indicated both the continuity of consensually conceived interests-driven foreign policy, *and* the ability of the new team to break with the Bush tramlines. The Bush years did not "change the weather" of foreign policy in such a way as to render subsequent policy departures either trivial or "merely" rhetorical.

Third, what of the "Bush revolution" as it related to enhanced presidential (or at least White House) domination of foreign policy? Was the foreign policy *process* changed in such a manner as to prevent a subsequent reversal in the trends set after 9/11? Clearly, the Bush White House did make some rather extraordinary claims—most particularly, in relation to preemptive war and to antiterrorist surveillance and detention.[33] These claims did not go unchallenged, but the docility of the post-9/11 legislature meant that the internal checks on power-accretion did not operate very effectively. Some commentators have seen the Bush power assertions, in domestic as well as in foreign policy, as achieving a tipping-point in executive-legislative relations. The constitutional balance between president and Congress is thus held to have become distorted to such a degree that subsequent rebalancing would prove near-impossible.[34]

It is impossible to predict exactly what will happen to executive power under the Obama administration. Some interesting dynamics made themselves apparent during its first year in office. At the level of rhetoric, Obama and his team were keen to jettison the baggage associated with the "new imperial presidency." In practice, however, incumbent administrations are not generally keen on ceding power. Testifying to this, Vice President Joe Biden was determined to play a strong foreign policy hand. Obama chose his fellow Senate Foreign Relations Committee colleague as his running mate in 2008 precisely to bolster his own lack of demonstrated foreign policy expertise. Yet

Biden was also acutely aware of the perils of appearing to emulate the example of Richard Cheney, easily the most influential foreign policy vice president in U.S. history and potent symbol of everything the Obama administration opposed. Rather than a semipermanent "Bush revolution" in executive power, the post-9/11 years seemed likely to stand (as the Nixon years did for an earlier generation) as the model of what should be avoided. Presidents tend to dominate in foreign policy crisis, real or manufactured. There are also significant inherent qualities in (at least crisis-oriented) foreign policy—primarily the need for speed of decision and unity of command—that encourage such domination. However, Congress also has its strengths, primarily involving the power of the purse. The pendulum certainly swung to the Bush White House after 9/11; it swung back a little during the second term, and no doubt will continue swinging in ways connected to particular foreign policy crises, as well as future to partisan alignments in the nation's capital.

American International Power

During the 2008 election campaigns, it was accepted by virtually all presidential candidates—Democrat and Republican—that the Bush years had witnessed a dangerous decline in America's international "soft power." The eventual Republican nominee, John McCain, promised to overhaul U.S. public diplomacy, "revitalize the transatlantic partnership," and "re-establish our moral credibility."[35] The slide in the international popularity of the United States between 2001 and 2005 was indeed striking. The Pew Global Attitudes survey in 2002 showed deepening international hostility to the United States, with public majorities in thirty-five out of forty-two countries surveyed appeared to harbor unfavorable opinions towards it.[36] The world metaphorically voted for John Kerry in the 2004 presidential elections. A *Globescan* survey of twenty-one countries reported only India, Poland, and the Philippines as seeing the world made safer by Bush's reelection.[37] However, the extremely personalized, anti-Bush nature of post-2001 global anti-Americanism made things easier for his successor. While Muslim countries remained a rather special case, it is scarcely an exaggeration to state that the world celebrated when Obama was elected. Polling in Britain, for example, showed a near-immediate transformation in public perceptions of the United States.[38]

The contemporary debate about the nature of American international power focuses less on "soft power" per se than on the relative distribution of power resources in a world witnessing the "rise of the rest." Fareed Zakaria articulated what had become the conventional wisdom by the end of the Bush presidency: "America remains the global superpower, but it is an enfeebled one." Change in relative power was already evident, as indicated by China having contributed more that the United States to global economic growth in 2007. According to Zakaria, "In the long run this secular trend—the rise of the rest—will only gather strength. At a military-political level, America still dominates the world, but the larger structure of unipolarity—economic, financial, cultural—is weakening."[39]

Foreign policy pundits vary in the degree to which they ascribe these changes to the overreaching, ally-offending, and economically counterproductive policies of the Bush administration. Zakaria linked at least part of his argument to the diminishing of soft power under Bush: "The Bush administration never seemed to understand the practical value of legitimacy in the run-up to the Iraq War."[40] Zbigniew Brzezinski, an early adviser to Obama in his nomination campaign, went so far as to postulate "the emergence of a more pointedly anti-US coalition led by China in East Asia and by India and Russia in Eurasia." In his estimate, the "crisis of American superpower" is linked to a "global political awakening," as well as to poor leadership in Washington—not only Bush's "self-righteously unilateral conduct" of foreign policy, but also Bill Clinton's reluctance to address "global social problems."[41] Leslie Gelb traced current power shifts—the "United States is in danger of becoming merely first among major powers"—to "the demons of ideology, politics and arrogance" that were so prominent in (though not confined to) the George W. Bush administration. In his estimate, another important element of the Bush legacy that could have significant implications for the erosion of American power was a public debt in excess of ten trillion dollars: "The United States is now the biggest debtor nation in history, and no nation with a massive debt has ever remained a great power."[42]

As in the later stages of the Cold War, the perception of military overstretch figured prominently in analyses of Bush 43's "hard power" legacy. A study produced in 2009 by a team of Pentagon insiders, retired military figures and professional defense analysts, painted a picture of military crisis. Retired marine colonel John Sayen, for example, described U.S. military forces as "high-cost dinosaurs" that in Iraq and Afghanistan had been stretched to cope with an enemy far less numerous than that encountered in Vietnam.[43] Cost overruns in weapon systems appeared, in inflation adjusted dollars, to be higher in 2008 than ever before.[44]

The U.S. military was undeniably exposed and stretched by the Bush wars, and suffered associated problems of morale and purpose, but invocations of "defense meltdown" are a little extreme. Defense scares, after all, have been part and parcel of many presidential electoral and transition debates. One thinks of the "missile gap" identified by Democratic presidential candidate John F. Kennedy to discredit the incumbent Republican administration in the 1960 election, and of Republican accusations forty years later that Bill Clinton had left a "hollow military" to his successor. The 1960 missile gap was more or less fictitious, and Clinton's hollow military was little more than a partisan slur. It is also the case that much of the debate concerning the defense meltdown left by George W. Bush reflects the bitterness attending Donald Rumsfeld's tenure at the Pentagon.[45] Robert Gates, who succeeded Rumsfeld in 2006, attempted to mend fences through a less abrasive sponsorship of the Revolution in Military Affairs. However, the reaction to Rumsfeld—involving skepticism about excessive reliance on technology as well as to what Gates himself called the "creeping militarization" of foreign policy[46]—continued to affect defense debates under Obama.

It would be foolish to maintain unreservedly that the Bush legacy to Obama was the imminent eclipse of American global power. Numerous commentators prior to the fall of the Berlin Wall and even in the early 1990s were proclaiming America's decline—evidencing military overstretch, unequalled federal deficits, and even (with the end of the Cold War) a general loss of national purpose. Such proclamations were spectacularly premature. The new, "legacy of Bush," declinism can also be overdone. Robert Kagan argues convincingly that the much-vaunted global "rebalancing" against the imperialism of Bush's America simply has not occurred. The transatlantic relationship, at least according to Kagan, was transformed by the post-2005 transfers of power in Paris, Berlin, and Washington, while Chinese and Russian opposition to American predominance remained spasmodic and uncoordinated.[47]

It is evident that the limits of U.S. global power were exposed under Bush, but it was equally evident that America was still the lone superpower when he left office. What Bush did bequeath to Obama, however, was an American military that was suffering the stresses of global reach; a China that was rapidly developing its naval power; and a near-universal consensus that the balance of global economic power was shifting away from America, even as the United States clearly remained the world's major economy. A not inconsiderable part of the legacy handed over by George W. Bush in 2009 was a degree of dependence on foreign (and disproportionately Chinese) holders of American debt. By 2009, it was estimated that non-U.S. creditors held about half of all U.S. Treasury debts, compared to 18 percent in 1990.[48]

Conclusion: The Future of American Internationalism

Besides leftover problems and immediate opportunities, longer-term constraints handed on by one president to his successors, and the state of U.S. global power, a foreign policy legacy may be seen as containing at least one more important element: the presence or absence of a domestic consensus in favor of effective American internationalism.

If we survey the contemporary elite debate over foreign policy options in the post-Bush era, we actually find a striking commitment to continuing American internationalism and global leadership. In 2008, Melvyn Leffler and Jeffrey Legro collected a series of essays from across the elite political spectrum, from Samantha Power to Robert Kagan, from John Ikenberry to Niall Ferguson. As Leffler and Legro noted, "not a single one of the experts is calling for disengagement from the international scene." All accepted the Madeleine Albright (U.S. Secretary of State, 1997–2001) formulation of the United States as the "indispensable nation."[49] The likely future for foreign policy partisan debate seems likely to be built around the opposition between Obama's pragmatic engagement and the kind of assertive conservative nationalism articulated by John McCain in his 2008 campaign for president. John McCain, as we have seen, broke with many of the rougher edges of the Bush record. He was also a committed internationalist and free trader. The 2008 candidates differed radically in policy outlook, but agreed on the need for American global reach and global leadership. Both candidates supported increasing the military budget.

The concept of America as the post–Cold War "indispensable nation" was arguably handed on from the Clinton administration to the Bush team, and eventually to Obama. The kind of global disengagement offered by Republican presidential nomination candidate Ron Paul has few elite proponents. The situation at mass, popular level, however, may be a little different. A 2006 Chicago Council on Global Affairs poll found only 10 percent of respondents prepared to agree that "as the sole remaining superpower the United States should continue to be the preeminent leader in solving world problems."[50] To the extent that Washington has, in truth since the close of the Bush 41 administration, been chary of precipitate military action, an "Iraq syndrome" does exist. However, contrary to many expectations, part of the Bush 43 legacy was a consensus in favor of engaged internationalism. Where the consensus is most precarious is undoubtedly in the trade arena. Protectionist pressures, bubbling up in the U.S. Congress, were sometimes (as in the case of farm bills) indulged but, on balance, were more or less resisted during the Bush years. They seemed likely to persist, and indeed possibly to thrive, in the dark economic conditions inherited by President Obama.

The Bush legacy in foreign policy was primarily negative: diminished soft power; military strains; the multifarious threats outlined in the 2008 McConnell reports; two wars, one of them (Iraq) the product of reckless choice and unreflective arrogance. The nature of the legacy, as we have seen, created opportunities as well as problems. The simple shift in partisan control of the White House gifted a foreign policy agenda to the Obama team: activism in the Israel-Palestine dispute, movement on climate change, pursuance of arms control agreements with Russia, support for the Comprehensive Nuclear Test Ban Treaty, easing of relations with Cuba. However, the extreme partisanship of the Bush era made this process of agenda-shifting actually easier. Obama wisely chose not to reject *everything* associated with Bush. His retention of Robert Gates at the Pentagon indicated his recognition that the "change" mantra of the campaign neither could nor should be absolute. However, the incoming team had no difficulty in mapping out a new identity in terms of a new spirit of pragmatic engagement, constantly bolstered by references to the more extreme stances and statements of the George W. Bush first term. In April 2009, Obama was asked if he had indeed abandoned the high ground of American exceptionalism. The president responded that national pride would not prevent him from "recognizing that we're not always going to be right, or that other people may have good ideas, or that in order for us to work collectively, all parties have to compromise. And that includes us."[51] Part of the Bush legacy was the simple fact that a twenty-first century American president felt it wise, necessary, and proper to make such a statement.

Notes

1. Colin Campbell and Bert A. Rockman, "Introduction," in Campbell and Rockman, eds., *The Clinton Legacy* (New York: Chatham House, 2000), ix–xviii, ix.
2. Ibid., emphasis in the original. For some interesting observations on the concept of political legacy, see Terrence Casey, "Introduction: How to

Assess the Blair Legacy?" in Casey, ed., *The Blair Legacy: Politics, Policy, Governance, and Foreign Affairs* (Basingstoke: Palgrave Macmillan, 2009), 1–19.
3. Michael Mandlebaum, "The Bush Foreign Policy," *Foreign Affairs*, 70, 1990–91, 5–22 (quotation p. 5).
4. "A Failure to Reflect," *Times*, January 13, 2009, 2.
5. H. W. Brands, *From Berlin to Baghdad: America's Search for Purpose in the Post–Cold War World* (Lexington: University Press of Kentucky, 2008), 301.
6. Derek Chollet and James Goldgeier, *America between the Wars: From 11/9 to 9/11* (New York: PublicAffairs, 2008), 318, 325.
7. See, in particular, John Mearsheimer and Stephen Walt, *The Israel Lobby and US Foreign Policy* (London: Allen Lane, 2007).
8. Richard N. Haass, *War of Necessity, War of Choice: A Memoir of Two Iraq Wars* (New York: Simon and Schuster, 2009).
9. See John Dumbrell, *Clinton's Foreign Policy: Between the Bushes, 1992–2000* (New York: Routledge, 2009), 6–10; Joseph S. Nye, *The Powers to Lead: Soft, Hard and Smart* (New York: Oxford University Press, 2008); Stanley A. Renshon and Deborah W. Larson, *Good Judgement in Foreign Policy: Theory and Application* (Lanham, MD: Rowman and Littlefield, 2003).
10. Gerard Baker, "He Wasn't Evil. Just the Epitome of Ineptitude," *Times*, January 16, 2009, 28.
11. See Jane Mayer, *The Dark Side: The Inside Story of How the War on Terror Turned into a War on American Ideals* (New York: Doubleday, 2008).
12. Thomas E. Ricks, *The Gamble: General David Petraeus and the American Military Adventure in Iraq, 2006–2008* (New York: Penguin Press, 2009).
13. David Frum, "Think Again: Bush's Legacy," *Foreign Policy*, September/October 2008, http://www.foreignpolicy.com.
14. *The 9/11 Commission Report: Final Report of the National Commission on the Terrorist Attacks on the United States* (New York: W. W. Norton, 2004), 199.
15. David Sanger, *The Inheritance: The World Obama Confronts and the Challenges to American Power* (London: Bantam Press, 2009), xv–xx.
16. *The 9/11 Commission Report*, 199, 340.
17. See Bronwen Maddox, *In Defence of America* (London: Duckworth Overlook, 2008), 82.
18. Elizabeth Pond, "The Dynamics of the Feud over Iraq," in D. M. Andrews, ed., *The Atlantic Alliance under Stress: US-European Relations after Iraq* (Cambridge: Cambridge University Press, 2005), 54–81.
19. "Remarks by Vice President Joseph Biden at 45th Munich Conference on Security Policy," February 9, 2009, www.America.gov (U.S. Department of State).
20. Ibid.

21. Barack Obama, "Remarks on U.S. Military and Diplomatic Strategies for Afghanistan and Pakistan," March, 27, 2009, *American Presidency Project*, www.pres.usbc.edu. See also Anthony H. Cordesman, *The Obama Administration and US Strategy: The First 100 Days*, Center for Strategic and International Studies, April 14, 2009, http://csis.org.files/media/csis/pubs/090414_Obama100.
22. Barack Obama, "Address to the Grand National Assembly of Turkey in Ankara, Turkey," April 6, 2009, *American Presidency Project*, www.pres.usbc.edu
23. Ivo Daalder and James M. Lindsay, *America Unbound: The Bush Revolution in Foreign Policy* (Washington DC: Brookings Institution Press, 2003).
24. John Lewis Gaddis, *Surprise, Security, and the American Experience* (Cambridge MA: Harvard University Press, 2005).
25. Timothy J. Lynch and Robert S. Singh, *After Bush: The Case for Continuity in American Foreign Policy* (New York: Cambridge University Press, 2008).
26. John Dumbrell, "American Leadership into the New Century," in Martin Halliwell and Catherine Morley, eds., *American Thought and Culture in the 21st Century* (Edinburgh: Edinburgh University Press, 2008), 35–48.
27. John Dumbrell, "The Neo-conservative Roots of the War in Iraq," in James P. Pfiffner and Mark Phythian, eds., *Intelligence and National Security Policymaking on Iraq: British and American Perspectives* (Manchester: Manchester University Press, 2008), 19–39.
28. Philip Gordon, *Winning the Right War: The Path to Security for America and the World* (New York: Times Books, 2007).
29. Stephen Hurst, "Is the Bush Revolution Over?" *International Politics*, 46, 2009, 157–76.
30. "Remarks by Richard B. Cheney," May 21, 2009, American Enterprise Institute for Public Policy Research, www.aei.org/speech/100050
31. John Bolton, "The Post-American Presidency," *Standpoint*, July/August 2009, 42–45 (quotation p. 42).
32. Secretary of State Hillary Clinton press conference in Seoul, South Korea, February 20 2009, www.American.gov (U.S. Department of State).
33. Andrew Rudalevige, *The New Imperial Presidency: Renewing Presidential Power after Watergate* (Ann Arbor: University of Michigan Press, 2005); Robert M. Pallitto and William G. Weaver, *Presidential Secrecy and the Law* (Baltimore: Johns Hopkins University Press, 2007).
34. John E. Owens, "Presidential Power and Congressional Acquiescence in the 'War' on Terror: A New Constitutional Equilibrium?" in John Dumbrell and John E. Owens, eds., *America's "War on Terrorism": New Directions in US Government and National Security* (Lanham MD: Rowman and Littlefield, 2008), 53–91; Bruce P. Montgomery,

The Bush-Cheney Administration's Assault on Open Government (Westport CT: Praeger, 2008).
35. John McCain, "An Enduring Peace Built on Freedom," *Foreign Affairs*, 86, 2007, 19–34 (quotations pp. 26, 33).
36. William Schneider, "Unilateralism Wins Few Friends," *National Journal*, January 4, 2003, 41.
37. BBC News, "Global Poll Slams Bush Leadership," January 19, 2005, www.news.bbc.co.uk.
38. Peter Riddell, "In a Week, Britain Learns to Love America Again," *Times*, November 12, 2008, 20.
39. Fareed Zakaria, *The Post-American World* (London: Allen Lane, 2008), 217–18. See also Timothy J. Lynch, "Whither American Power?" *British Journal of Politics and International Relations*, 9, 2007, 535–44; Richard N. Haass, "The Age of Nonpolarity," *Foreign Affairs*, 87, 2008, 44–56.
40. Zakaria, *The Post-American World*, 248.
41. Zbigniew Brzezinski, *Second Chance: Three Presidents and the Crisis of American Superpower* (New York: Basic Books, 2007), 210, 184–85.
42. Leslie H. Gelb, "Necessity, Choice and Common Sense: A Policy for a Bewildering World," *Foreign Affairs*, 88, 2009, 56–72 (quotations pp. 56–57, 58).
43. John Sayen, "The Overburden of America's Outdated Defense," in Winslow T. Wheeler, ed., *America's Defense Meltdown: Pentagon Reform for President Obama and the New Congress* (Stanford CA: Stanford University Press, 2009), 1–25.
44. "Preface" to Wheeler, ed., *America's Defense Meltdown*, i–xx, ix.
45. Andrew Cockburn, *Rumsfeld: An American Disaster* (London: Verso, 2007).
46. *Economist*, June 20, 2009, 56.
47. Robert Kagan, "End of Dreams, Return of History," in Melvyn P. Leffler and Jeffrey W. Legro, eds., *To Lead the World: American Strategy after the Bush Doctrine* (New York: Oxford University Press, 2008), 36–59.
48. Lexington, "Two Cheers for America," *Economist*, July 4, 2009, 42.
49. Leffler and Legro, "Dilemmas of Strategy," in Leffler and Legro, *To Lead the World*, 250–76 (quotation p. 251).
50. Samantha Power, "Legitimacy and Competence," in Leffler and Legro, *To Lead the World*, 133–56, 150.
51. Dan Fromkin, "White House Watch," *Washington Post*, May 29, 2009, www.washingtonpost.com

Chapter Eight

Bush and Big Government Conservatism

Alex Waddan

When George W. Bush entered the White House, it was widely assumed that his objective would be to consolidate and extend the conservative agenda in public policy started by Ronald Reagan in the 1980s. The fortieth president had enjoyed mixed success in his efforts to implement that agenda,[1] but the forty-third promised to buttress the initial building blocks of the Reagan revolution. Writing in 2003, Steven Schier reflected that Bush's ambition cast him, in Stephen Skowronek's typology, as a president of "articulation": "The primary project of the Bush presidency is the completion of the political reconstruction of national politics, government and policy begun by Ronald Reagan in 1981."[2] Using a slightly different terminology but to the same effect, Skowronek himself commented in the wake of Bush's election: "This first unified Republican government in the post-Reagan era is opening a pivotal episode in orthodox innovation."[3] In other words, one measure of the Bush presidency would be to examine his capacity both to implement conservative ideas and to develop them into a winning political brand. According to Gillian Peele, central to Bush's conservatism was "a determination to reduce the role of government."[4]

As it was, Bush's presidency came to be dominated by international affairs. The fiscal and economic crises that burst to the fore during his final months in office brought domestic matters back to the center of political debate in the 2008 election, but his foreign policy legacy is likely to remain more debated than his domestic one. Yet, the Bush presidency was a consequential one in the latter sphere. A series of measures deserve particular recognition including the huge tax cuts enacted in 2001 and 2003; the No Child Left Behind (NCLB) education reform; the creation of the Department of Homeland Security; the enactment of the Patriot Act; the Medicare Modernization Act (MMA) of 2003; and the bank bailout of 2008. Moreover, simply concentrating on explicit legislative outcomes misses the potential lasting importance of the appointment of conservative justices. Certainly the judgments of Chief Justice John Roberts and Justice Samuel Alito since their appointments to the Supreme Court suggest that they will prove more effective champions of judicial conservatism than Justice David Souter, who was nominated to the Court by President George H. W. Bush. In short, Bush's presidency merits careful scrutiny in domestic as well as foreign affairs. Yet, whatever its achievements, by the time he left office, the forces of conservatism were in confusion and the Republican Party was manifestly not a winning brand.

This disarray was most obviously manifested in electoral terms; there was also evidence of considerable intellectual turmoil on the right as leading conservatives accused Bush of having betrayed their creed.[5] Their primary complaint was that he had not reduced the size of government. Indeed, these critics worried that Bush had shown himself partial both to increasing government spending and the exercise of government power in a most un-conservative fashion. One response to this, from conservatives who remained loyal to the administration, was that these critics were too one-dimensional in their view of conservatism. Hence, commentators such as Fred Barnes and Daniel Casse argued that it was important to distinguish between the *size* of government and the *actions* of government. In their judgment, Bush had remained faithful to conservative principles but had recognized the political difficulty of a simple "slash and burn" approach. Instead, his solution had been to change the nature of public programs so that they empowered individuals rather than the administrative arm of the state. It was in this context that the phrase "Big Government conservative" entered the political lexicon.[6]

Dilemmas of Conservatism and the Emergence of Reaganism

Before assessing "Bushism," it is important to establish a framework within which to discuss contemporary conservative ideas. Analyzing the nature of American conservatism is more problematic than might be assumed. During the Reagan era the label of conservatism took on a more distinctive meaning on the American political stage than had been the case through the 1950s and 1960s, but even its modern usage has different, and not wholly consistent, strands.

Critics who lament that Bush was insufficiently conservative are not comparing him unfavorably to Dwight Eisenhower and Richard Nixon, who accommodated the New Deal state, but with Ronald

Reagan, who sought to roll it back. Indeed invoking Reagan and Reaganism has become a favorite ideological weapon of contemporary conservatism. As a tool of self-definition it overlooks some of the inconsistencies in Reagan's policymaking to present him as an unambiguous champion of the cause. Despite occasional deviations, however, there is no doubt that Reagan was the most ideological president of modern times. As Hugh Heclo notes, "Although political competition in America rarely descends into intellectual debate, Reagan's words spoke to a momentous contest of ideas that is nonetheless going on behind the scenes."[7] That contest is muddied by the political and legislative compromises that are necessary to get anything done in a political system so beset with veto points, both formal and informal. Yet, as Heclo persuasively argues, Reagan had a clear and consistent set of ideas, most notably his belief that the state exerted too much control in socioeconomic affairs. As he put it in his 1981 Inaugural Address, "In the present crisis, government is not the solution to our problem; government is the problem."[8]

During the heyday of the New Deal political order from the 1930s through the 1960s, conservatism had a less certain voice. In his seminal analysis, *The Liberal Tradition in America*, Louis Hartz considered it to have only a marginal role in the development of American political discourse.[9] This scholar used the term liberal not in its modern sense of liberal Democrat but in its classical sense pertaining to America's adherence to the ideal of rugged individualism. For Hartz, America's self-identity was bound up with the rags-to-riches fables of Horatio Alger, so there was little scope for alternative political ideas to the dominant liberal ideology. In his canon, therefore, conservatism was denied oxygen by the smothering historical blanket of liberalism.

Furthermore, conservatism suffered from identification either with totalitarianism or as a reactionary force protecting wealth and privilege in the midtwentieth century.[10] Until the 1960s, the two versions of liberalism—that is, New Deal liberalism with its commitment to a degree of state activism and rugged individualism—seemed to have reached a working accommodation whereby government compensated for some of the flaws and omissions of the free enterprise system without becoming a mechanism for enforcing socioeconomic equality. As a consequence, the legatees of Franklin D. Roosevelt dominated the American political scene at both an electoral and intellectual level. In the end this proved an unsustainable accommodation as the New Deal coalition, always inherently unstable with its mix of segregationists and civil rights advocates, imploded in the late 1960s over the Vietnam War, the expansion of the welfare state, and wider cultural divisions.[11] The economic crisis of the 1970s then undid the governing assumptions of the New Deal's neo-Keynesian economic arrangements.[12] This produced a gap in the ideological market, but it was not immediately obvious that this would be filled by a *coherent* American conservatism.

Determined to occupy a distinctive position on the American political map, midtwentieth-century conservative intellectuals both distanced themselves from the far right and appropriated rugged individualism as their own talismanic value. In establishing liberty and the free market as the core of modern conservatism, Friedrich Hayek's writings provided the intellectual foundation for the emergence of a new American right that attacked New Deal-Great Society liberalism as a violation of the American tradition of self-sufficiency.[13] The historical significance of Reaganism was that it gave political form to that intellectual movement.

Notwithstanding Reaganism's successful linkage of rugged individualism and the free market within a new conservative ethos that prized liberty above all else, significant challenges remain in any quest to define a clear conservative agenda. For example, Alan Brinkley commented: "American conservatism is not easy to characterize, even for those who view it sympathetically.... Individual conservatives find it possible, and at times perhaps even necessary, to embrace several clashing ideas at once."[14] In his broad examination of conservative ideology since World War II, George Nash acknowledged that in view of "its intriguing complexity," he had "to dispense with defining 'true' conservatism."[15]

In terms of conservatism's intellectual coherence, one problem has been that while conservatives have generally agreed on the merits of a Hayekian libertarian approach in the economic domain, generally taken to mean minimal government interference in terms of taxation and regulation of business, there is disagreement over whether this laissez faire attitude should carry over into what might broadly be termed the values domain.

On some issues, such as gun control, conservatives are in relative agreement that government should not intervene. On other questions, however, there is a clash between those who extend their libertarian beliefs to matters of individual lifestyle choices and those who adhere to a more traditionalist approach that emphasizes the defense of conventional social and religious values. In the Bush era the balance of political power within conservative ranks was very much with the latter group, as was evident in the 2004 presidential contest when

GOP political strategy centered on mobilizing cultural conservatives. Nevertheless there does remain an intellectual tension between those who are libertarian across the philosophical board and those whose primary concern is to make Americans live according to a particular moral code.[16] While there were rumblings of discontent among some conservative groups that Bush had not sufficiently pressed their sociomoral agenda,[17] he did seek to meet the expectations of the GOP Christian base in a number of high-profile cases. In 2005, presidential intervention in the dispute over whether Terri Schiavo, a Florida woman in a permanent vegetative state, should be kept alive or allowed to die, accorded with traditionalist conservative thinking that justifies government interference in "morality" issues. In similar vein, Bush cast his first veto to prevent liberalization of the laws governing stem cell research in 2006.

A further and related intellectual tension exists between libertarians concerned about the expanding power of the state that is justified in the name of fighting crime and terrorism and conservatives tolerant of big government for this purpose. The New Right that emerged in both America and Britain had a Hayekian view of the state's role in the socioeconomic world but held an authoritarian perspective on its purpose in the "law and order" domain.[18] In this context passage of the Patriot Act of 2001 and establishment of the Department of Homeland Security in 2002 were predictable conservative responses to the terrorist attacks of 9/11 and traded off the extension of government power for a purpose considered legitimate against consequent diminution of individual liberties.

Conservative criticism of the Bush White House's expansion of government centered not on its development of homeland security but its socioeconomic initiatives. Typifying such concern, Bruce Bartlett, a former Reagan administration official, asserted in his 2006 book, *Impostor: How George W. Bush Bankrupted America and Betrayed the Reagan Revolution*, "Bush clearly is not a Reaganite."[19] When the forty-third president had entered the White House, few could have anticipated the confusion that would overtake the right within a few years and its consequent vilification of him.

Compassionate Conservatism

During the 2000 election campaign Bush projected himself as a "compassionate conservative." This was never concisely defined, but hinted that the outcomes of the free market would be mediated to some extent for the most vulnerable Americans. Conservatives, however, had faith that Bush was their man and rallied to his cause. This was particularly apparent when he faced the challenge of Senator John McCain (R-AR) in the primaries. According to Gary Jacobson, many conservatives took comfort that the practicalities of running a general election campaign and the need to win over moderate and independent voters prevented Bush from giving free rein to his conservative principles.[20] Moreover, Bush left enough clues to satisfy them that he was on message. Cultural conservatives, for example, applauded his selection of Dick Cheney, a steadfast opponent of abortion, as his running mate. For economic conservatives there was the promise of massive tax cuts and partial privatization of Social Security.

Despite its effective disappearance from the forty-third president's political lexicon by the end of his first term, his "compassionate conservative" rhetoric signified that he was not simply offering a repeat prescription of Reagan's antistatism. In his acceptance speech at the 2000 Republican convention, Bush declared that government could not solve the ills of the poor and vulnerable but that benign neglect was not the answer either. He called instead for putting "conservative values and conservative ideas into the thick of the fight for justice and opportunity."[21] Returning to this theme in April 2002, Bush elaborated:

> Government cannot solve every problem, but it can encourage people and communities to help themselves and to help one another. Often the truest kind of compassion is to help citizens build lives of their own. I call my philosophy and approach "compassionate conservatism." It is compassionate to actively help our fellow citizens in need. It is conservative to insist on responsibility and results.[22]

During the 2000 campaign Bush enthusiastically promoted two policy ideas that he viewed as embodying this compassionate conservative agenda: the faith-based initiative through which government would provide financial support to religious-based organizations to deliver social services at a local level; and educational reform to improve schools. The former was confined to small-scale projects, but did change the manner in which some government money was distributed. For example, from 2002 to 2005, the Compassion Capital Fund, based in the Department of Health and Human Services, distributed $148.3 million to religious groups performing social services.[23] Moreover, as a policy instrument, the faith-based initiative appealed to conservatives across the board. Traditionalists appreciated its emphasis on "faith," while small-government conservatives approved of the dispersal of power away from federal bureaucrats.[24] In contrast, Bush's education initiative, the NCLB of 2001, elicited widespread conservative condemnation.

In hindsight it is possible to see the NCLB law as encapsulating some of the central confusions about the nature of Bush's conservatism. This is not to say that the bill typified his political style since it was enacted through a bipartisan process that was not the White House norm. The debate within conservative ranks over just how conservative NCLB has proved to be does, however, capture the essence of an ideological uncertainty: the measure also signified that the new president was prepared to disregard some traditional conservative nostrums in pursuit of *his* goals.

Essentially Bush's educational initiative proposed to "provide more money to states and more flexibility in spending it, but to require them to be accountable for improved performance, especially by instituting state testing plans and improving student test scores."[25] Interestingly he was prepared from the outset to compromise with leading Democrats, including liberals like Senator Edward Kennedy (D-MA), to attain reform. This ensured bipartisan support for NCLB in both chambers of Congress, but it also resulted in some features important to conservatives being stripped from the bill. In particular, the proposal for school vouchers, which conservative Republicans envisaged as enabling children in so-called failing schools to use at another school of their choice—even a private one—fell victim to Democratic insistence that it would take money from already underfunded public schools.[26] As finally enacted, NCLB only allowed parents of poor children in underperforming schools to use federal funds for afterschool tuition. In addition, while Bush celebrated the legislation for granting "unprecedented flexibility for states and school districts," he made it clear to conservative Republicans that it also increased the federal role in education.[27] In fact, as Peele notes, NCLB "was a major and novel extension of [national government] power into state and local control of education" that contrasted with traditional Republican wariness of federal regulation of education.[28]

Despite the compromises made to secure its enactment, the White House consistently portrayed NCLB as among Bush's most substantive presidential achievements. In his 2004 acceptance speech at the GOP convention, he called it "the most important federal education reform in history."[29] Bush also hoped that his appropriation of a traditionally Democratic issue would benefit his own reelection.[30] All this did little to appease disgruntled conservatives. Lawrence Uzzell of the libertarian Cato Institute castigated the NCLB for its centralizing tendencies that reflected a "top-down, Great Society model of reform."[31] Acknowledging that it ran counter to traditional conservative preferences on this score, Bush supporters like Fred Barnes argued that the measure more than made up for this in its promotion of other conservative principles of "high standards and accountability."[32]

Fiscal Conservatism

If the NCLB was ideologically ambiguous, Bush's profound commitment to tax cuts was not. This was the policy area in which he most aggressively articulated themes from the Reagan era. The fortieth president had sanctified massive reduction of the federal tax bill as a key tenet of conservative faith through promoting enactment of the Economic Recovery Tax Act (ERTA) of 1981, characterized by political commentator Thomas Edsall as the "centerpiece of the Reagan revolution."[33] Twenty years on, tax cuts were again a particularly effective ideological and political tool for a new conservative administration looking to assert control of the political agenda. Scholar Mark Smith has illustrated just how powerful a political message tax cutting became for Republicans in contrast to shifting and complex Democratic efforts to give life to their ideas on the economy:[34] in promoting tax cuts Bush proved to be a *more* faithful follower of the guiding principles of Reaganism than not only his father (who accepted tax increases in 1990) but also Reagan himself (who sanctioned tax increases in 1982, 1984, and 1986).

The tax cut proposals quickly gave Bush early domination of the political agenda and set aside all doubt about his legitimacy after the controversial circumstances of his election. The new president followed Reagan's example by framing tax reduction as a powerful engine of economic growth that would benefit all Americans, even though most neutral analysts contended that his initiative favored the wealthiest Americans.[35]

Clearly conservatives believe that tax cuts are "good" in their own right as they allow people to keep more of their own money. Traditionally, Republicans had looked to pay for tax cuts through expenditure retrenchment, but some conservatives came to appreciate the strategic benefits of the large Reagan-era deficit as an impediment to new program development. They knew too well the difficulties of cutting existing programs that had powerful recipient constituencies, but the capping effect of deficits on future expenditures did not provide such a clear focus for political opposition. The respected budget analyst Allen Schick contended that this so-called starve the beast strategy was central to the Bush administration's thinking. In his assessment, "Bush's revenue policy is actually a spending strategy. He wants revenue deprivation to force a truly fundamental change in the course of government."[36] In line with this, he noted that the 2001 tax initiative "immediately cut federal receipts by a half a percent of Gross Domestic Product," even though the biggest rate reductions were scheduled to come into effect only in later years.[37] Moreover, the quantifiable impact on the fiscal equation in the United States was much more direct than the complex budget deals negotiated in 1990, 1993, and 1997.[38] Furthermore, these cuts and the ones that followed in 2003 came at a time when federal revenues as a percentage of GDP were already at historically low levels. According to Congressional Budget Office estimates, federal revenues in 2004 would be at the lowest as a percentage of GDP since the 1950s. When Paul O'Neill expressed unease about promoting another large tax cut with federal finances deep in the red, Vice-President Dick Cheney retorted, "Reagan proved deficits don't matter."[39] The disgruntled Treasury secretary received his pink slip of dismissal from the administration shortly afterward for being off message.

O'Neill's concerns about the parlous state of federal finances proved well founded. As Bush took office, the Congressional Budget Office forecast that the federal government would run continuous surpluses aggregating $5.6 trillion in FY 2001–FY 2011. By 2004, its revised ten-year forecast predicted an aggregate deficit of $3 trillion.[40] When Bush unveiled his final budget in February of 2008, the administration's own figures predicted deficits of $400 billion per year for the following two years with interest on the national debt at approximately $260 billion.[41] By the summer of 2008 that estimate had gone up again to a deficit for fiscal 2009 of $482 billion.[42] Even this did not compute all the money then being spent on the wars in Iraq and Afghanistan and did not forecast the scale of emergency spending on protecting the banking system in the fall of 2008.[43]

The growing tide of budgetary red ink only partially explains conservatives' qualms regarding the Bush administration's fiscal priorities. After all, deficits had been a permanent feature of the Reagan era. The conservative critique damned not the deficits in themselves but the Bush White House's propensity to expand government spending. Stephen Slivinski of the Cato Institute calculated that the increase in spending in Bush's first term on nondefense and nonentitlement programs was higher than the increase under Lyndon Johnson.

Discretionary spending had also increased under Reagan, of course, but only because of the increases in defense spending. As Slivinski noted, the latter presided over "a real nondefense discretionary spending *cut* of 9.5 percent," while there had been "massive increases in nearly every category" under Bush.[44] Another Cato analysis produced similarly critical comparisons. Rather than looking at eventual budget outcomes, since these are resolved only after the budget has passed through the congressional mangle, it compared the first three budget plans proposed by both presidents. Bush sought increases in total federal outlays above baseline levels in each of his, while Reagan requested spending cuts to below baseline levels in each of his.[45] Hence, as Iwan Morgan noted, during his first term "Bush ranked with Democrats Lyndon Johnson and Jimmy Carter as one of only three presidents since 1950 to preside over the expansion of both the defence and domestic budgets."[46]

Speaking for many on the right, conservative activist Stephen Moore lamented, "The enormous build-up of government has been what I call the virus of the Bush presidency."[47] While supportive of his tax cuts as the agency of economic growth, he and other critics damned his spending record. The Bush initiative that angered them more than any other was the Medicare Modernization Act of 2003, which provided a new entitlement to prescription drugs to senior citizens under the Medicare program.[48]

Democratic presidential candidate Al Gore called for a new benefit in the 2000 campaign. In order to defuse a potential wedge issue, Bush too agreed that one was needed to help seniors with their out-of-pocket health care expenses. Ironically, GOP success in the 2002 midterm elections increased the pressure on him to honor this pledge since the congressional Democrats could no longer be blamed for inaction. Final passage of the legislation in late 2003 was a tortured affair with unprecedented scenes in the House where Republican leaders kept the vote open for three hours as they worked to overturn an initial vote of 219 to 215 to defeat the proposal into a 220 to 215 margin of victory. During this time Speaker Dennis Hastert (R-IL) and Health and Human Services Secretary Tommy Thompson patrolled corridors "persuading" reluctant Republicans to come onboard. Moreover, Bush's Legislative Affairs director David Hobbs awakened a jet-lagged president at 4.00 am so that he could telephone waverers.[49] As it was, the bill passed along highly partisan lines. In the House nearly 90 percent of Republicans voted in favor of the final conference bill with over 90 percent of Democrats against. In the Senate those numbers were 82 and 76 percent respectively.[50] The significance of the legislation was not in doubt. When signing it, Bush legitimately declared: "You are here to witness the greatest advance in health coverage for America's seniors since the founding of Medicare."[51]

At that point the projected ten-year cost of the new benefit was $400 billion, but it transpired that the administration had hidden the true estimates to keep fiscally conservative Republicans onside. Within two months of the president signing the law the estimated cost had risen to $534 billion over ten years.[52] Nevertheless Bush made it clear that he would veto any attempt to scale back the benefit that he continued to call a "landmark achievement."[53] Some Republicans, in contrast, could not hide their frustration. Senator Trent Lott (R-MS) lamented: "I think I made a big mistake...That's one of the worst votes I've cast in my 32 years in Congress."[54] Meanwhile, Bruce Bartlett charged that "the Medicare drug bill may well be the worst piece of legislation ever enacted" since it "will cost vast sums the nation cannot afford," inevitably leading to "higher taxes."[55]

Redefining Conservatism: Facing Up to Big Government

An expensive new commitment from government that expanded the state's role in social welfare provision, the MMA was a violation of small-government principles. So is it possible to reconcile the MMA, the NCLB, and other spending initiatives with a meaningful vision of Reagan-inspired conservatism? According to Fred Barnes, not only was Bush "a great admirer of what Reagan did and said" but he was also equally dedicated to conservatism. The different contexts of their presidencies had to be taken into account, however. Had Reagan been faced with the challenge of making government smaller in the early twenty-first century, Barnes avowed that he would have done "just what Bush has done: next to nothing."[56] In his assessment, latter-day conservatives had to accept that most Americans had grown comfortable with the protections provided by Big Government. Indeed, as early as summer 2003, *National Journal* analyst Jonathan Rauch reflected on how Bush had broken from the model of small-government conservatism from the start of his presidency. The rationale was simple. Rauch quoted a White House aide: "The Republican Party in 1994 tested a proposition...that people wanted government to be radically reduced. And they found out that people didn't want government to be radically reduced."[57] David Brooks, a conservative columnist, concurred with that analysis. "If you want to put a date on the tombstone of small-government Republicanism, it would be Nov. 14 1995. That was the day the new G. O. P. majority shut down the government."[58]

For these analysts, the lesson of the 1990s was clear. Attempts to retrench universal, as distinct from means-tested, programs, would run into well-organized opposition that made such reforms almost impossible to achieve. For conservatives, that conclusion presented a particular dilemma: if they were not to concede ideological defeat and permit further growth of the activist government on liberal terms, how could they reconstruct government in accordance with their values? According to Barnes, Bush's answer to this conundrum was to change the nature of Big Government through its adaptation to the "ownership society" concept. This might sound just as nebulous a phrase as "compassionate conservatism" but the effort to give the idea concrete form underlay Bush's most significant, if doomed, second-term legislative initiative, the partial privatization of Social Security. The promotion of Health Savings Accounts (HSAs) as part of the MMA was a further illustration of this philosophy.

HSAs are individually tailored health insurance packages that allow people to start up tax privileged savings accounts to pay for out-of-pocket health care expenses. In promoting such measures, Barnes argues, "Bush and his aides have embraced an insight lost on some other conservatives: what matters is not how 'big' government is, but what it does.... Bush realized that a conservative president can use government policies to expand personal freedom...and health savings accounts in Medicare aim to do that."[59] It is worth noting that Newt Gingrich, an icon for small-government conservatives, lobbied reluctant GOP legislators to vote for the MMA on grounds that HSAs were the way to personalize and hence transform the health insurance market.[60] George Edwards further explains that the key to understanding the forty-third president's philosophy is to appreciate that "Bush is not antigovernment in the tradition of Goldwater, Reagan and Gingrich." Instead, his basic strategy "is to put strong government in the service of conservative values."[61] As two other political scientists explain,

> in practical terms, this means re-working incentive structures, often through the tax system, to encourage people to seek individually tailored insurance packages rather than to rely on existing, government-organised, collectivist provision. Furthermore, it has meant encouraging the private sector to act as a provider of welfare services even though the funding for these services still comes from government.[62]

The boldest "ownership society" initiative was the attempted partial privatization of Social Security. Bush had been a consistent champion of Social Security reform. He had highlighted the possibility of establishing personal accounts within the Social Security system when formally announcing his presidential candidacy in 1999. Although national and homeland security took priority over Social Security reform after the 9/11 attacks, the idea remained on the president's future agenda. In the 2004 State of the Union address, he announced: "Younger workers should have the opportunity to build-up a nest egg by saving part of their Social Security taxes in a personal retirement account. We should make the Social Security system a source of ownership for the American people."[63]

The proposal that was made in 2005 would have done much to undermine the collectivist basis of the Social Security system by allowing people to divert some of their payroll tax into an individual retirement account. The scale of presidential ambition was soon shown to be hubristic. Indeed, Fiona Ross, among others, has argued that the deeply embedded features of the Social Security system meant that the reform attempt was doomed to fail.[64] Hindsight, however, should not obscure the ideological significance of Bush's initiative. From a conservative perspective it was the holy grail of politics as it challenged one of the steadfast foundations of New Deal liberalism. If successful, pension reform *might* have worked to reorder the political landscape since social policies can "powerfully affect citizens' relationship to government because they typically provide them with their most personal and significant experiences of government in action."[65] On this score, regardless of how desultory Bush's initiative was in retrospect, it presented a greater theoretical threat to the American welfare state than anything attempted by Ronald Reagan.

Conclusion

Conservative critics of Bush find evidence of his disbelief in Reaganite antistatism in a speech made in October 1999. In this, the future president remarked: "Too often, my party has confused the need for limited government with a disdain for government itself."[66] For one of his supporters, Daniel Casse, measuring Bush "by the Reaganesque barometer of conservative purity" is outdated and misguided.[67] Like Fred Barnes, he insisted that the forty-third president had to move beyond these tests of fidelity to the rhetoric of Reaganism in order to bring about real change. For Bush, transforming the nature of government activism in order to direct it toward promoting individual-level incentives rather than collectivist ones offered a better way of fulfilling conservatism's vision rather than slavishly following a blueprint simply to downsize government, which was politically unmarketable irrespective of its philosophical merits.

As it was, after the Democratic recapture of Congress in the 2006 midterm elections, Bush did try to reestablish some small-government credentials through use of the veto. If anything, Democratic control of Congress made it easier for a Republican president to act as a small-government advocate. In 2007, Bush remonstrated against Democratic spending bills, notably vetoing the State Children's Health Insurance Program (SCHIP) reauthorization bill that attempted to expand this program's remit. Although there was little political mileage in opposing such a popular program, he chose to emphasize concern about the growth of government-provided health care and backdoor-creeping socialization of medicine.

Yet the SCHIP and subsequent vetoes can hardly be construed as a positive legacy. There is much to study and ponder arising from the administration's domestic agenda but the notion that a coherent creed of 'big government conservatism' emerged during the Bush era is "problematic at best."[68] Too much was contradictory or unfulfilled. Hence, big tax cuts pleased the conservative faithful, but the deficits that resulted from the corollary absence of spending retrenchment did not. The NCLB law posed dilemmas for conservatives who simultaneously wanted to impose standards but wished to keep the federal government out of education policy. The faith-based initiative hinted at the possibility of spending government money through non-state channels and the 2003 Medicare reform illustrates a capacity to embrace big government-style spending along with subtle, but potentially significant, changes that shift the emphasis from the state and collective organization to the market and the individual. In the end, however, this is not enough evidence to put flesh on the intellectual skeleton drawn by Barnes and others.

Indeed, Bush's response to the banking crisis encapsulated some of the ideological inconsistencies about the role of government. The events at the close of 2008 were surreal in many ways as an outgoing administration struggled to prevent a systemic collapse of Wall Street institutions. Given the speed with which bad news piled up, it is perhaps not too surprising that at times Secretary of the Treasury Hank Paulson seemed engaged in impromptu policy-making. In the end the efforts to broker deals to save Bear Stearns and Merrill Lynch; the underwriting of Fannie Mae and Freddie

Mac; the effective nationalization of AIG; and the creation of the Troubled Assets Relief Program suggest Big Government writ large. Yet, in line with a more laissez faire ideology, Lehman Brothers was left to sink. This may have satisfied those concerned about moral hazard, but the real world consequences of that decision illustrated that as Bush left office the conservative movement faced an intellectual challenge about the role of government in a modern economy far greater than even his most vociferous conservative critics and supporters had anticipated.[69]

Notes

1. Paul Pierson, *Dismantling the Welfare State? Reagan, Thatcher, and the Politics of Retrenchment* (Cambridge: Cambridge University Press, 1994).
2. Steven Schier, "George W. Bush's Presidential Project and Its Prospects," *Forum* 1, 2003; Stephen Skowronek, *The Politics Presidents Make: Leadership from John Adams to Bill Clinton* (Cambridge MA: Belknap Press, 1997).
3. Stephen Skowronek, "The Setting: Change and Continuity in the Politics of Leadership," in Michael Nelson, ed., *The Elections of 2000* (Washington DC: Congressional Quarterly Press, 2001), 22.
4. Gillian Peele, "Electoral Politics, Ideology and American Social Policy," *Social Policy and Administration*, 39, April, 2005, 160.
5. Though this is not a comprehensive list, these works were amongst the more notable attacks on Bush from acknowledged conservatives: Bruce Bartlett, *Imposter: How George W. Bush Bankrupted America and Betrayed the Reagan Legacy* (New York: Doubleday, 2006); Michael Tanner, *Leviathan on the Right: How Big-Government Conservatism Brought Down the Republican Revolution* (Washington DC: Cato Institute, 2007); Richard A. Viguerie, *Conservatives Betrayed: How George W. Bush and Other "Big Government" Republicans Hijacked the Conservative Cause* (Los Angeles, Bonus Books, 2006); Stephen Slivinski, *Buck Wild: How Republicans Blew the Bank and Became the Party of Big Government* (Washington DC: Cato Institute, 2006), and Ryan Sager, *The Elephant in the Room: Evangelicals, Libertarians and the Battle to Control the Republican Party* (New Jersey: Wiley, 2006).
6. Fred Barnes, *Rebel-in-Chief: Inside the Bold and Controversial Presidency of George W. Bush*, (New York: Crown Forum, 2006); Daniel Casse, "Is Bush a Conservative?" *Commentary*, February 2004.
7. Hugh Heclo, "Ronald Reagan and the American Public Philosophy," in W. Elliot Brownlee and Hugh Davis Graham, eds., *The Reagan Presidency: Pragmatic Conservatism and Its Legacies* (Lawrence: University Press of Kansas, 2003), 32.

8. Ronald Reagan, "Inaugural Address," January 20, 1981, in John T. Woolley and Gerhard Peters, *The American Presidency Project*. Santa Barbara: University of California, www.presidency.ucsb.edu [hereafter cited as *APP*].
9. Louis Hartz, *The Liberal Tradition in America: An Interpretation of American Political Thought since the Revolution* (New York: Harcourt Brace, 1955).
10. Alan Brinkley, "The Problem of American Conservatism," *American Historical Review*, 99, April, 1994, 410–14.
11. Allen J. Matusow, *The Unravelling of America: A History of Liberalism in the 1960s* (New York: Harper and Row: 1984).
12. Iwan Morgan, *Beyond the Liberal Consensus: A Political History of the United States since 1965* (London: Hurst, 1994).
13. F. A. Hayek, *The Road to Serfdom* (London: Routledge and Kagan Paul, 1944). On Hayek's importance to the development of American conservative thought, see E. J. Dionne, *Why Americans Hate Politics* (New York: Simon and Schuster, 1992) and George Nash, *The Conservative Intellectual Movement in America since 1945*, 2nd ed. (Wilmington: Intercollegiate Studies Institute, 1996).
14. Brinkley, "The Problem of Conservatism," 414.
15. Nash, *The Conservative Intellectual Movement*, xv.
16. John Tierney, "South Park Refugees," *New York Times*, August 29, 2006. There was some evidence that libertarians moved away from Bush between 2000 and 2004. A Cato Institute study found that 13 percent of the population could be classified as libertarians. Of these 72 percent voted for Bush in 2000. By 2004 that figure had dropped to 59 percent (see Brink Lindsay, "Liberaltarians," *New Republic*, December 11, 2006, 15).
17. John Micklethwait and Adrian Wooldridge, *The Right Nation: Why America Is Different*, (London: Penguin Books, 2005), 412.
18. The term "New Right" is potentially confusing. In his authoritative account of American conservatism George Nash equates the New Right with the Religious Right (*The Conservative Intellectual Movement*, 331). That is not how the term is used here. This chapter takes a broader conception of the New Right that is perhaps still best understood through a classic work of British political scholarship—see Andrew Gamble, *The Free Economy and the Strong State: The Politics of Thatcherism* (Basingstoke: Macmillan, 1988).
19. Bartlett, *Impostor*, 1.
20. Gary Jacobson, *A Divider, Not a Uniter: George W. Bush and the American People* (New York: Pearson Education, 2007).
21. George W. Bush, "Address Accepting the Presidential Nomination at the Republican National Convention in Philadelphia," August 3, 2000, *APP*.
22. George W. Bush, *President Promotes Compassionate Conservatism* (Washington DC: Office of the Press Secretary, April 30, 2002).

23. Thomas Edsall, "Grants Flow to Bush Allies on Social Issues," *Washington Post*, March 22, 2006.
24. Daniel Beland and Alex Waddan, "Conservative Ideas and Social Policy in the United States," *Social Policy and Administration*, 41, December 2007, 768–86.
25. John Fortier and Norman Ornstein, "President Bush: Legislative Strategist," in Fred Greenstein, ed., *The George W. Bush Presidency: An Early Assessment* (Baltimore: Johns Hopkins University Press, 2003), 151.
26. Barbara Sinclair, "Context, Strategy, and Chance: George W. Bush and the 107th Congress," in Colin Campbell and Bert A. Rockman, eds., *The George W. Bush Presidency* (Washington DC: Congressional Quarterly Press, 2004), 115.
27. Adam Clymer with Lizette Alvarez, "Congress Reaches Compromise on Education Bill," *New York Times*, December 12, 2001.
28. Peele, "Electoral Politics, Ideology and American Social Policy," 160.
29. George W. Bush, "Address Accepting the Presidential Nomination at the Republican National Convention in New York City," September 2, 2004, *APP*.
30. Gary Jacobson, "The Bush Presidency and the American Electorate," in Greenstein, *The George W. Bush Presidency*, 214.
31. Lawrence Uzzell, "No Child Left Behind: The Dangers of Centralized Education Policy," *Policy Analysis*, 544 (Washington DC: Cato Institute, May 2005), 2–3.
32. Barnes, *Rebel-in-Chief*, 23.
33. Thomas Edsall with Mary Edsall, *Chain Reaction: The Impact of Race, Rights and Taxes on American Politics* (New York: W. W. Norton, 1991), 159.
34. Mark Smith, *The Right Talk: How Conservatives Turned the Great Society into the Economic Society* (Princeton: Princeton University Press, 2007).
35. Jacob Hacker and Paul Pierson, "Abandoning the Middle: The Bush Tax Cuts and the Limits of Democratic Control," *Perspectives on Politics*, 3, 1, 2005, 33–53.
36. Allen Schick, "Bush's Budget Problem," in Greenstein, *The George W. Bush Presidency*, 81.
37. Hacker and Pierson, "Abandoning the Middle," 33.
38. Barry Bosworth, "The Budget Crisis: Is It All *Déjà Vu*?" *Issues in Economic Policy*, 2 (Washington DC: Brookings Institution Press, February 2006).
39. Ron Suskind, *The Price of Loyalty: George W. Bush and the Education of Paul O'Neill* (New York: Simon and Schuster, 2004), 291.
40. Iwan Morgan, "The Bush Administration and the Budget Deficit," in Iwan Morgan and Philip Davies, eds., *Right On? Political Change and Continuity in George W. Bush's America* (London: Institute for the Study of the Americas, 2006), 113.

41. Michael Abromowitz and Jonathan Weisman, "Bush's Budget Projects Deficits," *Washington Post*, February 5, 2008.
42. Andrew Taylor, "US Deficit Zooming to Half-Trillion as Bush Leaves," *San Francisco Chronicle*, July 29, 2008.
43. By the summer of 2009 the CBO was anticipating an annual deficit of $1.2 trillion between 2009 and 2012. That compared with its long range forecast made in January 2001 that there would be an annual surplus of $800 billion in those years. Using CBO reports over the period from 2001 to 2009 an analysis of this $2 trillion dollar per annum shift by the *New York Times'* economic correspondent David Leonhardt found that "About 33 percent of the swing stems from new legislation signed by Mr. Bush." A further 20 percent came from policies initiated by President Bush but continued by President Obama such as the conflicts in Iraq and Afghanistan, the Wall Street bailout and tax cuts for household earning less than $250,000 (David Leonhardt, "America's Sea of Red Ink Was Years in the Making," *New York Times*, June 10, 2009).
44. Stephen Slivinski, "Bush Beats Johnson: Comparing the Presidents," *Tax and Budget Bulletin*, 26 (Washington DC: Cato Institute, October 2005).
45. Veronique de Rugy and Tad DeHaven, "On Spending, Bush Is No Reagan," *Tax and Budget Bulletin*, 16 (Washington DC: Cato Institute, August 2003).
46. Morgan, "The Bush Administration and the Budget Deficit," 116.
47. Stephen Moore, "We Are All Post-Reaganites Now," *American Spectator*, April 2006, 33.
48. The details of how the benefit was to be provided were complex. Seniors would still have to pay a monthly premium, an annual deductible and some coinsurance. See *CBO Report for Congress: Overview of the Medicare Prescription Drug, Improvement and Modernization Act of 2003* (Washington DC: Congressional Research Service, 2004).
49. Robert Pear and Robin Toner, "A Final Push in Congress: The Overview; Sharply Split House Passes Broad Medicare Overhaul; Forceful Lobbying by Bush," *New York Times*, November 23, 2003; Robert Draper, *Dead Certain: The Presidency of George W. Bush* (New York: Free Press, 2007), 280.
50. Douglas Jaenicke and Alex Waddan, "President Bush and Social Policy: The Strange Case of the Medicare Prescription Drug Benefit," *Political Science Quarterly*, 121, 2, 2006, 235–36.
51. George W. Bush, "Remarks by the President at Signing of the Medicare Prescription Drug, Improvement and Modernization Act of 2003," December 8, 2003, *APP*, www.presidency.ucsb.edu
52. Joel Aberbach, "The Political Significance of the George W. Bush Administration," *Social Policy and Administration*, 39, 2, 2005, 141.
53. Robert Pear, "As Deadline Nears, Sorting Out the Medicare Drug Plan," *New York Times*, October 11, 2005.
54. Mary Agnes Carey, "Lott Laments His Medicare Vote," *CQ Weekly*, March 27, 2005, 726.

55. Bartlett, *Impostor*, 80.
56. Fred Barnes, "Strong Government Conservatism: How George W. Bush Has Redefined the American Right," *Weekly Standard*, January 23, 2006, 27.
57. Jonathan Rauch, "The Accidental Radical," *National Journal*, July 26, 2003.
58. David Brooks, "How to Reinvent the G. O. P," *New York Times*, August 29, 2004.
59. Barnes, *Rebel-in-Chief*, 176.
60. There was in fact much in the small print of the MMA that was decidedly conservative in nature. For example, one of the reasons the estimated costs were so high was that the administration explicitly refused Democratic suggestions that the government use its bargaining power to force pharmaceutical companies to offer discounted prices as part of the new benefit scheme. For a full discussion of the ideological complexities contained in the MMA and the apparently counterintuitive partisan behavior. See Jaenicke and Waddan, "President Bush and Social Policy," 217–40.
61. George Edwards, *Governing by Campaigning: The Politics of the Bush Presidency* (New York: Pearson, 2007), 16–17.
62. Daniel Beland and Alex Waddan, "Taking 'Big Government Conservatism' Seriously? The Bush Presidency Reconsidered," *Political Quarterly*, 79, 1, 2008, 115.
63. George W. Bush, "State of the Union Address," January 20, 2004, *APP*.
64. Fiona Ross, "Policy Histories and Partisan Leadership in Presidential Studies: The Case of Social Security," in George Edwards and Desmond King, eds., *The Polarized Presidency of George W. Bush* (Oxford: Oxford University Press, 2007), 419–46.
65. Suzanne Mettler, "The Transformed Welfare State and the Redistribution of Political Voice," in Paul Pierson and Theda Skocpol, eds., *The Transformation of American Politics: Activist Government and the Rise of Conservatism* (Princeton: Princeton University Press, 2007).
66. Transcript of a speech by Governor George W. Bush, "A Culture of Achievement," at the Manhattan Institute Forum on the Future of Educational Reform, October 5, 1999, http://www.manhattan-institute.org/html/bush_speech.htm
67. Casse, "Is Bush a Conservative?" 25.
68. Beland and Waddan, "Taking 'Big Government Conservatism' Seriously?" 116.
69. The turmoil was well illustrated by the opposition of many congressional Republicans to the $700 billion Troubled Assets Relief Program enacted in the fall of 2008 despite the strong push given to the bill by President Bush and Treasury Secretary Henry Paulson. See David Herszenhorn, "Bailout Plan Wins Approval; Democrats Vow Tighter Rules," *New York Times*, October 3, 2008.

Chapter Nine

Bush's Political Economy: Deficits, Debt, and Depression

Iwan Morgan

When George W. Bush became president, America's economic future seemed bright. Thanks to new technology and massive expansion of investment, productivity growth had reached levels not seen since the 1960s as the twentieth century drew to a close. The creation of over 18 million new jobs during Bill Clinton's presidency effectively produced a full-employment economy with the jobless level at just 4 percent in 2000. The tax revenues harvested from boom times ended the twenty-eight-year unbroken cycle of budget deficits to produce four consecutive balanced budgets in Fiscal Years (FY) 1998–2001, the longest sequence of federal surpluses since the 1920s. Confidence that economic growth would continue apace generated expectation that the federal government would have the surplus income to pay off the public debt within a decade.

When Bush departed the White House, however, the United States was in the grip of the worst economic crisis since the Great Depression. The future of everlasting, debt-eliminating budget surpluses proved a mirage. Bush presided instead over the return of chronic fiscal deficits that were instrumental in the precipitous decline of national saving. As a result America became dependent on borrowing from abroad to make good this shortfall. The willingness of foreigners to loan it money helped to keep interest rates low but distorted the operations of the private economy. With Americans stocking up on cheap credit, the United States experienced a real estate boom and consumer spree of epic proportions. Whereas economic growth had ridden the crest of the high-tech wave during the Clinton era, it became increasingly dependent in the Bush years on a level of private indebtedness that proved unsustainable. The collapse of the subprime mortgage market in 2007 set off a chain of events that nearly resulted in financial system meltdown and precipitated the worst recession since the 1930s.

While his administration's foreign policy was the subject of much controversy, the forty-third president and his defenders could at least argue that he would be vindicated in the eyes of history if his objectives in Afghanistan and Iraq were ultimately realized and the Bush Doctrine strengthened America's security against Islamic terrorism.[1] In contrast, his economic record had seemingly little prospect of positive reevaluation in the future. For critics on the right, Bush had betrayed the free-market legacy of Reaganomics in allowing the renewed expansion of domestic programs and running huge deficits that would eventually threaten his tax reduction program.[2] Liberals decried his tax program for exacerbating the income inequality in American society that had narrowed in the 1990s. They also feared that the Bush-era legacy of massive public and private indebtedness would ultimately threaten the American Dream.[3] Joseph Stiglitz, formerly chair of Bill Clinton's Council of Economic Advisers (CEA), charged that Bush was a worse steward of the economy than even Herbert Hoover. In his assessment, "The economic effects of Bush's presidency are more insidious than those of Hoover, harder to reverse, and likely to be long-lasting."[4]

The American economy is too large, complex, and globally interdependent to be subject to presidential control. Its fundamental strengths and weaknesses tend to be structural, deep rooted, and shaped more by the decisions of banks, business, and consumers than those of the White House. Accordingly, George Bush cannot be held solely responsible for the economic difficulties that occurred on his watch, any more than his predecessor can be uniquely credited for the boom of the 1990s. Nevertheless every president has significant influence on the nation's economic agenda through the political and policy tools at his disposal.[5] It is reasonable, therefore, to assess Bush's economic record against the goals that he set for his administration and evaluate the extent that his policies contributed to the problems of the American economy on his watch.

Supply-Side Economics Mark II

As Bush took office, the Congressional Budget Office (CBO) issued a long-term fiscal projection anticipating a ten-year baseline budget surplus of $5.6 trillion for FY2002–FY2011 on the expectation that economic growth would continue at the high levels of Clinton's second term. It also estimated that the reducible public debt (excluding securities that investors wanted to retain) would be paid off in FY2006. The new president expressed even greater confidence about the nation's economic possibilities. "We can do better than that in America," he declared, "We've got some unbelievable productivity gains to be achieved in our economy." Tax cuts that could be delivered "without fear of budget deficits" were to be the agency of enhanced expansion.[6] Bush's belief in the economic elixir of lower taxes matched that of Ronald Reagan and sparked renewal of the supply-side crusade associated with the fortieth president.

Bush's outlook on taxes derived intellectual legitimacy from the work of a new generation of supply-side theorists, dubbed "neoconomists" by financial journalist Daniel Altman. Seeing labor force expansion and technological innovation as fixed elements in the economy, the first-wave proponents of this doctrine had pinned their hopes for long-term growth on boosting capital expenditure to expand productive capacity. In their estimate, a taxation system that diminished virtually every type of return on the individual saving that financed investment simply encouraged people to spend their money to keep it from government's grasp. These early supply-siders anticipated that the economy would experience a growth spurt from investment-boosting tax cuts before settling back to its normal rate of expansion, but now from a higher base that allowed for permanent improvement in living standards. Taking this theory a stage further amidst the 1990s boom, their successors believed that tax cuts could also generate technological change, whose economic potential outstripped what was possible through capital expenditure growth alone. According to the new logic, if more money were available to invest in research and development, it would produce a constant flow of technological innovation that would continuously boost economic growth.[7]

Instinct and his own entrepreneurial experience as an oilman (in truth a failed one) were sufficient to make Bush "a neoconomist in the flesh," but an academic guru honed his understanding of the message while he was governor of Texas. Once his presidential ambitions took shape, he sought advice from Harvard economist Martin Feldstein, who visited him in Austin to impart the gospel that high taxes were the chief cause of low saving. Feldstein was a prominent critic of the marginal tax rate hikes in Bill Clinton's deficit reduction program of 1993 because they "substantially exacerbated the inefficiency—that is, the deadweight loss—of the income tax system." In his opinion, the real cause of the revenue surge that eventually balanced the budget was "the increase in economic growth driven by the new technology that raised taxable personal incomes, corporate profits, and capital gains." Feldstein had authored the tax reduction plan on which Bob Dole campaigned as Republican candidate for president in 1996. His influence with Bush was manifest in the appointment of his former graduate students, Larry Lindsey and Glenn Hubbard, as chairs respectively of the National Economic Council and the CEA in the new Republican administration.[8]

Bush was remarkably successful in promoting tax reduction during his first six years in office. The most important initiatives were the Economic Growth and Tax Relief Reconciliation Act (EGTRRA) of 2001 that provided $1.35 trillion tax reduction (including a $100 billion rebate) over ten years and the Jobs and Growth Tax Relief Reconciliation Act (JGTRRA) of 2003 that provided $350 billion tax reduction over five years. These were the second and third largest tax cuts in U.S. history behind Reagan's Economic Recovery Tax Act of 1981. No president had hitherto asked for such large tax cuts in quick succession to each other. Moreover, the JGTRRA, enacted at the outset of the Iraq war, broke a tradition going back to the Civil War that taxes were raised not reduced in wartime.

In the 2000 presidential election, Bush had characterized his tax cut proposals as a case of returning "the people's money" now sitting in government coffers in the form of the Clinton surpluses.[9] Despite this populist rhetoric, the common feature of EGTRRA and JGTRRA was that their distributive benefits overwhelmingly advantaged the very affluent. The former trimmed the top marginal rate of income tax from 38 percent to 35 percent and the bottom rate from 15 percent to 10 percent. It also provided a host of other benefits, including child credits, raised limits on contributions to Individual Retirement Accounts, the elimination of the estate tax by 2010, and removal of the limits on itemized deductions from 2006 to 2010. Even though the new 10 percent tax bracket accounted for one-third of EGTRRA's revenue cost, the affluent received the largest portion of its aggregate relief since they had more income on which they paid taxes. Consequently, taxpayers in the lowest income quintile gained $827 in aftertax income over ten years from the measure, those in the middle quintile got $6,516, and those in the top quintile received $46,243.[10] The 2003 tax cut was even more heavily skewed toward the affluent in its provision of relief to the investor class from capital gains and dividend taxes. According to a liberal fiscal watchdog, the Center on Budget Policy and Priorities, 46 percent of its benefits went to the 0.2 percent of households with annual incomes over $1 million and nearly three-quarters went to the 3.1 percent making more than $200,000 a year.[11]

Other Bush tax cuts manifested the same distributive skew. The Working Families Tax Relief Act of 2004 renewed the EGTRRA benefits scheduled for expiry at the end of the year at an estimated revenue cost of $146 billion. The measure sailed through Congress far more easily than the 2001 and 2003 measures because the administration succeeded in framing it during an election year as a middle-class tax cut. In reality, households in the top income quintile got 70 percent of the benefits compared with just 9 percent for those in the middle quintile. Shortly afterward, the president signed another Republican bill providing corporate tax breaks for manufacturers, energy producers, and agribusinesses.[12] Bush's hopes of making his 2001 and 2003 tax cuts permanent following his reelection fell victim to growing concern among congressional Republicans about the budget deficit. After prolonged wrangling, however, he secured enactment of the Tax Increase Prevention and Reconciliation Act of 2005 extending the five-year EGTRRA capital gains and dividend tax cuts by two years. A case of half a loaf being better than none, this locked in the administration's two major tax initiatives to the same expiry date of 2010.[13]

The partisan rewards of this tax program for the president and his party were self-evident. It not only pleased the conservative activists and moneyed interests that were their first line of electoral support but also appealed to the growing investor class that was a natural GOP constituency. In line with the Bush administration's privatization and enhanced choice initiatives in fields like pensions and education, the tax cuts supported its efforts to expand the so-called ownership society that had more interest in the private economy than the public sector. According to pollster John Zogby, 46 percent of voters in the 2004 presidential election were self-identified investors, and this group went for Bush by 61–39 percent, whereas noninvestors backed the Democratic candidate, Senator John Kerry (D-MA), by 57–42 percent.[14]

Whatever its electoral benefits, there is little evidence that Bush's tax program made a significant contribution to America's economic well-being. JGTRRA was enacted against the backdrop of recession precipitated by the collapse in overvalued dot.com stocks. In addition to bringing to an end a ten-year cycle of continuous economic growth, the downturn ushered in a new cycle of huge deficits. As Federal Reserve chair Alan Greenspan commented, "Just as the bull market of the tech boom had generated the surplus, the post-dot.com bear market took it away."[15] While the recession was a problem that Bush had inherited, his policies did little to speed recovery. To ease congressional passage of EGTRRA, complex phase-in rules delayed the bulk of tax relief for top-band taxpayers until the latter part of its ten-year duration, which minimized its stimulus effect amidst the downturn. Bush's onetime mentor, Martin Feldstein, contended that immediately reducing the top rate to 33 percent or even 28 percent would have had greater economic benefits for relatively little revenue loss. Other analysts claimed that the economy would probably have grown faster without the tax cuts because the phase-ins induced wealthier taxpayers to defer income accumulation until it was taxed less.[16]

The Bush administration's proposal for a ten-year $726 billion tax cut in 2003 was also of dubious economic utility. Half the projected revenue costs flowed from the elimination of the tax on stock dividends, which would have ended the double taxation on investors initiated by the New Deal. The administration's goal was to boost the stock market that was still in the doldrums following the dot. com collapse. However, critics questioned this rationale because half the dividends eligible for this tax break went to nontaxpaying entities such as pension funds and retirement accounts. "This is beyond Voodoo Economics," declared *Newsweek* analyst Allan Sloan, "It's just a mistake. Call it Booboo Economics." Worried about the effect on the deficit, GOP legislators offered a $350 billion counterproposal that included a five-year reduction in both capital gains and dividend taxes to 15 percent (from 20 percent and 38.6 percent respectively). Though critical that this did not provide sufficient stimulus to investment, Bush eventually accepted its enactment as the JGTRRA for fear that he would otherwise end up without a new tax cut.[17]

The surge in economic growth at the start of Bush's second term appeared to vindicate his tax program. A congressional Joint Economic Committee report showed that nonresidential business investment, having declined at an annual rate of 5.6 percent from mid-2000 through mid-2003, had grown by 9.2 percent over the next three years. Linking this development to the enactment of JGTRRA, Treasury Secretary John Snow exulted, "It was as if a light had been thrown on. Rarely has a piece of policy been so effective, with the effects so evident and immediate."[18] Skeptics contended instead that it resulted from a belated recovery disproportionately benefiting corporations, investors, and upper-income groups. Nevertheless, the consequent expansion of tax revenues, which rose from 16.4 percent GDP in FY2004 to 18.5 percent GDP in FY2006, enabled Bush to declare mission accomplished two years early on his 2004 promise to halve the budget deficit by the time he left office. "Some in

Washington say we had to choose between cutting taxes and cutting the deficit," he declared in July 2006, "[The budget numbers] show that that was a false choice. The economic growth fueled by tax relief has helped to send our tax revenues soaring."[19] Accordingly, Bush sought to make the 2006 elections a referendum on the extension of his tax cuts against opposition party demands for their expiry on schedule as vital for restoration of fiscal responsibility. The economic choice facing the nation was a simple one, he affirmed: "Do we keep taxes low so we can keep this economy growing, or do we let the Democrats in Washington raise taxes and hurt the economic vitality of this country?"[20]

The severe recession that blighted Bush's final year in office did nothing to diminish his belief that making the 2001 and 2003 tax cuts permanent was essential for economic renewal. Worried that the newly ascendant Democrats would undo his legacy, he affirmed in his last presidential press conference: "Sound economic policy begins with keeping taxes low." Nevertheless, Bush's promotion of the largest tax cuts since 1981 had generated meager economic returns. One critic, Wall Street economist Mark Zandi, characterized his period in office as "almost a lost decade," a term conventionally used to describe Japan's economic experience in the 1990s. Far from supply-side tax relief transforming the economy into a dynamic engine of growth, GDP rose at a modest annual rate of 2.6 percent during the 24 quarters of consecutive expansion between the recession of 2001 and the downturn that began in late 2007. This compared with 3.7 percent in the previous expansion cycle that had lasted 38 quarters from mid-1991 through 2000. Even factoring out the effect of recession, total civilian employment growth during the Bush years amounted only to 6.6 percent, a lower level than any eight-year period since 1945 and far below the 15.5 percent expansion under Clinton.[21]

Bush's claims that his tax cuts would be self-funding thanks to the economic growth they generated flew in the face of the evidence. Interest rate reductions were far more significant in generating the business-cycle recovery from the 2001 recession. As conservative economist Bruce Bartlett observed, "Much revenue was sacrificed to achieve not very much in terms of improving the tax code or stimulating economic growth."[22] In confirmation of this, the congressional Joint Committee on Taxation reported that the annual cost of tax cuts enacted since 2001 amounted in FY2006 to $251 billion (including interest payments on higher government borrowing necessitated by revenue loss), $3 billion more than the actual deficit.[23] In other words, this budget would have been in balance but for the tax cuts, even allowing for the costs of the Iraq and Afghanistan wars and the emergency response to the Hurricane Katrina disaster. A Treasury Department report also disproved Bush's claims regarding the expansionary benefits of making his tax cuts permanent. In its calculation, this would at best increase annual economic output by a mere 0.7 percent over ten years. Meanwhile the CBO calculated that the consequent revenue loss would add $143 billion to the aggregate deficit through FY2010 and $1.5 trillion in FY2011–FY2015.[24]

Indebted America

Economic policy had featured a mix of expansionary fiscal policy and tight monetary policy in the Reagan era and the reverse in the Clinton era. In the Bush years, by contrast, both monetary policy and fiscal policy were expansionary, which had significant consequences for public and private indebtedness in the United States and America's position in the global economy.

Government finances swung sharply from a surplus of 2.6 percent GDP in FY2000 to a deficit of 3.4 percent GDP in FY2004, a fiscal deterioration of 6 percent GDP that was unmatched in peacetime since the early stages of the Great Depression.[25] In such circumstances, monetary policy would normally have become tighter either to counter inflationary pressures or to attract foreign capital to make good the deleterious effect of government borrowing on national saving. This had been the pattern of the 1980s. Monetary policy had tightened in 1979–82 in response to high inflation that was commonly attributed in part to growing budget deficits. Once inflation was brought under control, interest rates remained high in comparison to those of other industrial nations in 1983–85 to attract foreign capital at a time of mammoth budget deficits. A brief period of monetary relaxation then gave way to a new period of restraint from 1987 to 1990 as inflation rose once more.[26] In contrast, the Fed aggressively lowered the short-term Federal Funds interest rate from 6.5 percent in late 2000 to a historical low of 1 percent in 2003. Reversing course in mid-2004 to counter house price inflation, the central bank steadily increased the rate to a peak of 5.25 percent in mid-2006. Nevertheless this was hardly tight money in comparison to the recent past since the monetary authorities had held short-term interest at or above this level for all but some thirty months of Clinton's presidency.

Fed chair Alan Greenspan was publicly critical of Bush's 2003 tax cut out of concern that it would deplete federal coffers just as new spending demands built up from the impending retirement of the huge postwar baby-boom cohort born between 1945 and 1965. Testifying before the Senate Banking Committee, he warned: "Faster economic growth alone is not likely to be the full solution to the currently projected long-term deficits."[27] The Federal Reserve's displeasure at large budget deficits had caused Bush's three immediate predecessors to sanction revenue-enhancing tax increases as a trade-off for monetary relaxation, but he did not have to follow suit. Despite concern about America's fiscal future, Greenspan had his hands full dealing with the present state of the economy because of the depressing effects of the stock market collapse, the recession, and the 9/11 terrorist attacks. To the detriment of his 1990s reputation as monetary maestro, the Fed chair mitigated the consequences of one bubble bursting through an aggressive policy of monetary relaxation, which did much to create a bigger bubble that would implode even more spectacularly.[28]

Cheap credit fueled a real estate boom that drove the recovery of the entire economy. By mid-2004, house price inflation was running at a twenty-five–year high. The aggregate market value of single-family homes in the United States rose by $8 trillion from 2000 through 2005. In the expectation that prices would continue to rise, large numbers of Americans accrued huge levels of debt to trade up for a better dwelling, buy a second home, or improve their existing one. Speculators also saw real estate inflation as a way to make a quick fortune. According to the National Association of Realtors, investors accounted for 28 percent of home purchases in 2005, whereas they had rarely been responsible for more than 10 percent annually in the second half of the twentieth century. Furthermore, many families with dubious credit histories or unstable income sources, particularly those living in economically declining, predominantly black, inner-city neighborhoods, were tempted to enter the real estate market or refinance their existing homes to raise cash loans through the availability of subprime mortgages. Of the nearly $3 trillion of home mortgage originations in 2006, a fifth fell into this category.[29]

The availability of cheap credit depended on two factors that were outside the Fed's purview but these carried threats as well as opportunities. When government competed with private borrowers, the usual consequence was to push up interest rates. Instead of tight money conditions, however, America experienced a glut of cheap credit in the early twenty-first century thanks to the unprecedented willingness of foreigners to loan it vast sums. In particular, East Asian central banks, led first by Japan's and later China's, rushed in to buy U.S. Treasury securities with the consequence that their countries' exports benefited from currency exchange rates favorable to their competitiveness in the giant American market. Foreigners held just over 50 percent of the U.S. public debt by the time Bush left office, with China's portion amounting to some $1.4 trillion. Meanwhile, the United States became a magnet for capital investment by European private banks, businesses, and wealthy individuals looking to take advantage of the rising value of the Euro and other currencies against the dollar. In 2006, more than two-thirds of the capital buying in America came from across the Atlantic. As a result of these parallel developments, the United States absorbed an estimated 80 percent of the savings that the rest of the world did not invest at home.[30]

To the Bush administration and the Federal Reserve, the world's appetite for U.S. assets was a sign of America's strength. In the assessment of Fed governor Ben Bernanke (later chair of the Bush CEA before being appointed to head the central bank on Greenspan's retirement), global capital flowed to those countries that could turn it to most productive use and provide the best combination of investment return and security.[31] Pessimistic analysts worried, in contrast, that the United States was sacrificing its economic future for the sake of current gratification.

The flow of cheap goods—mainly from Asia—sent America's trade deficit ballooning from $454 billion in 2000 to $847 billion in 2006, well over a quarter of it in bilateral trade with China. This development further accelerated the decline of employment in American manufacturing, whose labor costs disadvantaged it against foreign competition. Conversely, European purchase of U.S. assets meant that over 5 million Americans worked for domestic affiliates of foreign companies in 2007, making them fundamentally subject to commercial decisions taken abroad.[32]

What was even more worrying was that America—the world's largest creditor for nearly forty years after World War II—had become by far the world's largest debtor. Its current account deficit (comprised primarily of the trade deficit, net interest payments to foreign investors, and the costs of foreign transfer programs like economic and military aid) rose to $857 billion in 2006, equal to 6.5 percent of its own GDP and 1.7 percent of global GDP. This imbalance, which first emerged in the Reagan years, had a pre-Bush era peak of 3.5 percent GDP in 1987. Recent history suggested that nations operating external deficits in excess of 4 percent GDP suffered self-correcting financial crises. Of course, the United States enjoyed two unique advantages against this danger—the appeal of its huge market, and its capacity to refinance its debt in its own money owing to the dollar's status as global reserve currency. Nevertheless, critics worried that the Bush administration, in contrast to its preemptive foreign policy, was running risks with the nation's economy that no great power should be taking. In their view, the more indebted the United States grew, the greater its exposure to a massive economic crisis in the event of a slowing down or reversal of capital flows from abroad.[33] Voicing such concerns, Senator Barack Obama (D-IL) warned, "[T]his easy credit won't continue for ever. At some point, foreigners will stop lending us money, interest rates will go up and we'll spend most of our nation's output paying them back."[34]

The president could not ignore the massive trade imbalance, particularly when the rise of protectionist sentiment in Congress early in his second term threatened the possibility of tariff penalties against nations that manipulated their currencies for import advantage. Nevertheless, there was little he could do to get China to revalue its currency. Bush raised the issue with Chinese premier Hu Jintao at the 2003 Asia Pacific Economic Conference but received a firm rebuff. Nor did the United States get any further by enlisting the support of its partners at the 2004 G-7 meeting, which Chinese officials attended for the first time. According to some estimates it would have required a 25 percent revaluation in the Chinese currency to narrow the bilateral trade gap appreciably. Beijing finally relented to allow a 6.5 percent shift in 2005–6, but it had no interest in meeting American targets—not least because this would have severely devalued its massive holdings of U.S. dollars.[35]

In essence, the best way that America had of reducing its dependency on foreign debt was to transform its budget deficit into a surplus, but Bush's dedication not only to preserving his tax cuts but also expanding them ruled out this approach.[36] Despite this, the day of reckoning in the form of a foreign retreat from the dollar foretold by doomsayers never dawned on his watch. What occurred instead was a standoff. The United States had little leverage to force the Chinese to be more accommodating on currency revaluation but Beijing and the rest of the world could not afford to cut off the supply of cheap credit to America because the entire global economy had become dependent on its consumption to sustain growth.[37] Nevertheless, the U.S. current account deficit did decline to 4.6 percent GDP by the end of 2008 as a result of declining demand in economic hard times, a downward trend that reflected the pattern in past recessions.[38]

If America's external indebtedness was not directly responsible for the economic crisis, it facilitated the domestic indebtedness that was the root cause. The implosion of the subprime mortgage market that began in August 2007 resulted from a combination of cheap credit, financial institution competitive pressures, and lax government regulation, all of which generated massive lending to borrowers with low income, limited assets, and troubled credit histories. As interest rates rose to cool house price inflation, many holders of these mortgages could not make repayments, which led to a glut of foreclosures. In Cleveland, the subprime capital of America, one in ten homes was repossessed in 2007. Meanwhile, many homeowners with stable income who had bought at the peak of the boom in housing hot spots, notably California and Florida, also had difficulty meeting higher interest rates. By September 2008, one in ten of all mortgage holders nationally was either delinquent or in foreclosure.[39]

The bursting of the housing bubble also impacted on the rest of the economy to produce rapidly rising unemployment. Hardest hit was the construction industry that accounted for 15 percent of the entire labor force, but manufacturers of home appliances, automobile makers, and financial institutions were not far behind. Financial institutions, many holding mountains of bad debt, now became reluctant to lend money to individuals, businesses, and each other. The credit crunch spelled bad news for an economy dependent on borrowing for growth. Private sector debt had spiraled from $22 trillion in 2000 (222 percent GDP) to $41 trillion (294 percent GDP) in 2007. While financial sector borrowing accounted for the bulk of increased indebtedness, virtually all the rise in nonfinancial debt was among households rather than business. The United States consequently slid into the longest and deepest recession of the postwar era in December 2007, even though the existence of the downturn was not formally recognized until a year later.[40]

Democratic presidential candidate Barack Obama and party leaders in Congress lined up to blame Republican free-market prejudice for the catastrophe. Senator Charles Schumer (D-NY) typically proclaimed, "Eight years of deregulatory zeal by the Bush administration, an attitude of 'the market can do no wrong,' have let us down." However, the reality was more complex. Certainly the public dissaving consequences of Bush's tax program helped to generate the massive inflows of foreign loan capital that underwrote the easy credit responsible for the unsustainable booms in housing and consumer spending. Moreover, the White House strongly supported financial deregulation but predominantly in terms of implementing current provision put in place with bipartisan support since the late 1970s rather than development of further initiatives. Particularly critical to the onset of the financial crisis was the Clinton-backed Financial Services

Modernization Act of 1999 that removed the limitations imposed by the Glass-Steagall Act of 1933 on the ability of banks, investment firms, and insurance companies to enter each others' markets. Despite his attacks on Bush, Charles Schumer was an enthusiastic supporter of this measure and later supported review of the Sarbanes-Oxley Act of 2002 that required greater financial disclosure by corporations in the wake of the Enron and WorldCom bankruptcies. Moreover, Alan Greenspan, who had twice been reappointed to office by Clinton and once by Bush, had added his influential and nonpartisan voice to legitimize the cause of economic deregulation.[41]

The fact that shortsightedness toward the financial danger signals was not confined to the administration does not excuse its culpability, of course. Bush did not uphold his own standards in this regard. As political scientist Charles Jones observed, he was one of the most executive-oriented presidents (and the only one to hold a Harvard MBA). In his canon, political leaders were to be judged by the success of the long-term solutions they proposed for the nation's problems. Before assuming office, Bush had declared that "the role of the chief executive of the country, the president, is to anticipate."[42] As president, however, he engaged in a politicized economic policy that mismanaged the risks of excessive reliance on credit for short-term gain and failed to promote sustainable growth.

Bush and the Economic Crisis

Franklin D. Roosevelt and Ronald Reagan defined themselves as strong presidents during economic crisis. Bush had little prospect of emulating them because lame-duck status constrained his capacity for leadership. To make matters worse, he had become trapped in political time as a president committed to the outdated ideas of a once ascendant political regime.[43]

Unlike Roosevelt and Reagan, Bush faced economic crisis during his final rather than first year in office. It was, therefore, difficult for him to ring the alarm bell of national emergency without casting doubt on his promise that tax reduction would generate prosperity. The hope that financial market self-correction was possible also made him reluctant to sound too pessimistic for fear of further undermining confidence. Until the crisis engulfed Wall Street, Bush only conceded that the economy faced "a rough patch." He also resisted the proposal of House Speaker Nancy Pelosi (D-CA) to convene a top-level bipartisan meeting to address the mortgage crisis. On September 5, two days before events dramatically proved otherwise, the White House released a fact sheet entitled *American Economy Is Resilient in the Face of Challenges.*[44]

Bush's statements made him look out of touch with reality. Consequently, his poll ratings for economic leadership were consistently lower throughout his final year than even his dire overall job approval ratings. Nor could the president reap popular credit for the significant initiatives that were undertaken to mitigate the crisis. Despite his rhetorical optimism, the administration was active in addressing economic problems. Bush devolved policy leadership to Treasury Secretary Henry Paulson in his capacity as chair of the President's Working Group on Financial Markets, a quadriad that included the chairs of the Federal Reserve, the Securities and Exchange Commission, and the Commodity Futures Trading Commission. This delegation was logical in view of the complex nature of the economic threats, but it led to accusations that Bush had gone AWOL in the crisis. Even a friendly critic, Representative Peter King (R-NY), observed, "[I]t would be better if the president himself was more out front, rather than leaving it so much to Paulson. When there is a perceived national crisis, it's important for the president to be the point man."[45]

Though not to the fore in policy development, Bush still had to approve what his lieutenant recommended and showed flexibility in doing so. In cooperation with Nancy Pelosi and House Minority Leader John Boehner (R-OH), Paulson crafted a proposal for an immediate tax rebate of $100 billion for 130 million households to boost consumer spending. To reach a deal, Bush agreed that income caps on full rebates should be set at $75,000 for individuals and relinquished the opportunity to press for renewal of the 2001 and 2003 tax cuts as part of the package. It transpired, however, that recipients spent only 15–25 percent of the money and either saved the rest or used it to pay off debt.[46]

More significantly, the Treasury Secretary put together the Troubled Assets Relief Program (TARP) to preempt the collapse of the financial system after Lehman Brothers went bust on September 13. This committed the Treasury to take up to $700 billion of toxic private mortgages onto its books. Combined with the costs of the Fanny Mae and Freddie Mac nationalizations and of the effective nationalization of insurance giant AIG, TARP's enactment meant that gross federal liabilities had expanded over the course of the single month of September 2009 by $1 trillion, almost twice the cost hitherto of the Iraq war. Previously insistent that financial institutions take responsibility for their high-risk loans, the president agreed to support the measure in recognition that the alternative might be meltdown of the banking system. On September 26, in his first address to the nation on the economic crisis, he urged the public to support congressional approval of the plan.[47]

Like his father's effort to promote adoption of the tax-raising 1990 bipartisan budget agreement, Bush's rhetoric initially fell on deaf ears. He had not used the teaching function of the presidential podium to prepare Americans for the necessity of bailing out the financial houses whose recklessness had caused the crisis. With polls showing lack of public support, the House of Representatives rejected TARP on September 29 by 228–205. Some two-fifths of Democrats voted nay on grounds that it did not include help for homeowners. Demonstrating that lame-duck status limited Bush's influence as party leader, two-thirds of Republicans also rejected TARP, most doing so in support of free-market principles. An amended version was finally enacted on October 3, but this owed little to presidential influence. A stock market collapse following the initial rejection of TARP wiped out a trillion dollars in paper wealth in a single day, including a large chunk of retirement savings. Painful evidence that the crisis endangered Main Street as well as Wall Street induced congressional acceptance of a modified bill that included more generous insurance for individual bank deposits and stronger financial regulation.[48]

Though TARP averted financial catastrophe, it did little to revive consumer spending because the flow of credit, on which many American depended to fund their shopping habit, had largely dried up. Some 1.2 million jobs were lost from September through November as demand slumped.[49] With private lenders unwilling to incur more bad debt, one means of reviving consumption was through a new fiscal stimulus that combined spending measures and further tax cuts. Victorious Democratic presidential candidate Barack Obama announced support for this option, but Bush refused to countenance it. In essence, there were limits to the forty-third president's flexibility. Despite endorsing a greater level of intervention in the economy than had any of his Republican predecessors, he drew the line against a solution based on public spending.

In essence, Bush was trapped in the same dilemma as Herbert Hoover in the early 1930s and Jimmy Carter in the late 1970s, both classified by political scientist Stephen Skowronek as disjunctive presidents because of their affiliation to a decaying political regime. These presidents recognized that the policy commitments of the regime with which they were identified were no longer relevant in the face of economic crisis, but could not break free of them without destroying the political order on which their leadership authority was dependent. Bush was affiliated to the Reagan-initiated conservative regime that had been political ascendant for nearly three decades. One of the core principles of this political order was opposition to big-government intervention in the economy. Now, however, amidst the worst economic downturn since the Great Depression, Reagan's famous dictum that government was the problem rather than the solution had been turned on its head. Recognizing as much, Bush declared in his final *Economic Report* that in the current "extraordinary circumstances...a systemic, aggressive and unprecedented Government response was the only responsible policy action." Unable to embrace the full implications of this reality, on the other hand, he insisted that federal antirecession initiatives could be only a temporary palliative because the surest means of sustained recovery was tax cuts to encourage individual initiative.[50]

Conclusion

George Bush may prove to be the last president of what some historians termed the "Age of Reagan." The conservative political order initiated by the fortieth president rested on belief in the free market to legitimize reduced government involvement in the economy, diminution of tax progressivity, and socioeconomic deregulation. In political terms, Bush displayed strong and effective leadership in pursuit of his core economic goals, namely tax cuts that were supposed to benefit the investor class and build sustainable foundations for twenty-first–century economic growth. However, the outcomes of this renewed commitment to the free market fell far short of delivering the prosperity that he had promised. Instead, it produced at best only short-term gains that evaporated amidst economic crisis in his final year.

Rightly or wrongly, every president since Franklin D. Roosevelt has been judged by history in part on the well-being of the economy that he bequeathed to his successor. It is too soon to make a definitive pronouncement on Bush's economic legacy, but the early returns do not look good. The common feature of the American economy under Ronald Reagan and George Bush was that its growth became excessively dependent on credit and consumption rather than productive investment that strengthened the foundations of the economy for the long term. The economy under the fortieth president did not experience the unraveling that many liberal critics of the free market had predicted, but the forty-third president was not so lucky. In 2009, the United States faced a difficult economic future encompassing massive public debt, huge growth of entitlement spending as the population ages, and structural unemployment in parts of the country because of the decline of key industries, notably automobile manufacturing. For Bush's successor, the renewal of America's prosperity required the restoration of the state as an important economic actor. If Barack Obama succeeds in establishing this as the core principle of a new political economy, it will entail a repudiation of the old order that could make George Bush's economic presidency look like the twenty-first–century version of Herbert Hoover's. In this regard, Bush's historical reputation will likely be shaped by the success—or otherwise—of the forty-fourth president's economic leadership.

Notes

1. See, for example, Timothy Lynch and Robert Singh, *After Bush: The Case for Continuity in American Foreign Policy* (New York: Cambridge University Press, 2008).
2. Bruce Bartlett, *Impostor: How George W. Bush Bankrupted America and Betrayed the Reagan Legacy* (New York: Doubleday, 2006); Michael D. Tanner, *Leviathan on the Right: How Big-Government Conservatism Brought Down the Republican Revolution* (Washington DC: Cato Institute, 2007).
3. Daniel Altman, *Neoconomy: George Bush's Revolutionary Gamble with America's Future* (New York: PublicAffairs, 2004).
4. Joseph Stiglitz, "The Economic Consequences of Mr. Bush," *Vanity Fair*, December 2007, 228.
5. John P. Frendreis and Raymond Tatalovich, *The Modern Presidency and Economic Policy* (Itasca IL: F. E. Peacock, 1994); B. Dan Wood, *The Politics of Economic Leadership: The Causes and Consequences of Presidential Leadership* (Princeton: Princeton University Press, 2007). For studies of specific presidents, see Allen J. Matusow, *Nixon's Economy: Booms, Busts, Dollars & Votes* (Lawrence: University Press of Kansas, 1999); W. Carl Biven, *Jimmy Carter's Economy: Policy in an Age of Limits* (Chapel Hill: University of North Carolina Press, 2002); John W. Sloan, *The Reagan Effect: Economics and Presidential Leadership* (Lawrence: University Press of Kansas, 1999).
6. Congressional Budget Office (CBO), *The Budget and Economic Outlook: Fiscal Years 2002–2011* (Washington DC: CBO, 2001), 2; "Remarks to the National Conference of State Legislatures," March 2, 2001, in John T. Woolley and Gerhard Peters, *The American Presidency Project* (Santa Barbara: University of California), www.presidency.ucsb.edu [hereafter

cited as *APP*]. For fuller discussion of the politics of Bush's tax program, see Iwan Morgan, *The Age of Deficits: Presidents and Unbalanced Budgets from Jimmy Carter to George W. Bush* (Lawrence: University Press of Kansas, 2009), Chapter 7.

7. Altman, *Neoconomy*, 21–30, 32–34, 38–39. For exposition of new supply-side theory, see Robert Barro and Xavier Sala-I-Martin, *Economic Growth* (New York: McGraw Hill, 1995).
8. Altman, *Neoconomy*, 40; Martin Feldstein, "The Effect of Marginal Tax Rates on Taxable Income: A Panel Study of the 1986 Tax Reform Act," *Journal of Political Economy*, 103, June 1995, 551–72, and "Comments," in Jeffrey Frankel and Peter Orszag, eds., *American Economic Policy in the 1990s* (Cambridge MA: MIT Press, 2002), 124–25, 136 (quotation p. 125); David Leonhardt, "Scholarly Mentor to Bush's Team," *New York Times*, December 1, 2002.
9. "The 2000 Campaign: Exchanges between the Candidates in the Third Presidential Debate," *New York Times*, October 18, 2000, A26.
10. Altman, *Neoconomy*, 237; Citizens for Tax Justice, "Year-by-Year Analysis of the Bush Tax Cuts' Growing Tilt to the Very Rich," June 2, 2002, www.ctj.org.html/gwb0602.htm.
11. Joel Friedman, "Dividend and Capital Gains Tax Cuts Unlikely to Yield Touted Economic Gains," *Center on Budget Policy and Priorities* [*CBPP*], March 10, 2005.
12. Jonathan Weisman, "Congress Votes to Extend Tax Cuts," *Washington Post*, September 24, 2004, A1; Robert Greenstein, "New 'Middle Class' Tax Cut Bill Represents Cynical Policymaking," *CBPP*, September 24, 2004; Associated Press, "Bush Quietly Signs Corporate Tax-Cut Bill," October 22, 2004, www.msnbc.msn.com/id/6307293/
13. Morgan, *The Age of Deficits*, 229–30.
14. Jacob S. Hacker and Paul Pierson, *Off Center: The Republican Revolution and the Erosion of Democracy* (New Haven CT: Yale University Press, 2005), 48–49; Thomas B. Edsall, *Building Red America: The New Conservative Coalition and the Drive for Permanent Power* (New York: Basic Books, 2006), 43–44; John Zogby, "Investors for Bush: How Social Security Reform Can Bring About a Republican Realignment," *Wall Street Journal*, March 15, 2005, 25.
15. Alan Greenspan, *The Age of Turbulence: Adventures in a New World* (New York: Penguin Press, 2001), 224.
16. Martin Feldstein, "The 28% Solution," *Wall Street Journal*, February 28, 2001, www.nber.org/feldstein/wsj021601.html; Christopher House and Martin Shapiro, "Phased-In Tax Cuts and Economic Activity," *National Bureau of Economic Research Working Paper*, No. 14015, April 2004.
17. Allan Sloan, "This Cut Won't Pay Dividends," *Newsweek*, January 20, 2003, 25–28, 29; "Nobel Laureates, 450 Other Economists Fault Bush Tax Plan," *Economic Policy Institute Press Release*, February 10, 2003; John P. Burke, *Becoming President: The Bush Transition 2000–2003* (Boulder CO: Lynne Rienner, 2003), 136–37, 154.

18. Jonathan Weisman and Paul Blustein, "GOP Reaches Deal on Tax Cuts: $70 Billion Would Extend Breaks," *Washington Post*, May 10, 2006, A1; Jim VandeHei and Nell Henderson, "Economy Gained Muscle Last Year, Expanding Jobs: In Chicago Bush Rejoices and Says Policies are Working," *Washington Post*, January 7, 2006; Robin Toner, "Holding Fast to a Policy of Tax Cutting," *New York Times*, February 7, 2006, A1.
19. George W. Bush, "Remarks on the Office of Budget and Management Mid-Session Review," July 11, 2006, *APP*.
20. Michael Abramowitz and Peter Baker, "Painting a Rosy Picture: Bush Touts Rising Deficit, but Long-Term Outlook Is Dimmer," *Washington Post*, October 11, 2006, A6.
21. "The President's Press Conference," January 12, 2009, *APP*; "The Frat Boy Ships Out," *Economist*, January 17, 2009, 28; Neil Irwin and Dan Eggen, "Economy Made Few Gains in Bush Years," *Washington Post*, January 12, 2009, A1. For economic data, see *Economic Report of the President 2009* (Washington DC: Government Printing Office, 2009), 4, 285, 320, 328.
22. Bartlett, *Impostor*, 62. For other critical evaluations, see Lori Montgomery, "Lower Deficits Spark Debate Over Tax Cuts' Role," *Washington Post*, October 17, 2006, D1.
23. Richard Kogan and James Horney, "Deficit Announcement Masks Bigger Story: Long-Term Outlook Remains Bleak," *CBPP*, October 11, 2006.
24. U.S. Treasury, "A Dynamic Analysis of Permanent Extension of the President's Tax Relief," July 25, 2006, www.treas.gov/press/reports/treasurydynamicanalysisreporjuly252006pdf; Congressional Research Service, *The Budget for FY2006* (Washington DC: CRS, August 30, 2006); James Horney, "A Smoking Gun: President's Claim that Tax Cuts Pay for Themselves Refuted by New Treasury Analysis," *CBPP*, July 27, 2006.
25. Richard Kogan and Robert Greenstein, "President Portrays Social Security Shortfalls as Enormous, but His Tax Cuts and Drug Benefit Will Cost at Least Five Times as Much," *CBPP*, February 11, 2005.
26. Sloan, *The Reagan Effect*, 237–44; Iwan Morgan, "Reaganomics and its Legacy," in Cheryl Hudson and Gareth Davies, eds., *Ronald Reagan and the 1980s: Perceptions, Policies and Legacies* (New York: Palgrave, 2008), 101–18.
27. Edmund Andrews, "Greenspan Throws Cold Water on Bush Argument for Tax Cut," *New York Times*, February 12, 2003, A1; Greenspan, *The Age of Turbulence*, 234–40.
28. Stephen Roach, "Think Again: Alan Greenspan," *Foreign Policy*, January/February 2005, 19–20; Ashley Seager, "Solid Foundations or House of Cards? America Awaits Greenspan's Legacy," *Guardian*, January 31, 2006, 25.
29. Greenspan, *The Age of Turbulence*, 229–33.
30. William Cline, *The U.S. as a Debtor Nation* (Washington DC: Institute for International Economics, 2005); Brad Sester and Nouriel Roubini,

"Our Money, Our Debt, Our Problem," *Foreign Affairs*, 84, 4, 2005, 198–206; William Bonner and Addison Wiggin, *Empire of Debt: The Rise of an Epic Financial Crisis* (Hoboken NJ: John Wiley, 2006); Iwan Morgan, "The Public Budget and the US Current Account Deficit," in Diego Sanchez-Ancochea and Iwan Morgan, eds., *The Political Economy of the Public Budgets in the Americas* (London: Institute for the Study of the Americas, 2008), 82–103.

31. Ben Bernanke, "The Global Saving Glut and the U.S. Current Account Deficit," *The Sandridge Lecture*, March 10, 2005, www.federalreserve.gov; *Economic Report of the President 2006* (Washington DC: Government Printing Office, 2006).
32. Bureau of Economic Affairs, "U.S. International Trade in Goods and Services May 2009," www.bea.gov/newsreleases/international/trade/tradenewsrelease.htm; Menzie Chinn and Ben Steil, "Why Deficits Matter," *International Economy*, Summer 2006, 18–23; Peter Goodman, "Two Outcomes When Foreigners Buy Factories," *New York Times*, April 7, 2008.
33. Lawrence Summers, "America Overdrawn," *Foreign Policy*, July/August 2004, 47–49; L. J. Bivens, "Debt and the Dollar: The United States Damages Future Living Standards by Borrowing Itself into a Deceptively Deep Hole," *Economic Policy Institute Brief*, 203, December 14, 2004; W. Godley, D. Papadimitriou, C. Dos Santos, and G. Zezza, *The United States and Her Creditors: Can the Symbiosis Last?* (The Levy Institute of Bard College: September, 2005), www.levy.org. For a review of the debate, see Iwan Morgan, "The Indebted Empire: America's Current Account Deficit problem," *International Politics*, 45, January 2008, 92–112.
34. Barack Obama, *The Audacity of Hope: Thoughts on Reclaiming the American Dream* (New York: Crown, 2006), 188.
35. Fred Bergsten, "Foreign Economic Policy for the Next President," *Foreign Affairs*, 83, 2, 2004, 88–101; A. Heath, "China Dashes G-7 Hopes of Currency Revaluation," *Business*, October 4, 2004, 1; Council of Foreign Relations, *US-China Relations: An Affirmative Agenda, A Responsible Course*, Task Force Report, April, 2007.
36. Kenneth Rogoff, "America's Current Account; A Deficit of Judgment," www.globalagendamagazine.com/2005/kennethrogoff.asp; Robert Rubin, Peter Orszag, and A. Sinai, "Sustained Budget Deficits: Longer-Run U.S. Economic Performance and the Risk of Financial and Fiscal Disarray," Allied Social Science Meeting, The Andrew Brimmer Policy Forum, *National Economic and Financial Policies for Growth and Stability*, January 4, 2004; Peter G. Peterson, "Old Habits Must Change," *Banker*, 1, 2005, 12–13.
37. "The Passing of the Buck," *Economist*, December 4, 2004, 77–80; William Mead, "America's Sticky Power," *Foreign Policy*, 83, 2, 2004, 46–53; Congressional Budget Office, "Will the US Current Account Have a Hard or Soft Landing?" (Washington DC: CBO, 2007).

38. "Economic and Financial Indicators," *Economist,* January 3, 2009, 76; E. M. Truman, "Budget and External Deficits: Not Twins but the Same Family," *Federal Reserve Bank of Boston Annual Research Conference,* January 14–16, 2004.
39. For development of the crisis, see Charles Morris, *The Trillion Dollar Meltdown: Easy Money, High Rollers, and the Great Credit Crash* (New York: PublicAffairs, 2008); Robert Shiller, *The Subprime Solution: How Today's Global Financial Crisis Happened and What to Do About It* (Princeton: Princeton University Press, 2008); Mark Zandi, *Financial Shock: A 360 Degree Look at the Subprime Mortgage Implosion, and How to Avoid the Next Financial Crisis* (Upper Saddle River NJ: FT Press, 2009).
40. "Worse than Japan," *Economist,* February 14, 2009, 83–84.
41. Joseph Goldstein, "Pro-Deregulation Schumer Scores Bush for Lack of Regulation," *New York Sun,* September 22, 2008; James L. Gattuso, "Meltdowns and Myths. Did Deregulation Cause the Financial Crisis?" *Heritage Foundation,* October 22, 2008, www.heritage.org/Research/Economy/htm2109.ctm; Greenspan, *The Age of Turbulence,* 374–76, 430–31. For a critical assessment of Bush's efforts to gut deregulatory agencies, see Philip J. Cooper, *The War against Regulation: From Jimmy Carter to George W. Bush* (Lawrence: University Press of Kansas, 2009).
42. Charles O. Jones, "Governing Executively: Bush's Paradoxical Style," in John C. Fortier and Norman J. Ornstein, eds., *Second-Term Blues: How George W. Bush Has Governed* (Washington DC: Brookings Institution Press/AEI, 2007), 109–30; George W. Bush, *A Charge to Keep: My Journey to the White House* (New York: William Morrow, 1999), 118–19; Bush remarks on *60 Minutes* (CBS), December 6, 2000, quoted in Altman, *Neoconomy,* 40.
43. For "political time" see Stephen Skowronek, *The Politics Presidents Make: Leadership from John Adams to Bill Clinton* (Cambridge MA: Belknap, 1997).
44. Sheryl Gay Stolberg, "In Economic Drama, Bush Is Largely Offstage," *New York Times,* April 3, 2008; Irwin and Eggen, "Economy Made Few Gains in Bush Years"; "Address to the Nation on the National Economy," September 24, 2008, *APP.*
45. Douglas McIntyre, "Henry M. Paulson Jr. for President," March 28, 2008, 247 wallst.com; Stolberg, "In Economic Drama, Bush Is Largely Offstage;" Marc Gunther, "Paulson to the Rescue," September 19, 2008, http://money.cnn.com. For the Treasury Secretary's memoir of the crisis, see Hank Paulson, *On the Brink: Inside the Race to Stop the collapse of the Global Financial System* (New York: Business Plus, 2010).
46. David Herszenshorn, "Bush and House in Accord for $150 Billion Stimulus," *New York Times,* January 25, 2008, A1; Christian Broda and Jonathan Parker, "The Impact of the 2008 Rebate," www.vocu.org/index.php?q=node/1541.

47. Clive Crook, "Nationalization in All but Name," *Financial Times*, September 8, 2008, 6; "The Doctor's Bill," *Economist*, September 27, 2008, 92–94.
48. David Herzenshorn, "Bailout Plan Wins Approval: Democrats Vow Tighter Rules," *New York Times*, October 4, 2008, A1; "The Politics of the Bailout," *Economist*, October 4, 2008, 56–58.
49. Louis Uchitelle and others, "U.S. Loses 533,000 Jobs in Biggest Drop since 1974," *New York Times*, December 6, 2008, A1; Ron Lieber and Tara Siegel Bernard, "U.S. Consumer Loan Aid Will Trickle Only So Far," *New York Times*, November 27, 2008.
50. Skowronek, *The Politics Presidents Make*, 260–85, 361–406; *Economic Report of the President 2009*, 3.

Chapter Ten

Bush's Partisan Legacy and the 2008 Elections

Philip John Davies

In 2004, George W. Bush became the first Republican president since Calvin Coolidge in 1924 to be reelected with his party retaining control of both the House of Representatives and the Senate. This appeared to mark an important staging post in the attainment of what political pundits dubbed "the Rove Revolution." With the decline of the New Deal party system in the late 1960s, American politics had lacked a clear-cut majority party for the remainder of the twentieth century. To fill this vacuum, senior presidential adviser Karl Rove embarked on a project to create a new Republic majority under the aegis of the Bush presidency. The 2004 vote seemingly indicated that this venture was on the brink of success. Testifying to Republican optimism on this score, House Majority Leader Tom DeLay (R-TX) asserted that the GOP had become "a permanent majority party for the future.... We are going to be able to lead this country in the direction we've been dreaming of for years." Seeing a hard road ahead for his party, Ed Kilgore of the Democratic Leadership Council commented, "We've got to become credible on issues where the people don't trust us."[1]

Belying the optimism of 2004, electoral trends in Bush's second term suggested that visions of a new Republican ascendancy were a mirage. GOP loss of both houses of Congress in the 2006 midterm elections and the presidency in 2008 signified that the party was stuck in the wilderness rather than approaching the promised land of majority status. The Republican decline was a rapid one by historical standards. In the past, parties that suffered erosion of power were in the latter stages of extended electoral-coalition decay. Even the so-called Republican Revolution that saw the GOP effectively replace the Democrats as the congressional majority party in 1994 had fallen short of gaining control of the presidency as well. In truth, no party had experienced such a swift transformation from putative majority to new minority in modern times. Instrumental in this development was the parallel transformation of George Bush from electoral asset to his party in 2002–4 to electoral liability in 2006–8. Accordingly, this essay considers why Republican fortunes declined so quickly in Bush's second term, assesses what part Bush played in this development, and evaluates what the 2008 elections signify about future GOP prospects.

Writing in 2004, political scientist Steven Schier asserted, "The primary project of the Bush presidency is to complete the political reconstruction of national politics, government and policy begun to Ronald Reagan in 1981."[2] Central to this was the establishment of the GOP's status as the majority party that could enact the forty-third president's agenda and sustain it after his departure from office. Guided by Karl Rove, Bush adopted what a contributor to this volume has dubbed a strongly presidentialist and highly partisan strategy that linked Republican fortunes with those of the White House.[3] Whatever benefits this approach had for the task of governing, the assumption that it would lay the foundations for the long-term success of the GOP rested on questionable logic.

Bush's electoral value to his party was debatable from the very outset of his presidency. In 2000, having won 540,000 fewer votes than Democratic rival Al Gore, he became the first president since Benjamin Harrison in 1888 to attain office without a popular-vote majority. Bush narrowly carried the Electoral College by 271 votes to 266, thanks in part to the more widespread distribution of his popular vote—he ran ahead of Gore in 240 of the 435 House districts.[4] Nevertheless, his victory was ultimately dependent on the Supreme Court's *Bush v. Gore* decision that effectively allocated him Florida's disputed Electoral College votes.

In such circumstances it was hardly surprising that Bush lacked discernible coat-tail effects that helped his party in Congress. In this regard, however, he was no different from all but one president of the past thirty years—the exception being Ronald Reagan. As a result of the 2000 elections, the Republican majority over the Democrats shrank slightly from 223–211 to 221–212 in the House of Representatives. More significantly, the loss of five seats in the Senate turned the GOP majority of 55–45 in the previous Congress into a 50–50 balance. Republican control of the upper chamber now depended on the casting vote of Vice President Dick Cheney, but proved short-lived. Already holding misgivings about the new administration, Senator James Jeffords (R-VT) fell out with it over agricultural policy. The disagreement led him to assume Independent status in May 2001, thereby giving the Democrats control of the Senate.

If Bush's worth to his party was not immediately apparent in the 2000 elections, his supporters felt that he could help to strengthen and consolidate its position over time. The presidential contest always looked like being a close run thing, and Bush's candidacy certainly gave the GOP ticket advantages that none of his rivals for the nomination could offer. As the son of the forty-first president defeated by Bill Clinton, he made a potent symbol for the reaffirmation of Republicanism in the wake of the political conflicts of the 1990s. The Bush family network of contacts provided an important source of political support and fundraising. As a born-again Christian who identified strongly with his Southern roots as a Texan, Bush also had great personal appeal to the increasingly important fundamentalist base of his party, even if that potential was not fully exploited in 2000.[5]

The $91.3 million in individual contributions that the Federal Election Commission reported Bush as having received in the 2000 primary campaign season was more than three times the total raised by his closest rival, Senator John McCain (R-AR), and twelve times more than any of the other Republican presidential hopefuls. Supported by this web of financial interest, Bush had been able to make the then unusual decision to decline federal matching funds, and thereby liberate his primary campaign from the limits that accompanied their acceptance. By the time Bush left office, presidential candidate refusal of federal funds had become much more common in recognition of the constraints imposed by their acceptance.

While the 2000 campaign had been skilful, the fundraising network continued to work well, and the new president's pragmatic style in office was not without success, it was not clear in the early days of his administration that Bush could lead the GOP toward its longed-for majority status. However, the September 11, 2001, terrorist attacks on New York and Washington DC transformed the context of his presidency. After an uncertain start, Bush's public responses to the perceived threat of further strikes against the American homeland achieved a combination of reassurance and reaction that met with the approval of most Americans, and public support for the way he was doing his job grew to the highest levels ever recorded Even though voters had many other issues on their minds, this level of approbation for the president continued to work to GOP advantage in the 2002 and 2004 elections.

Bush's public campaign for popular support of his leadership in the war on terror effectively turned the midterm elections of 2002 into a referendum on this. One exit poll showed that 43 percent of voters had cast their ballot as a vote for the president, with only 17 percent taking the contrary position. This undoubtedly worked to GOP advantage in a number of tight contests.[6] The party consequently increased its House majority from nine to twenty-four and won three additional Senate seats to give it a majority of two in that chamber. This was the first occasion since the heyday of the New Deal in 1934 that a president's party had increased its congressional strength in the midterm elections of his first term in office.

A rarity since the late 1960s, single party control of the federal government was a common feature of mid-twentieth-century politics. Party leaders of recent times yearn for its restoration. Despite the tradition of cross-party bargaining and voting in the American polity during periods of single party control, partisan elites are convinced that policy aims can be achieved more efficiently in such a situation. Not since the 1920s had the Republicans been in this position of power. Apart from a tantalizingly brief ascendancy in 1953–54, they did not simultaneously control the presidency, House, and Senate again in the twentieth century. Bucking this dismal record, Bush led his party to a position where it held such triumvirate authority in the 2002 midterm elections. The 2004 presidential and congressional elections reaffirmed GOP single party control of government for the first time since 1928. On this occasion Bush won a popular-vote majority, even if his 2.5 percent margin of victory over Senator John Kerry (D-MA) was the narrowest ever for a reelected president. Moreover, the GOP extended its House and Senate majorities to thirty and ten respectively. The party had not held a higher aggregate number of congressional seats since the late 1920s. Moreover, all but 32 of the 232 victorious House Republicans had won majorities above 55 percent, which seemingly gave them safe seats in the next election.

Instead of marking a new era of Republican ascendancy, the 2004 elections constituted the party's high water mark under Bush. Other than in 1998, the historical record indicates that the president's party does not fare well in the midterm elections of his second term. In 2006, however, the GOP majority would be sunk by a "perfect storm" of adverse circumstances.

The Republicans had hitherto benefited from Bush's reputation for competence, notably as displayed in his response to the 9/11 attacks. In August 2005, this was blown away when Hurricane Katrina made landfall on the Gulf Coast, flooding New Orleans and leaving a trail of damage and destruction across the region. The Bush administration's faltering and inadequate response to the disaster severely undermined public confidence in the president's leadership capacity to the consequent detriment of his party.

The taint of scandal and corruption further damaged the GOP. In January 2006, Jack Abramoff, a lobbyist closely associated with the Republican Party, pleaded guilty in federal court to charges that included corruption of public officials. In November 2005, Representative Randy "Duke" Cunningham (R-CA) also pleaded guilty in an unrelated case to fraud, bribery, and tax evasion charges. Representative Bob Ney (R-Ohio) withdrew his candidacy in the 2006 elections in the face of corruption charges to which he would eventually plead guilty. Tom DeLay, once the cheerleader of the golden Republican future, also suffered an embarrassing end to his political career. Indicted by a Texas federal grand jury for alleged breaches of campaign finance law, he maintained his innocence but his position became increasingly untenable. DeLay decided not to seek reelection when two former aides, Tony Rudy and Michael Scanlon, pleaded guilty to charges relating to the Abramoff affair. Adding to GOP woes, Representative Mark Foley (R-FL) stepped down after revelations concerning messages sent to male congressional pages. This litany of individual wrongdoing undermined the Republican claim to be the party of moral probity.

On the foreign policy front there was growing public anxiety about the continued occupation of Iraq. Failure to find the "weapons of mass destruction" supposedly possessed by Saddam Hussein had already raised doubts as to the quality of the intelligence gathering and analysis on which the original decision to go to war was based. As American casualties mounted in the effort to reconstruct Iraq into a democracy, popular concern about the clarity of the U.S. mission and apparent lack of an exit strategy correspondingly increased. Just as the public had increasingly seen Vietnam as Lyndon's Johnson's war when hopes of speedy victory diminished, it now thought of Iraq as Bush's war. In one of his last public appearances in 2003, the late Richard Neustadt predicted that Bush would come to regret his decision to decry the attacks of September 2001 as "war" rather than adopting the construction offered by others, including Pope John Paul II, of "a crime against humanity," which allowed for greater flexibility of policy response. If there was no evidence that the president ever had such doubt, Neustadt's other observation that Americans were intolerant of long wars was borne out in Iraq.[7] The prolonged and costly occupation of that country was a critical factor in the steep decline of Bush's job approval rating to 38 percent on the eve of the 2006 elections, the lowest for any president at midterm since Harry S. Truman in 1946.[8]

In 2006, the Republicans experienced a steep and abrupt fall from the heights they had ascended in 2004: the thirty-seat loss in the House was their worst since 1974, while the six-seat loss in the Senate was their worst since 1986. The last time the GOP had suffered losses on this scale in both chambers simultaneously was in 1958. The picture was almost as grim at state level, with the loss of 6 governorships (Arkansas, Colorado, Maryland, Massachusetts, New York, and Ohio) and around 300 seats in state legislatures. In historical context, however, these losses for the presidential party in the sixth year of an administration were not as bad as they looked. Political analyst Rhodes Cook identified nine "six-year plus" administrations since the election of Woodrow Wilson in 1912, a list including Harding/Coolidge, Kennedy/Johnson and Nixon/Ford composites. In terms of the number of House seats held at the six-year mark, the Bush administration lies fifth, exactly halfway down the table but only bested by one Republican administration (Harding/Coolidge). According to the number of Senate seats held, loss of House seats since the start of the administration, and loss of Senate seats since the start of the administration, the Bush presidency lay consistently in third place, with a better showing than any other Republican administrations in the sample period.[9]

Howsoever mitigated by historical comparisons, the Republican defeat in 2006 still carried ominous portends. The party no longer controlled at least one branch of the legislature for the first time since 1994. Over half of Democratic gains in both houses came in seats that Republican incumbents previously held with majorities above 55 percent. In the Senate especially the GOP had limited opportunity for recovery, since two-thirds of the seats due for election in 2008 were ones it already held. At executive level the unlimited commitment to the war on terror and its practical consequences continued to strain against the American antipathy for long wars that Neustadt had identified. The depressing effect that Iraq continued to exert on Bush's poll ratings also meant that he would be a hindrance rather than help to his party in the 2008 elections.

The 2008 presidential election was the first since 1928 not to feature an incumbent president or vice president among the main party nominees. Expanding its historical uniqueness even further, political scientist Michael Nelson commented, "Not since George Washington was unanimously chosen as the first president in 1788 had there been an election in which it was clear from the outset that neither the incumbent president nor the incumbent vice president would be on the ballot."[10] Memories did not have to be that long for political hopefuls to recognize that the 2008 race could provide unusual opportunities.

A goodly number of Republicans threw their hat into the ring but most were no-hopers. The contest quickly boiled down to a three-cornered one between Senator John McCain, former Massachusetts governor Mitt Romney, and the populist former Arkansas governor Mike Huckabee, but the race proved a sprint rather than a marathon. McCain's name recognition and national reputation, superior organization and solid funding base brought him extensive victories in the Super Tuesday primaries, an outcome that persuaded his two main rivals to withdraw their candidacies.

A similarly long list of Democratic hopefuls rapidly boiled down to two serious candidates, Senator Barack Obama (D-IL) and Senator Hillary Clinton (D-NY), but theirs was a tough and lengthy battle. It was not clear until the final primaries on June 3, and with super delegates increasingly declaring their voting intentions, that Obama would take the nomination at the Democratic National Convention. The historic significance that an African American male or a white woman was in line to run for president heightened popular interest in the Democratic contest. Whereas Clinton based her appeal on the party's blue-collar, female, and senior citizen constituencies, Obama's campaign attracted support from an eclectic coalition of younger voters, African Americans, Latinos, and the college-educated.

Bush's ratings continued their steady decline amidst the battle to succeed him. The fifteen polls recorded by the Roper Center at the University of Connecticut in January 2008 showed between 27 percent and 34 percents of respondents approving his performance in office, with the median figure at 32 percent. Nevertheless Bush had further to fall from an already woefully low position. Of the eleven Roper-recorded polls in the run up to the party conventions in August, the president had a median approval rating of 30 percent—two slipping as low as 25 percent—but had still not hit bottom. In twenty-seven polls from early October to the eve of polling, Bush had a median approval rating of 25 percent, with his lowest tally at 20 percent.[11] With voters increasingly seeing the president as a failure, he was daily becoming a greater encumbrance for McCain and Republican candidates for other offices.

The president's travails cast a shadow over the entire election campaign. Without doubt, McCain's maverick reputation and his clear dissociation from the administration on a number of issues, notably the use of torture against war-on-terror detainees and campaign finance reform, was a factor in his successful campaign for the nomination.

Obama, meanwhile, benefited from establishing that Clinton was not as distant from Bush as he was. A freshman senator first elected in 2004, he repeatedly condemned the invasion of Iraq to highlight Clinton's 2002 Senate vote in favor of the Iraq war resolution. The New York senator's defense on *Meet the Press* that she "thought it was a vote to put the [UN nuclear weapons] inspectors back in" hardly inspired confidence in her political judgment.[12] In a primary race that was decided by the slimmest of margins, any advantage was important to victory. Obama's ability to link Clinton in this instance with Bush policies was of clear benefit when appealing for support in the Democratic primaries.

On the other hand, the reaction against Bush was helpful to both Democratic candidates in making "change" such an appealing and emotive issue in 2008. This not only had an impact on the issue agenda of the party's campaign but also the opportunities presented to its far from traditional presidential candidates The nomination of either an African American or woman to head a main-party ticket would represent a significant first in the annals of American political history. The factors that brought about change had been long in the making. Popular resistance to a candidate on the grounds of his or her race or gender has declined substantially over time. Nevertheless, the anti-incumbent context of the 2008 election may have provided a particularly fertile opportunity for these nontraditional candidates to emerge in this year.

In spite of Bush's unpopularity, the Republican nominee's cause appeared far from hopeless at the time of the party conventions. In late June, the Obama organization's own polling showed the Democrat leading 49–44 percent among voters who had already made their choice but trailing McCain 48–36 percent among the still undecided voters, who were mainly independents. Moreover, the Republican got a far bigger bounce from the GOP convention than Obama did from the Democratic one. Looking to shore his candidacy up against charges of inexperience and lack of foreign policy expertise, Obama selected six-term Maryland senator Joe Biden as his running mate. In contrast, McCain made the headline-grabbing selection of little known Alaska governor Sarah Palin for his ticket. The choice reinforced his maverick reputation, added to the "not Bush" image of the Republican ticket, appealed to many Republican conservatives who had suspicions about McCain, and scored a propaganda victory in putting a woman on the ticket as a counterbalance to the change personally embodied by Obama. By the end of the convention, McCain held an overall lead in the polls for the first time and had a 15 percent margin among independents. Not since 1952 had a candidate from the incumbent party achieved such good showing in the polls in the face of such low presidential approval ratings. Nonetheless, this had not proved sufficient to save Adlai Stevenson nearly sixty years earlier and it would not be enough to save McCain in 2008.[13]

As had been the case in 2006, the Bush administration's mismanagement of its domestic and foreign policy portfolios dragged down the Republican ticket in 2008. The effect of Katrina had certainly not entirely disappeared and concerns over Iraq had increased. Furthermore, American voters have shown a new inclination to change party control of the White House very regularly. Since Harry Truman's election in 1948, only once has the same political party held the White House for more than eight years. The Reagan-Bush 41 Republican continuum was the solitary exception. With Bush 43's approval rating at an all-time low, McCain had only a slim chance of bucking that trend. However, a banking crisis of historic proportions effectively put paid to his prospects of doing so.

There were indications of growing financial instability in the summer of 2008, but in September, the bankruptcy of Lehman Brothers, the need for rapid and massive emergency government intervention to protect other financial institutions, and a startling fall in the stock market sharpened the focus on financial and economic matters. In February 2008, Gallup recorded that 41 percent of respondents considered the economy "extremely important" when making their judgments on the candidates, a figure that had increased to 55 percent by late October.[14] At no point had McCain impressed the public with his grasp of economic matters, while polls consistently showed Obama inspiring more confidence on this score. As this issue became more salient, it overshadowed those of terrorism and defense on which the Republican candidate had greater expertise, further boosting Obama's appeal.

McCain's reaction to the economic crisis also managed to associate him more closely with the Bush administration. He trumpeted the health of the economy while the evidence of its ills was growing. When its fragility became obvious, he sought to suspend the campaign and rushed to Washington in an ill-judged move that only served to demonstrate his incapacity and lack of knowledge on economic issues. Meanwhile Governor Palin may have proved attractive to the conservatives in the party, but she did not stand up well to the rigours of a national campaign, particularly by failing to demonstrate a strong grasp of complex domestic and foreign policy issues. This further brought into question McCain's judgment. There is a point where maverick behavior shifts from endearing to worrying, and the Republican's decisions in this phase of the campaign came close to that line.

McCain's hitherto advantage of being seen as the stronger leader had effectively evaporated by October. A Gallup poll asking whether the presidential candidates had "a clear plan for solving the country's problems" found that affirmative responses for the Republican constituted only two-thirds of those for his opponent.[15] Meanwhile the issue concerns of swing voters increasingly matched those of Obama supporters rather than McCain supporters. While the economy ranked top for all groups, Obama supporters and swing voters agreed that jobs, health care, education, and energy were next in importance, but McCain voters included only one of these—energy—alongside taxes, terrorism, and Iraq in their top five.[16]

As the issue base of the campaign slipped away from them, the Republicans also found themselves outgunned in the field. Taking more than a leaf out of the Bush election handbook, Obama became the first candidate since the introduction of federal government grants for presidential general election campaigns to eschew that source of funding. The federal grant, $84.1 million in 2008, has become an increasingly modest part of the overall spending on presidential elections, with party committees providing an expanding proportion over the years. However, party expenditure in support of the campaign is technically separated from the presidential candidate's campaign, and not subject to the direction of that campaign's managers. In refusing the federal grant, the Obama campaign took on the burden of having to raise all its own funds, but gained the advantage of total direct control of the subsequent expenditure. Proving the most successful fundraising machine in U.S. electoral history, it followed in Bush's footsteps in redefining the parameters of American campaign finance.

Testifying that this was an expensive presidential race, the Center for Responsive Politics reported that the failed candidates alone raised $598 million, with tallies of $222 million for Clinton, $107 million for Romney, $59 million for former New York Republican mayor Rudi Giuliani, and $57 million for former Democratic North Carolina Senator and 2004 vice-presidential candidate John Edwards. The campaign chests of the two major candidates were reported by the same source as $368 million for McCain and $745 million for Obama.[17] Early in the campaign there was excited comment that 2008 was likely to be the first presidential election when the candidate campaigns spent a billion dollars. By the time it had finished, the total was closer to two billion dollars. Prior to the 2000 race, concerns had been raised about the financial viability of presidential election campaigns dependent on taxpayer-funded public money. However, the increasing number of serious candidates that followed Bush's example in opting out of public support reduced that danger. In 2008, Clinton, Obama, Giuliani, Romney, Ron Paul, and, after some dithering, McCain all refused primary election public funds, and the Obama campaign made the groundbreaking decision to refuse general election funds as well.

By 2008, all candidates were also using the Internet as an important part of their fundraising. In this regard the Obama campaign's success in soliciting modest but repeated donations was particularly significant. The Campaign Finance Institute identified about 580,000 individual contributors of over $200 to Obama by October 15, 2008, compared to 475,000 donors to all campaigns in 2004. In addition, it is estimated that around 2.5 million people gave donations of less than $200 to Obama, compared with a similar number of small donors to all campaigns in 2004. Around half of all Obama's campaign donations amounted to less than $200, but repeat donors meant that these constituted about one quarter of his total funds, about the same ratio as George W. Bush managed in 2004. A distinction does become evident in totals raised from higher-level donors, however. Obama obtained 47 percent of his funds from donors who gave a total of $1,000 or more, compared with McCain's tally of 59 percent. Nevertheless, this was a smaller proportion than Kerry and Bush's respective shares of 56 percent and 60 percent in 2004.[18] To claim that the driving engine of the Obama campaign was a grassroots community of small donors is an overstatement. What cannot be disputed, however, is that the Democratic candidate engaged an unusually large number of donors, kept many sufficiently involved to give repeat donations, and enthused supporters to maintain a personal stake in the race.

Obama emerged the winner over McCain with some 53 percent of the vote, a lead over McCain of about 7 percent. In the context of the twenty-nine presidential elections since 1896, conventionally regarded as the first modern campaign, he came fourteenth in the size of his popular vote and nineteenth in terms of his popular vote majority. While this was no landslide, Lyndon Johnson was the only Democratic candidate to win a larger share of the vote than Obama in post–World War II elections. Moreover, Obama had won the presidency without the historical advantage of having a "solid" South in the Democratic column. Instead, he turned the Northeast, the upper

Midwest, the Mid-Atlantic, the Pacific Northwest, and the Southwest into a blue zone on the map. In addition to winning the largest ever Democratic share of the vote in California and Illinois since 1936, he won the party's biggest vote in twenty-two other states (winning all but Montana and Nebraska) since 1964.

This was also a significant result for the first African American presidential candidate in American history. Obama's race probably dragged down his support from white voters, but estimates vary between 1 percent and 5 percent as to its actual effect. What is not in doubt is that his 43 percent share of the overall white vote was only 2 percent higher than Kerry's in 2004 in spite of the economic climate. Compensating for this, Obama ran much better with other demographic groups, taking 66 percent of voters aged under thirty, a similar proportion of Hispanics, and 95 percent of African Americans in comparison with Kerry's respective tallies of 54 percent, 53 percent and 88 percent in 2004. Turnout among black and Hispanic voters also grew, reducing the overall proportion of non-Hispanic white voters from 77 percent in 2004 to 74 percent in 2008. In broad terms, therefore, Obama's principal gains were made in demographic groups that were increasing as a proportion of the population—some of whom, especially the young, manifested greater racial tolerance, greater support of active government, a rising level of antiwar sympathies, and more liberal political views.[19]

The elections also confirmed the ascendancy of the Democrats at congressional level. This was a party victory more than one reliant on Obama's coattails. In the aggregate national vote for the House of Representatives, the Democrats ran 11 percent ahead of the Republicans. Taking the 2006 and 2008 elections together, the party registered an aggregate gain of fifty-eight seats in the House and fourteen in the Senate (boosted by the defection of Pennsylvania's Arlen Specter to its ranks in early 2009). The Democratic majorities in the House were significantly smaller than those of the past (the party had a hundred seat advantage as recently as the 102nd Congress of 1991–92), but comparable or better than had been the case in the Senate since the late 1970s. In comparison with these earlier times, however, the Democrats were more politically homogenous, thanks to the diminution of conservative Southerners in their ranks. As such, the congressional party was seemingly more capable of supporting Obama's presidential agenda than its precursors had been with regard to Jimmy Carter and even Bill Clinton in 1993–94.

The Republicans had few crumbs of comfort in the election result. Most significantly, they retained a strong base in the South, the rural

Midwest, and the Mountain states. In places they even pushed back the Democratic tide, notably increasing their presidential vote in the South and other loyal regions where voters tended to be "heavily white and older, with lower levels of educational attainment."[20] All this was little consolation for the GOP's loss of national power and the diminished appeal of its antistatist values in the current economic climate. The party ended the Bush era in much worse condition than at its start. McCain won 0.9 percent less of the popular vote and ninety-nine fewer Electoral College votes than Bush in the disputed election of 2000. The number of Republicans in the U.S. House declined from 221 to 176 and in the U.S. Senate from 50 to 41 (not including Specter's later defection) over the same period; the number of Republican state governors also declined from 29 following the 2000 election to 21 as a result of the 2008 vote; meanwhile the number of states in which the Democrats controlled both houses of the legislature rose from 16 to 27.

Accordingly, the Democratic Party was as hopeful for its future in the wake of the 2008 elections as the Republican Party had been when Bush was reelected four years previously—but whether with better cause remained to be seen. What the 2008 vote for president manifested most clearly was a popular repudiation of George W. Bush rather than a positive endorsement of Obama and the Democrats. On election eve, polls showed 75 percent of respondents thought that the country was on the wrong track, the highest level ever recorded. Exit polls also showed that one in three voters considered the need for change to have been the main influence on their ballot—and these went for Obama by a massive margin of 89–9 percent. The challenge facing the Democratic victor was to meet these aspirations when his choices were constrained by the domestic, economic, and international problems that he had inherited.

The long-term impact of the Obama victory will become apparent only with the electorate's subsequent judgment on the record of his administration in 2010 and 2012. Political realignments do not come about with one election, but consolidate over time. The evidence from the 2008 vote does not clearly indicate any strong ideological shift within the population as a whole, nor the identification of an issue so salient as to alter significantly the cleavages within the electorate. "Bush's War" (in Iraq) and "Bush's recession" destroyed the forty-third president's hopes of creating a Republican majority as part of his legacy. Obama has the opportunity to lay the foundations for an alternative partisan majority, but the experience of his predecessor indicates that the task is fraught with difficulty.

Notes

1. Karl Rove, "What Makes a Great President?" Address to the University of Utah's Rocco C. Siciliano Forum, November 12, 2002, http://hnn.us.articles/1529.html; John Harris and Jim VandeHei, "Doubts about Mandate for Bush, GOP," *Washington Post*, May 2, 2005, A1; J. Bresnahan, "Centrist Democrats Search for Direction," *Roll Call*, February 14, 2005. For scholarly analysis, see Philip Davies, "A New Republican Majority?" in Iwan Morgan and Philip Davies, eds., *Right On? Political Change and Continuity in George W. Bush's America* (London: Institute for the Study of the Americas, 2006), 184–203.
2. Steven Schier, "George W. Bush's Project," in Schier, ed., *High Risk and Big Ambition: The Presidency of George W. Bush* (Pittsburgh: University of Pittsburgh Press, 2004), 4.
3. See John E. Owens, "Bush's Congressional Legacy and Congress' Bush Legacy," Chapter 3.
4. For discussion, see Gary C. Jacobson, "Polarized Politics and the 2004 Congressional and Presidential Elections," *Political Science Quarterly*, 120, 2, 2005, 199–218.
5. Martin Durham, "Evangelicals and the Politics of Red America," in Morgan and Davies, *Right On?* 210.
6. *New York Times*/CBS News Poll, November 5, 2002.
7. Richard Neustadt, "Challenges Created by Contemporary Presidents," in George C. Edwards and Philip John Davies, eds., *New Challenges for the American Presidency* (New York: Pearson Longman, 2004), 15–16.
8. "Job Performance Ratings for President Bush," Roper Center Public Opinion Archives, http://webapps.ropercenter.uconn.edu/CFIDE/roper/presidential/webroot/presidential_rating_detail.cfm?allRate=True&presidentName=Bush
9. *The Rhodes Cook Letter*, 7, 6, December 2006, 8. The author thanks Rhodes Cook for kind permission to draw on this publication.
10. Michael Nelson, "The Setting: Diversifying the Presidential Talent Pool," in Nelson, ed., *The Elections of 2008* (Washington DC: CQ Press, 2010), 1.
11. http://webapps.ropercenter.uconn.edu/CFIDE/roper/presidential/webroot/presidential_rating_detail.cfm?allRate=True&presidentName=Bush
12. "Hillary Clinton Defends 2002 Iraq War Vote on Meet the Press," http://www.huffingtonpost.com/2008/01/13/hillary-clinton-defends-2_n_81261.html
13. Ryan Lizza, "Battle Plans," *New Yorker*, November 17, 2008; Lydia Saad, "McCain Now Winning Majority of Independents," September 9, 2008, http://www.gallup.com/poll/110137/McCain-Now-Winning-Majority-Independents.aspx; James E. Campbell, "An Exceptional Election: Performance, Values, and Crisis in the 2008 Presidential Election," *Forum*, 6, 4, 2008, article 7, 12.

14. Gallup Organization, "Election 2008 Topics and Trends," http://www.gallup.com/poll/17785/Election-2008.aspx#2.
15. Ibid., http://www.gallup.com/poll/17785/Election-2008.aspx#3.
16. Pew Research Center, "Obama's Lead Widens," October 21, 2008, 24, http://people-press.org/reports/pdf/462.pdf. My thanks to Sir Robert Worcester for pointing out this reference at the Eccles Centre U.S. presidential election debate, the British Library conference centre, October 2008.
17. Figures from the Center for Responsive Politics based on Federal Election Commission data, http://www.opensecrets.org/pres08.
18. Michael Malbin, "Reality Check," November 24, 2008, Campaign Finance Institute, http://www.cfinst.org/pr/prRelease.aspx?ReleaseID=216.
19. See Andrew Kohut, "Post-Election Perspectives," remarks at the Pew Research Center, 2nd Annual Warren J. Mirofsky Award Dinner, November 13, 2008, http://pewresearch.org/pubs/1039/post-election-perspectives; and Philip A. Klinkner and Thomas Schaller, "LBJ's Revenge: The 2008 Election and the Rise of the Great Society Coalition," *Forum*, 6, 4, 2008, article 9.
20. Ibid., 12.

Index

Abelson, Don, 131
Abortion, 21, 89–91, 170
Abramoff, Jack, 211
Abu Ghraib, 6, 108–10, 115
Adams, Gerry, 129
Adams, John, 19, 63
Adams, John Quincy, 15
Addington, David, 63, 65, 70, 102–103
Afghanistan, war in, 2, 22, 60, 128, 152, 154, 157, 173, 186, 190
Albright, Madeline, 115, 119
Alito, Samuel, 79, 82, 84, 85–86, 90–91, 93, 166
Al-Qaeda, 2, 150, 152
Altman, Daniel, 187
American Bar Association, 104–105
American Civil Liberties Union, 104
American Medical Association, 106–107
Anti-Ballistic Missile Treaty, 22, 133
Ashcroft, John, 33, 109
Australia, 133

Baccus, Rick, 106
Baker, James, 146
Balanced Budget and Emergency Deficit Control Act, 69
Barnes, Fred, 166, 172, 175–76, 177, 178
Bartlett, Bruce, 169, 175, 191
Beaver, Diane, 106
Bennett, William, 103
Berman, Paul, 130
Bernanke, Ben, 194
Betsy, Hurricane, 35
Betts, Roland, 45

Biden, Joe, 132, 151–52, 155–56, 214
Big-Government Conservatism, 3, 7, 165–79
Bin Laden, Osama, 24, 150
Black, Cofer, 107
Blasi, Vincent, 81
Blix, Hans, 110
Boehner, John, 43, 198
Bolton, John, 134, 154
Bork, Robert, 81
Boumediene v. Bush (2008), 92–93
Bovard, James, 123
Boxer, Barbara, 67
Brands, Hal, 146
Brennan, William, 80
Breyer, Stephen, 84, 93
Brinkley, Alan, 168
Brooks, David, 124, 175
Brown, Michael, 24
Brown, Sarah, 121
Brzezinski, Zbigniew, 126, 157
Buchanan, James, 18,19, 20
Buchanan, Patrick, 123
Budget
   deficit in, 7, 24, 173, 190–91, 192
   surplus in, 173, 185, 186, 192
Burger, Warren, 81
Burnham, Walter, 71
Buruma, Ian, 130
Bush Doctrine, 110–11, 131, 133, 134, 186
Bush, George H. W., 19, 44, 56, 81, 82, 84, 104, 132, 136, 146, 166
Bush, George W.
   big government conservatism and, 165–84
   congressional relations of, 51–78
   economic record of, 185–206

Bush, George W.—*Continued*
  ethical record of, 99–120
  foreign policy record of, 145–64
  impact on partisan and electoral politics, 207–22
  judicial record of, 79–98
  legacy of, 1–9
  neoconservatism and, 121–44
  presidential ratings and, 11–30
  presidential style of, 31–50
Bush, Prescott, 45
Bush v. Gore (2000), 208
Bybee, James, 66

Campbell, 145, 145
Card, Andrew, 58
Carothers, Thomas, 138
Carter, Jimmy, 4, 15, 37, 46, 82, 174, 199
Casse, Daniel, 166, 167
Cato Institute, 172, 173–74
Center for Responsive Politics, 160
Center on Budget Policy and Priorities, 188
Central Intelligence Agency (CIA), 65, 83, 84, 106, 107, 108, 111–13
Chalabi, Ahmed, 136
Chavez, Hugo, 149
Cheney, Dick, 26, 42, 52, 56, 61, 63, 65–66, 70, 102, 109, 114, 127, 128, 131–32, 137, 138, 149, 154, 155, 170, 173, 208
China, 132, 134, 137, 139, 157, 158–59, 193, 194–95
Chollet, Derek, 147
Christian Right, 169
Christopher, Warren, 129
Civil Rights Acts
  of 1964, 94
  of 1991, 94
Clarke, Jonathan, 122–23
Clean Air Act, 67
Climate change, 151
Clinton, Bill, 4, 7, 15, 17, 19, 59, 61, 66, 81, 82, 83–84, 90, 104, 129, 132, 134, 136, 147, 150–51, 157, 158, 185–86, 187, 188, 192, 196, 197, 209
Clinton, Hillary, 132, 155, 213–14, 216–17
Coleman, Dan, 108
Compassionate conservatism, 7, 52, 169–72
Comprehensive Nuclear Test Ban Treaty, 160
Congress, 5, 22, 26, 33, 40–42, 155, 178
  and Bush presidency, 51–78
Congressional Budget Office (CBO), 173, 186, 190
Conyers, John, 105
Cook, Rhodes, 212
Coolidge, Calvin, 19, 207, 212
Corwin, Edward, 129
Council of Economic Advisers, 194
Cuba, 147, 160
Cunningham, Randy, 211
Current account deficit, 194–95

Danforth, John, 130
Daniels, Mitch, 8
Dean, John, 101
DeLay, Tom, 43, 207, 211
Desert Storm, Operation, 136
Detainee Treatment Act, 93, 107
Dobriansky, Paula, 132
Dole, Bob, 188
Dorrien, Gary, 127, 128
Drury, Shadia, 124
Dworkin, Ronald, 79, 87

Edsall, Thomas, 172
Edwards, George, 176
Edwards, John, 206
Eisenhower, Dwight, 12, 59, 80, 166
Elections, 8, 15, 175
  of 2000, 52, 208–209
  of 2002, 53, 209
  of 2004, 210
  of 2006, 8, 59, 62, 212, 215

of 2008, 59, 62, 212–19
  campaign finance in, 209, 216–17
Emanuel, Rahm, 14–15, 145
Executive orders, 33
Executive privilege, 66–68
Extraordinary rendition, 105–107, 121

Federal Bureau of Investigation, 103–104, 107, 108
Federal Election Commission, 209
Federal Emergency Management Agency (FEMA), 24
Federal Reserve, 189, 192–93, 194, 198
Federalist Papers, 33–34
Federalist Society, 14, 18–19, 79
Feldstein, Martin, 188–89, 190
Felzenberg, Alvin, 14, 17
Ferguson, Niall, 159
Financial crisis, of 2007–2008, 24, 150, 165, 173, 178–79, 185, 195–200, 215–16, 219
Financial Services Modernization Act, 196–97
Foley, Mark, 211
Foley, Michael, 139
Ford, Gerald, 59
Foreign Intelligence Surveillance Act, 60
Franklin, Benjamin, 128
Franks, Tommy, 111
Freeden, Michael, 39
Friedberg, Aaron, 132
Friedman, Thomas, 130
Frum, David, 137, 149
Fukuyama, Francis, 100, 110–11, 124, 125–26, 129–30, 131
Funston, Richard, 81

Galston, William, 12
Gates, Robert, 158, 160
Gelb, Leslie, 157
Geneva conventions, 40, 65, 106, 115
Genovese, Michael, 15, 16, 26
Gerken, Heather, 88

Germany, 35, 137
Gingrich, Newt, 52, 176
Ginsberg, Ruth Bader, 84, 93
Giuliani, Rudi, 216, 217
Gold, Philip, 123
Goldgeier, James, 146
Goldsmith, Jack, 67
Goldwater, Barry, 176
Gonzalez, Alberto, 108
Gonzalez v. Carhart (2007), 89–90
Gorbachev, Mikhail, 38
Gore, Al, 15, 35, 134–35, 151, 174, 208
Graham, Bob, 66
Grant, Ulysses S., 19, 100
Gratz v. Bollinger (2003), 88–89
Gray, Boyden, 85
Greenburg, Jan Crawford, 90
Greenspan, Alan, 189, 192–93, 197
Gregg, Judd, 43
Grutter v. Bollinger (2003), 88–89
Gunatanamo Bay, 22, 105–107, 109, 121

Halper, Stefan, 122–23
Hamdan v. Rumsfeld (2006), 93
Hamilton, Alexander, 70
Hance, Kent, 35
Harding, Warren, 18, 19, 100, 212
Hardy, Thomas, 14
Harrison, Benjamin, 208
Hartz, Louis, 167
Hastert, Dennis, 174
Hayek, Friedrich, 168–69
Haynes, Willian, 106
Health Savings Accounts, 176
Heclo, Hugh, 44, 167
Heilbrun, Jacob, 130
Hendrickson, David, 133
Hobbs, David, 174
Holbrooke, Richard, 132
Homeland Security, Department of, 22, 59–60, 165, 169
Homeland Security Act, 65
Hoover, Herbert, 15, 20, 37, 61, 186, 199, 200

Huckabee, Mike, 213
Hurst, Steven, 128
Hutchison, Tim, 43

Ignatius, David, 107
Ikenberry, John, 159
Immigration, 4, 61
India, 35, 149, 156, 157
Intelligence Identities Protection Act, 113
Intelligence Reform and Terrorist Prevention Act, 22, 60, 65
Iran, 24, 134, 150, 152
Iran-Contra scandal, 56, 90
Iraq Study Group, 48
Iraq War and Occupation, 11, 23–24, 32, 38–39, 48, 60, 69, 90, 110, 114, 128, 134, 136, 139, 148–49, 153, 154, 157, 159–60,173, 188, 190, 211, 212, 214, 219
Isikoff, Michael, 111
Israel-Palestinian dispute, 153–60

Jackson, Andrew, 19, 134
Jackson, Robert, 71–72
Jacobson, Gary, 170
Japan, 137, 193
Jefferson, Thomas, 18, 19, 136
Jeffords, James, 52, 62, 208
Jintao, Hu, 195
John Paul II, Pope, 211
Johnson, Andrew, 18
Johnson, Lyndon B., 11, 17, 33, 35, 38, 59, 103, 145, 173–74, 211, 212
Jones, Charles O., 41, 197
Judicial Selection Committee, 84–85
Justice Department, 59

Kagan, Frederick, 124
Kagan, Robert, 110, 114, 124, 137, 158, 159
Katrina, Hurricane, 8, 24, 32, 34–35, 37, 39, 44, 48, 53, 190, 210–11, 215

Keane, Jack, 149
Kennedy, Anthony, 6, 81, 85–86, 87–93, 94
Kennedy, Edward, 43, 171
Kennedy, John F., 19, 36, 59, 147, 158, 212
Kennedy v. Louisiana (2008), 91
Kerry, John, 156, 189, 210, 217
Kilgore, Ed, 207
King, Peter, 198
Kohlberg, Lawrence, 100
Korean War, 149
Kosovo War, 132, 134
Krauthammer, Charles, 124
Kristol, Irving, 123, 125, 130

Lammers, William, 15, 16
Landy, Marc, 18
Leffler, Melvyn, 135, 159
Lego, Jeffrey, 159
Lehman Brothers, 179, 198
Libby, Lewis, 113, 115, 132
Libya, 22, 133
Lincoln, Abraham, 15, 18, 19, 51, 67
Long, Russell, 35
Lott, Trent, 175

McCain, John, 107, 130, 154, 156, 159, 170, 209, 213–17
McConnell, Michael, 150, 160
McKinley, William, 20
McLaughlin, John, 112
Madison, James, 34, 70
Mandelbaum, Michael, 146
Marquand, David, 38
Mayhew, David, 59
Medicare Modernization Act, 60, 62, 165, 174–75, 176, 178
Meese, Edwin, 85
Meredith v. Jefferson Co. (2007), 87–89
Micklethwait, John, 130
Miers, Harriet, 84
Military Commissions Act, 22, 93
Milkis, Sidney, 18

Millennium Development
   Corporation, 21
Miller, Geoffrey, 108–109
Miller, George, 43
Miller, Judith, 112
Moore, Stephen, 174
Mora, Albert, 106
Moravcsik, Andrew, 130
Morgan, Iwan, 174
Murray, Douglas, 127
Musharraf, Pervez, 38

Nash, George, 168
National Interest, 124–25
National Journal, 175
National Security Act, 22
National Security Agency, 40, 65, 66
National Security Letters, 103–104
Nelson, Michael, 212
Neoconservatives, 3, 6, 121–39
Neustadt, Richard, 5, 11, 12,
   31–32, 33, 34, 38, 43, 44, 47,
   52, 67, 211, 212
New Deal political order, 167–68,
   177
New Right, 169
New York Times, 65, 66, 107, 112
Ney, Bob, 211
Nixon, Richard, 2, 17, 18, 19, 33,
   40, 47, 56, 59, 67, 81, 82,
   100–101, 104, 128, 166
No Child Left Behind Act, 21,
   42–43, 165, 171–72, 178
North Korea, 21, 24, 134, 149,
Norton, Anne, 124
Novak, Michael, 137
Novak, Robert, 111

Obama, Barack, 7, 24, 32, 52, 71,
   85, 92, 95, 121, 132, 134, 145,
   146, 147, 151–52, 153–56,
   158, 159, 160, 195, 196,
   200, 213–19
Obama, Michelle, 121
O'Connor, Sandra day, 79, 85–86,
   87–91, 92, 93
Office of Legal Counsel, 65

Ogletree, Charles, 110
O'Neill, Paul, 101, 173
Ownership society, 176–77

Paine, Thomas, 99
Pakistan, 35, 38, 137, 150, 154
Palin, Sarah, 214, 215
Parents Involved v. Seattle (2007),
   87–89
Partial Birth Abortion Act, 89–90
Patriot Act, 22, 59, 90, 103–104,
   165, 169
Patriot Reauthorization and
   Improvement Act, 65, 68, 104
Paul, Ron, 159, 217
Paulson, Henry, 60, 178, 198
Peele, Gillian, 165, 171
Pelosi, 68, 113, 197
Perle, Richard, 136, 137
Perry, Barabra, 79, 87
Petraeus, David, 149
Pfiffner, James, 26, 40
Pierce, Franklin, 18
Pipes, Daniel, 149
Plame, Valerie, 111, 115
Plamegate affair, 5, 90, 110–13
Planned Parenthood v. Casey
   (1992), 90
Podhoretz, Norman, 124
Polk, James, 19
Powell, Lewis, 86, 88, 94
Power, Samantha, 159
Project for a New American
   Century, 130–32
Protectionism, 150, 160
Public debt, 193–95
Public Interest, 124–25
Public opinion, 23–24, 37, 39,
   52–53, 59, 67, 156, 213, 215,
   216

Rasul v. Bush (2004), 92–93
Rauch, Jonathan, 175
Rawls, John, 130
Reagan, Ronald, 3, 8, 18, 20, 38,
   40, 52, 56, 61, 82, 83–84, 85,
   90, 104, 146, 160, 166–69,

Reagan, Ronald—*Continued*
  170, 172, 173–74, 175, 176, 177, 188, 192, 197, 199, 200, 208
Regents of the University of California v. Bakke (1978), 89
Rehnquist, William, 81, 85, 90
Reid, Harry, 68, 113
Ricci v. DeStefano (2009), 94
Rice, Condoleezza, 109, 122, 127–28, 131–32, 137, 138
Richards, Ann, 144
Roberts, John, 82, 85–86, 87–89, 166
Rockman, Bert, 145
Roe v. Wade (1973), 90
Romney, Mitt, 213, 216, 217
Roosevelt, Franklin D., 8, 15, 18, 19, 52, 67, 79, 80, 134, 146, 167, 197, 200
Roosevelt, Theodore, 18, 19, 36
Roper v. Simmons (2005), 91
Ross, Fiona, 177
Rove, Karl, 1, 26, 58, 59, 68, 207–208
Rudalevige, Andrew, 43
Rudy, Tony, 211
Rumsfeld, Donald, 16, 63, 93, 106, 109, 122, 127, 128, 136, 137, 138, 158
Russia, 134, 137, 157, 160

Saddam Hussein, 22, 90, 110, 111–12, 128, 138, 132, 211
Sands, Philippe, 106
Sarbanes-Oxley Act, 197
Saudi Arabia, 66,
Sayen, John, 157
Scalia, Antonin, 80, 81, 84, 85–86
Scanlon, Michael, 211
Scheurer, Michael, 108
Schiavo, Terri, 169
Schick, Allen, 173
Schier, Steven, 165, 208
Schlesinger, Jr., Arthur, 13, 14, 18, 100–101, 105

Schlesinger, Sr., Arthur, 13, 14
Schmitt, Gary, 131
Schumer, Charles, 196–97
Scowcroft, Brent, 126, 128
Shane, Peter, 70
Sharansky, Natan, 137
Shenon, Philip, 36
Signing statements, presidential, 104–105
Skowronek, Stephen, 15, 52, 165, 199
Slivinski, Stephen, 173
Sloan, Alan, 190
Smith, Tony, 124, 130
Sniegoski, Stephen, 124
Snow, John, 190
Social Security, reform of, 4, 24, 41, 61, 170, 177
Soderberg, Nancy, 129
Somalia, 146
Sotomayor, Sonia, 85, 92
Souter, David, 81, 85, 90, 93, 166
Specter, Arlen, 217
State Children's Health Insurance Program (SCHIP), 178
Stenberg v. Carhart (2000), 90
Stevens, John Paul, 85, 93
Stewart, Potter, 14
Stiglitz, Joseph, 186
Strauss, Leo, 124, 129
Strauss, Robert, 103
Supply-side economics, 187–88
Supreme Court, 5–6, 52, 104
  and abortion, 89–91
  and death penalty, 91–92
  and detainee rights, 92–93
  and racial issues, 87–89
Suskind, Ron, 101
Swift, Charles, 105

Taguba report, 109
Taiwan, 35
Taliban, 2, 22, 38, 128
Tax reduction, 21, 42, 62, 165, 172–73,186–92

Tenet, George, 109, 112
Thomas, Clarence, 80, 84, 85–86
Thompson, Tommy, 174
Times, The (London), 11, 12, 146
Tocqueville, Alexis de, 115
Toobin, Jeffrey, 90
Torture, America's use of, 24, 47, 65–66, 107–10, 115
Trade, deficit in, 194–95
Troubled Assets Relief Program, 179, 198–99
Truman, Harry S., 4, 11, 33, 33–34, 145, 146, 211, 215
Tucker, Robert, 133
Twain, Mark, 15

Unitary executive doctrine, 63–67
United Nations, 10–11, 126, 132, 133
Use of force resolutions, 59, 62, 69
Uzzell, Lawrence, 171–72

Vietnam war, 11, 38, 68, 69, 133, 149, 157, 211

Wall Street Journal, 14, 18–19, 22
War Powers Resolution, 40–41, 64

Warren, Earl, 80, 81
Washington, George, 15, 18, 19, 212
Washington Community, 31–32, 35, 37–39, 41, 47, 48
Washington Post, 109
Watergate, 56, 68, 101, 113
Wesley, Charles, 46
Wilentz, Sean, 13
Wilson, James Q., 137
Wilson, Joseph, 111–13
Wilson, Woodrow, 11, 17, 40, 46, 67, 212
Wolfowitz, Paul, 126, 127, 151
Woodward, Bob, 2, 131
Wooldridge, Adrian, 130
Wygant v. Jackson Board of Education (1986), 94

Yoo, John, 66, 70, 71, 102–103, 105
Youngstown Sheet & Tube Co.v. Sawyer (1952), 34, 71

Zakaria, Fareed, 157
Zandi, Mark, 191
Zogby, John, 189